Hi-Tech Toys for Your TV:

Secrets of TiVo™, Xbox®, ReplayTV™, UltimateTV™, and More

Steven D. Kovsky

Contents
at a Glance

Introduction   **1**

1 The Revolution in Your Living Room   **5**

2 Intelligent Television—The Boob Tube Wises Up   **15**

3 Video IEDs: More Than Just Appliances   **41**

4 Playing the Field: Other Video IED Convergence Devices   **95**

5 Intelligent Game Consoles—Gaming Goes Global   **115**

6 Choosing the Right Gaming IED for You   **131**

7 Intelligent Audio—Teaching Your Stereo New Tricks   **179**

8 Choosing the Right Audio IED for You   **189**

9 Other "Convergence" Devices   **223**

10 Customizing Your Digital Entertainment Experience   **237**

11 Hacking Your IED   **255**

12 How Did You Ever Live Without It?   **273**

Index   **289**

201 W. 103rd Street
Indianapolis, Indiana 46290

High-Tech Toys for Your TV: Secrets of TiVo™, Xbox®, ReplayTV™, UltimateTV™, and More

Copyright © 2002 by Steven D. Kovsky

International Standard Book Number: 0-7897-2668-8

Library of Congress Catalog Card Number: 2001096309

Printed in the United States of America

First Printing: March 2002

05 04 03 02   4 3 2 1

Trademarks

Warning and Disclaimer

Associate Publisher
Greg Wiegand

Executive Editor
Rick Kughen

Acquisitions Editor
Rick Kughen

Development Editor
Todd Brakke

Technical Editor
James F. Kelly

Managing Editor
Thomas F. Hayes

Project Editor
Tricia Liebig

Copy Editor
Karen A. Gill

Indexer
Mandie Frank

Proofreader
Melissa Lynch

Interior Designer
Alan Clements

Cover Designer
Anne Jones

Page Layout
Ayanna Lacey
Stacey Richwine-DeRome

Photography
Steve Kovsky

Contents

Introduction 1

1 The Revolution in Your Living Room 5

Why Buy an Interactive Entertainment
Device (IED)? 6
The Cost Justifies the Means 8
The Down Side of IEDs 9

Video IEDs: A Better Mousetrap 10

Gaming IEDs Get Real 11

Audio IEDs: Finding a Home 12

The Living Room of Tomorrow 14

**2 Intelligent Television—The Boob Tube
Wises Up 15**

Overview of Video IEDs 16
A VCR on Steroids 16
What's Still Missing 17
What's Coming Next 19

Getting Hooked (Up) with Intelligent
Television 23
Pre-Installation Considerations 24
Cables: Which Wire Should You Use? 27
Putting It All Together 29

Video IED Recording Options 32
Timeshifting TV 32
Random Access 33
Pausing, Zapping, and Deleting 33
Playback and Recording Strategies 35
Internet Access and Interactivity 36

Flies in the Soup: Known Bugs and Glitches 38

3 Video IEDs: More Than Just Appliances 41

Choosing the Right Video IED for You 42

ReplayTV 43
Hardware 44
The "Hidden" Menu 48

ReplayTV Rerun 49
Software Highlights 51
The User Interface 52
Dumb ReplayTV Trick (Easter Eggs) 63

TiVo 64
Reaching Out to the Consumer 65
Hardware 68
Software 70
The Operating System 71
The User Interface 73
TiVo's Hidden Backdoor 75
Conclusions 80

UltimateTV 80
Hardware 81
Software 86
UltimateTV's Ultimate Future 92

**4 Playing the Field: Other Video IED
Convergence Devices 95**

Can My PC Be My IED? 96

Thinking Inside the Box: PC Hardware
Requirements 97
Processor and Memory 97
Hard Disk 99
Displays 101
TV Tuner Cards 101

Video IED Software for Your PC 106
ShowShifter 108
SnapStream PVS 109
VCR 110
CinePlayer DVR Plus 110
WinDVR 111

Buying Off the Rack: The Sony Digital Studio
PC 112

What's Coming Next? 113

5 Intelligent Game Consoles—Gaming Goes Global 115

Overview of Gaming IEDs 116
Is the PC Passé? 116
Separating PCs from Consoles 117

The Winds of War: Console Versus Console 119

What's in a Game? 121
Hard Drives 122
Modems 123

What's Still Missing 128

6 Choosing the Right Gaming IED for You 131

Overview 132
Performance 132
Software 135
Features 136
Price 137
That Certain Je Ne Sais Quoi 138

Nintendo GameCube 138
Hardware 140
Software 149
Tips, Tricks, and Modifications 150

Microsoft Xbox 152
Hardware 154
Software 163
Tips, Tricks, and Modifications 166

Sony PlayStation2 169
Hardware 171
Software 172
Tips, Tricks, and Modifications 176

What's Coming Next 176

7 Intelligent Audio—Teaching Your Stereo New Tricks 179

Overview of Audio IEDs 180
The Basics 180
MP3 and Your Stereo 182

Bring On the IEDs 185
Where Are the Big Brands? 185

What's Coming Next 187

8 Choosing the Right Audio IED for You 189

Overview 190

SonicBlue Rio Digital Audio Receiver 192
Hardware 193
Software 197

Turtle Beach AudioTron 198
Hardware 198
Software 203

iPaq Music Center 204
Hardware 206
Software 209

AudioReQuest Pro Digital Music System 211
Hardware 212
Software 214

Additional Audio IEDs and Related Components 217
Perception Digital's PD Hercules 217
DigMedia's MusicStore 219
Bose Wave/PC Interactive Audio System 220

Coming Attractions 221

9 Other "Convergence" Devices 223

What Else Is There? 224

ZapStation 224
Hardware 225
Software 226
Conclusions 226

Internet-Enabled Set-Top Boxes 227
  Open Season for Set-Tops 227
  Integrated Devices 229
  SurfReady NTV-2500 230
  A TASTE for Tuxia 231
  *Motorola Digital Convergence Platform 500
  Series* 233
  *Simple Devices SimpleFi Wireless Broadband
  Audio Player* 234

Conclusions on Convergence 235

**10 Customizing Your Digital Entertainment
    Experience 237**

Understanding the Pieces of the Puzzle 238

How Does It All Fit Together? 239
  Overprotective Copy Protection? 242
  All About Macromedia and Fair Use 244
  The A/V Receiver 246
  Seeing Infrared 247

Making Web Connections 249
  The Value Proposition 250
  How to Connect 251

Future Trends 252

11 Hacking Your IED 255

Are You a "Tweaker?" 256
  Weighing the Risks 257
  Weighing the Benefits 258

Tweaking Your Video IED 258
  Does It Work? 260
  Adding Storage Space to a TiVo 260
  Where to Go from Here 265

Game IEDs 266
  Audio IEDs 268

Final Options 271

12 How Did You Ever Live Without It? 273

Overview 274

Video IEDs 274
  Video IED Outlook 275
  What About "Surf TVs"? 276
  Where's the Service? 278

Gaming IEDs 281
  Gaming IED Outlook 282

Audio IEDs 284

And The Hits Keep Coming 287

A Final Rant 288

Index 289

Foreword

The first time that I knew ReplayTV was something special was a morning in January 1999. I was at the Consumer Electronics Show in Las Vegas, and this particular morning I had to get up really early. I was meeting a TV crew from *Good Morning America* at 5 a.m. for a live demo of ReplayTV. This was a new experience for me then, although it did become very common over the next few years.

CES is huge, with more than 100,000 exhibitors, dealers, industry analysts, reporters, and enthusiasts converging in Las Vegas to see what's going to be hot. And these were heady times for ReplayTV, the company I had founded less than two years earlier. A small group of us had spent the past year and a half working on ReplayTV, the world's first digital video recorder. We thought we had something pretty cool, but what would the world think? We were a tiny company in the world of consumer electronics that was dominated by mammoths such as Panasonic, Sony, and RCA. Would anyone notice us? Our booth was packed for the entire show. We won "Best of Show." TV crews lined up to tape in the booth. They were pretty exciting times for a small company from California. The world of television was changed forever.

The story of the genesis of ReplayTV began in 1991 when I was an avid fan of *Star Trek: The Next Generation*. I began thinking about how difficult it was to make regular recordings of my favorite television show.

Being an engineer by education and training, I easily mastered the complexities of programming a VCR. But still, there always seemed to be a few problems: the tape was full, the wrong tape was in the VCR, I didn't know I was going to be late, the timer wasn't set up correctly, the power was in the wrong state, and so on. And after the show was recorded, the problems kept coming. How do I find the show on an unlabeled tape? Which unlabeled tape is the show on? It seemed that there had to be a better way.

A few years earlier, I had designed and built what would turn out to be one of the most popular audio digitizers for personal computers, and I understood well the power of digitizing media and then storing and playing it back from hard drives. It seemed obvious that the right combination of storage and compression technology, coupled with some software to tie it all together, could result in a huge breakthrough in the way people watch television. With this combination, people would be able to personalize their television viewing experience. They could watch the shows they wanted to watch whenever they wanted. It would be television-on-demand that actually worked! It could change everything.

Of course, in 1991, hard drives were far too expensive to be used in consumer video products, as was the compression technology that was needed to squeeze large video files down to a size that could be managed by a consumer electronics device. Over time, however, prices spiraled downward, storage capacities dramatically increased, and video compression technologies made significant advancements. In August 1997, when the prices of storage and compression technology had crossed into the consumer price range, I formed ReplayTV. And on April 26, 1999 we shipped the early *Star Trek*-inspired vision: ReplayTV, the world's first DVR.

Much has changed since those early days of DVRs. ReplayTV was bought by SonicBlue (makers of the Rio MP3 players). As I write this, we are launching the ReplayTV 4000, the world's first networked DVR. With its Ethernet connection and broadband support, the ReplayTV 4000 connects your TV to the Internet in ways never before possible. Users can send their recordings to their friends, store and view digital photos, and download Internet delivered TV (IPTV).

How will you receive your TV in the future? It seems likely that, over time, proprietary cable networks and satellite networks will give way to IP standards-based delivery protocols. With IPTV, broadband TV content will be "trickle" downloaded to your DVR. Combine this with the terabyte storage capacity just around the corner in DVRs, and pretty soon every movie ever made will be waiting on your TV's hard drive, available to view on demand. Not only will this be "a movie store in a box," but other content such as TV shows and news will also be available.

How big are the hard drives going to grow in your DVR? When we launched ReplayTV in 1999, the largest model had 28GB of storage (enough for about 28 hours of TV). The ReplayTV 4000 line now has a model with 320GB of storage. That's enough for 320 hours of TV, or about 160 movies. Storage increases even faster than Moore's law. You can expect DVRs with a terabyte (1,000GB) of storage in a couple of years.

These are exciting times. The combination of low-cost but tremendously fast computing power and vast quantities of digital storage are powering the creation of new and cool ways to watch TV, listen to music, and play games. When you combine this with the broadband Internet, you could say we're in the early stages of a revolution. Costs are still coming down, and most consumers are still just learning about these new types of devices. But user satisfaction is very high. More than 85% of ReplayTV owners recommend their ReplayTV to a friend. They can't imagine giving up the convenience, power, and control that their DVR brings.

In this book, you'll learn about DVRs, as well as other types of entertainment appliances for video, audio, and gaming. Much is going on in this industry. Every day, the frontiers are being pushed forward as incredible new technology makes its way to the market.

Anthony Wood
Founder of ReplayTV
September 14, 2001
Palo Alto, California

Preface

"Never give up. Never give up. Never *ever* give up."

Those are the words of Sir Winston Churchill, as quoted to me by Sir Arthur C. Clarke when I interviewed him in September 2001, two weeks after the unspeakable terrorist attacks on the World Trade Center and the Pentagon.

Conversing over an Internet voice connection while a video camera rolled in his home in Sri Lanka, the man who many recognize as the greatest science fiction writer of all time was offering words of hope and compassion to his friends, far away in a shell-shocked nation. But I also found another type of encouragement in the words of this visionary octogenarian and author of more than 80 books and 500 short stories and articles.

The world changed on the day that Clarke referred to as Black Tuesday. Was it still a world that had time to watch television, listen to music, and play video games? However engaging these new high-tech devices were, could they really compete for our attention when the very foundations of our society were under violent and deadly attack? At least in terms of this book, "giving up" seemed at that moment like an attractive prospect.

Despite my doubts, I followed Churchill's advice, as did the editors and publishers at Que and the vast majority of Americans who took to heart their president's plea to simply "live your lives, and hug your children." We continue to work and to play. We do this not because we've forgotten the thousands of innocents who lost their lives on Sept. 11, 2001, but because we remember them, and living a normal life while enjoying the unprecedented freedoms of this country is the best way we can pay them homage.

Just as this preface lends a serious note to a book on tech toys, there is a serious side to these intelligent entertainment devices (IEDs), as I learned during those dark September days. I was voracious for news about the attack, about the rescue effort, about the criminals who were responsible, about new threats such as bioterrorism, about our resolve to fight back. These tech toys quickly demonstrated their worth as serious tools for information gathering. With my computerized video recorder, I scoured the news channels and paused the live broadcast of George W. Bush's historic September 20 address to a joint session of Congress and the American people, so that my family could gather to watch it together. With my computerized, Web-connected audio console, I was able to tune in Internet radio stations from around the world for a fresh perspective on the conflict.

As 2002 dawned, life in America seemed almost back to normal in many ways. We have lost much, but not our freedom, our tolerance, our desire for a rich life that balances duty and fun, or even our sense of humor. Entertainment, with its ability to renew the human spirit, is as important as ever.

That's a good thing because the technology discussed in this book is way too much fun to pass up. And the fun has only just begun. New advances promise to vastly improve our ability to customize and tailor our entertainment experiences in ways we never dreamed of. I hope you enjoy learning about these intelligent entertainment devices as much as I have.

Steve Kovsky
January 2002

About the Author

Steve Kovsky is executive editor for *CNET Radio* (AM910 KNEW in San Francisco, AM890 WBPS in Boston, XM Satellite Channel 130, www.CNETRadio.com) and the daily tech commentator for CBS Radio's *KFWB/LA Times Noon Business Hour with Ron Kilgore and Cindy Dole* (AM980 KFWB in Los Angeles).

In his 16 years as a professional journalist, he has covered every aspect of high technology for television, radio, magazines, newspapers, and the World Wide Web. His credits and bylines have appeared in a wide variety of media, including *CNET News.com*, *ZDNet*, *Tom's Hardware Guide*, *ZDTV* (now *TechTV*) and *ZDTV Radio*, *PC Week* and *PC Week Radio*, *Computer Sources*, *Electronic Components*, *Digital Review*, *Computer Systems News*, and the *San Jose Business Journal*.

Kovsky lives in Northern California with his wife and three children.

Dedication

For my wife, Julie, and my children Nicholas, Aaron, and Jenna. They seem to think I can do anything, and because of that, I frequently can.

Acknowledgments

There are many people without whom this book would never have made it into your hands.

I owe a great debt to PC hardware maven and Web site impresario Larry Barber from `AnandTech.com`, who introduced me to Que Publishing acquisitions editor Rick Kughen. After Rick invited me to work as a reviewer on *The AnandTech Guide to PC Gaming Hardware* by Anand Lal Schimpi, we started kicking around ideas for a tech title of my own. Rick and I exchanged lists of book project ideas. A book about the new generation of computer-based consumer appliances appeared on both our lists.

The entire team at Que—Rick, dedicated development editor Todd Brakke, associate publisher Greg Wiegand, and others—have been tremendously patient, gracious, and supportive as they gently initiated me into the world of book publishing. I also thank technical editor Jim Kelly for his insights and encouragement.

I'd like to acknowledge Candy Meyers, Brian Cooley, and all my colleagues at CNET Radio, CNET Broadband, and CNET News.com for their support and good wishes during a year that was surprisingly turbulent.

Many of the vendors discussed in this book worked tirelessly to lavish me with products and information. They are too numerous to thank individually, but their efforts are deeply appreciated.

Finally, thank you to my family and friends, including my father Brian (who has promised not to begrudge me the fact that I managed to get a book published before he did) and Chuck Smith, who was the first person to convince me that I could write a book.

In particular, I want to thank my world-class product testing team and pit crew: Nick, Aaron, Jenna, and Julie. It is as much your book as it is mine. I hope you take as much pride in it as I do in you.

Tell Us What You Think!

As the reader of this book, *you* are our most important critic and commentator. We value your opinion and want to know what we're doing right, what we could do better, what areas you'd like to see us publish in, and any other words of wisdom you're willing to pass our way.

As an Associate Publisher for Que, I welcome your comments. You can fax, e-mail, or write me directly to let me know what you did or didn't like about this book—as well as what we can do to make our books stronger.

Please note that I cannot help you with technical problems related to the topic of this book, and that due to the high volume of mail I receive, I might not be able to reply to every message.

When you write, please be sure to include this book's title and author as well as your name and phone or fax number. I will carefully review your comments and share them with the author and editors who worked on the book.

Fax: 317-581-4666

E-mail: feedback@quepublishing.com

Mail: Greg Wiegand
            Que
            201 West 103rd Street
            Indianapolis, IN 46290 USA

Introduction

The Revolution in Your Living Room

For couch potatoes, these are truly salad days. In fact, the new computerized entertainment devices designed for living rooms could make the notion of couch potatoes obsolete. Why lounge in front of a television in a vegetative state when you have at your fingertips the ability to get involved, be immersed, and control and customize a viewing experience that exactly suits your individual tastes?

The era of intelligent entertainment has arrived. For the purposes of this book, *intelligent entertainment devices* (IEDs) are defined as electronic appliances that are designed to provide a customizable entertainment experience through the integration of computer logic and circuitry. An IED might look like a VCR, TV, stereo, or game console on the outside, but don't be fooled—it is nothing less than a state-of-the-art, multimedia-capable personal computer masquerading as a conventional living room appliance.

Just take a look at the specifications for Microsoft's UltimateTV video IED:

- 40GB hard drive (capable of storing 35 hours of video data)
- Dual USB ports
- Printer port

- 56K modem
- Windows CE operating system

Only the addition of a dual-satellite TV receiver and a surplus of A/V jacks signals that this is a dedicated audio/visual subsystem rather than a high-end desktop PC.

It's a quantum leap forward from the analog appliances with which society grew up.

Some of us are old enough to remember TVs and radios that relied on glass vacuum tubes. I can recall helping my dad carefully label and remove the delicate tubes from the back of our television, and then accompanying him down to the Thrifty Drug Store, where we placed each one in a tester and then bought replacements for those that had burned out. I even recall earning a perfectly cylindrical scoop of Thrifty's pistachio ice cream as a reward for my participation in the venture.

Today, you would practically need a degree in electrical engineering to perform similar repairs on the digital components of your video or audio IED. However, that hasn't stopped some intrepid souls from opening up those boxes and, displaying total contempt for their warranties, adding disk drives and software to upgrade their devices far beyond what the manufacturer envisioned.

Where This Book Comes In

Chances are, this book lies open in your hands because you either have a computerized entertainment appliance in your home, or you're thinking about getting one. Either way, there's a lot to learn. These devices strive to make our lives easier and more fun, but they frequently fall short of those goals. We should welcome these advanced computers into our homes, winking at their feeble attempts to masquerade as ordinary appliances, but with full knowledge of what they are, what makes them tick, and how to get from them the results we desire.

Although innovative new devices are constantly redefining any attempts to categorize the technology, I have separated IEDs into three main categories:

- Video IEDs (primarily ReplayTV, TiVo, and UltimateTV)
- Gaming IEDs (primarily GameCube, Xbox, and PlayStation 2)
- Audio IEDs (primarily Turtle Beach Audiotron, Rio Receiver, AudioRequest ARQ Pro, and Compaq iPaq Music Center)

Video IEDs (also called *personal video recorders* and *digital video recorders*) made significant inroads into our living rooms in 2001, and that trend is set to accelerate rapidly in 2002. In Chapter 1, "The Revolution in Your Living Room," we'll discuss the pricing and positioning of these and other important IED products. In Chapter 2, "Intelligent Television—The Boob Tube Wises Up," we'll drill down on how these smart video recorders work, how to hook them up, and how to get the most out of them. Chapter 3, "Video IEDs: More Than Just Appliances," goes in-depth on each of the major products, with blow-by-blow descriptions of what's inside and how their designs and features stack up, along with tips and tricks to bring out their best qualities. Chapter 4 "Playing the Field: Other Video IED Convergence Devices," takes a hard look at hardware alternatives, such as refitting your PC to behave like a dedicated video recorder.

The new generation of game consoles takes center stage in Chapters 5 and 6. Chapter 5, "Intelligent Game Consoles—Gaming Goes Global," looks at the phenomenal forces at work in the electronic gaming arena, including the introduction of three new technically advanced gaming IED platforms in 2001, and how they will shape the world of online and offline entertainment moving forward. Chapter 6, "Choosing the Right Gaming IED for You," delves into the pros and cons of each console, helping you understand the technical nuances in the hardware as well as the subtle variations between the design and business philosophies of blood rivals Microsoft, Sony, and Nintendo. You will come away with your own set of answers to the question of which gaming IED offers the ideal balance between imaginative software, heart-stealing heroes, mind-blowing graphics, and gut-wrenching arcade action.

What do you get when you cross a computer with a home stereo? Find out in Chapter 7, "Intelligent Audio—Teaching Your Stereo New Tricks," as we look at the market forces that are shattering the age-old commercial music industry and allowing consumers to effortlessly collect and administer huge collections of songs using the latest technology. Chapter 8, "Choosing the Right Audio IED for You," explores each of these divergent products designed to feed your ears with digitally perfect copies of your favorite tunes. From network nodes that route music from your PC to your stereo via phone lines, to standalone Linux machines that sit in your stereo cabinet, there is an audio IED to suit every taste and budget.

Chapter 9, "Other 'Convergence' Devices," looks at those digital entertainment products that defy categorization, from set-top boxes with a karaoke flair, to digital audio receivers that pluck songs directly from the online libraries of your broadband cable provider.

How do these disparate pieces of the digital entertainment puzzle fit together? You'll find out in Chapter 10, "Customizing Your Digital Entertainment Experience," as we attempt to integrate these systems with our existing analog appliances. Buckle up—getting these smart devices to play nicely together can be a bumpy ride.

Still not getting the results you want? Or has becoming a TiVo/ReplayTV/UltimateTV junky left you panting for more—more power, more capacity, more everything? If you think you're ready to pick up a screwdriver and take matters into your own hands, you're ready for the hands-on advice in Chapter 11, "Hacking Your IED."

Finally, Chapter 12, How Did You Ever Live Without It?, looks at the technological advances that are conspiring to fundamentally change the way we entertain ourselves at home. Find out what new features are waiting in the wings to enliven your video, audio, and gaming experiences in the months and years to come.

Chapter 1

The Revolution in Your Living Room

Why Buy an Interactive Entertainment Device (IED)?

Let's face it. The new array of digital video, gaming, and audio devices now being offered for your entertainment pleasure will take their toll on you. Apart from the "wasted" hours spent gleefully watching, playing, and listening, the cost alone is enough to make most consumers shudder.

Take video IEDs. These include UltimateTV, TiVo, and ReplayTV designs, none of which have been seen for less than $199 MSRP, even after $100 rebates. A fully configured UltimateTV, including a satellite dish and wireless keyboard, represents at least a $500 investment. And don't forget the cost of dish installation (figure at $100 to $200, conservatively), and the monthly service charges. Microsoft's offering will require a $9.99 monthly commitment for the UltimateTV service, plus another $5 to $20 per month for Internet access. Then, of course, you'll want some actual television programming, so tag on another $21.99 to $82.99 per month, payable to DirecTV. You're easily looking at an initial layout of over $800 for the first month. After one year of watching your UltimateTV, you could be about $2,000 poorer (see Table 1.1).

Table 1.1 – Typical Costs Associated with Setting Up UltimateTV Service in 2001			
First Month Investment			
	Minimum*	Maximum**	Average
UltimateTV purchase	$399.00	$500.00	$449.50
Installation	$100.00	$200.00	$150.00
UltimateTV service	$9.99	$9.99	$9.99
UltimateTV Internet Access fee	$5.00	$20.00	$12.50
DirecTV service	$21.99	$82.99	$52.49
Total	$535.98	$812.98	$674.48

Table 1.1 – Continued

	One Year Investment		
	Minimum*	**Maximum****	**Average**
UltimateTV purchase	$399.00	$500.00	$449.50
Installation	$100.00	$200.00	$150.00
UltimateTV service	$119.88	$119.88	$119.88
UltimateTV Internet Access fee	$60.00	$240.00	$150.00
DirecTV service	$263.88	$995.88	$629.88
Total	$942.76	$2,055.76	$1,499.26

*Excludes dish and wireless keyboard; requires use of separate ISP account

**Includes dish and wireless keyboard, bundled Internet access, and DirecTV Platinum programming package*

Any way you look at it, that's a lot of cash to spend on watching TV, an activity that few people view as being of any particular benefit to society or one's personal well being. Can it possibly be worth it? Most people who own a video IED (alternatively called a PVR for *personal video recorder* or a DVR for *digital video recorder*), for instance, will answer the question with a resounding "Yes!"

Why? Because the unique features of the video IED completely transform the experience of viewing commercial television. Storing video from your satellite or cable provider on a hard disk in real-time gives the viewer complete independence from the whims of network programmers.

For example

- Pause the live TV signal while you answer a phone call (or nature's call), or put the kids to bed.
- Record your favorite show at 8 p.m., and watch it at 8:20… the next day (or week, or whenever you like).
- Missed some dialog, or a key plot development in the show you're watching? Just hit rewind.

- Want to see a football player's amazing sideline catch again in slow motion without relying on the TV networks to do it? No problem.

- Tired of commercials? Pause the show while you grab a sandwich, then come back and fast forward right past the ads.

- Construct "virtual channels" with only the shows you like, regardless of which station aired them.

➡ For details on these specific features of video IEDs, see sections on "Timeshifting TV," p. 32, "Pausing, Zapping, and Deleting," p. 33, and "Playback and Recording Strategies," p. 35.

The Cost Justifies the Means

The ability to manipulate live video in the same way we control a videotape is a breakthrough capability, and for many consumers, enough to justify the investment. Add superb, "lossless" quality (the recording is digitally exact, so there is no degradation from the original to the copy) and advanced personalization and search features, and you have a brand new entertainment experience.

Likewise, owners of audio IEDs—devices such as the IPAQ Music Center, the SONICblue Rio Digital Audio Receiver, the Turtle Beach AudioTron, and others—will attest to the degree of control they can exercise over their music collections. These computerized stereo components store hundreds of songs, all instantly accessible and programmable, with superb sound quality. Add to that the native support for the popular and compact MP3 music file format, which can be easily copied from PC to portable player to home stereo. What's not to like? Retail prices of $300 to $400 are not out of line with more conventional high-end home stereo components.

Finally, the new "connected" video game consoles—Microsoft's Xbox, Nintendo's GameCube, and Sony's retooled PlayStation 2—aim to offer gamers the ultimate in electronic recreation. In addition to serving up on-the-fly animation at quality that approaches motion picture special effects, these gaming IEDs promise online access to a worldwide community of potential opponents and teammates. As Microsoft's chief Xbox officer Robbie Bach stated in a frenzy of pre-launch hype: "Xbox is going to change video games the way MTV changed music. Your games are never going to be the same." Will hard-core gamers willingly pay up to $299 for the Xbox, GameCube, or PS2? Just try to cut in line ahead of some scraggy Xbox-toting customer at the electronics store. Go ahead, make his day (and quite possibly the evening news).

The Down Side of IEDs

Aside from the generally high costs of IEDs, there are other draw-backs. Consider the learning curve.

Right now in America, tens of thousands of videocassette recorders are dumbly blinking "12:00," their owners having given up after repeated attempts to set the machines' internal clocks. If we routinely fail in that simple task, what hope is there for us to gain mastery over a new generation of devices that are vastly more complicated?

Thankfully, these digital devices can, in most cases, set their own clocks. But despite the designers' best efforts to create a simple and intuitive user interface, they do represent a much greater degree of complexity than their analog predecessors do (and that's *after* getting them hooked up properly—no small task). Even after months of using a TiVo video IED in my home, I occasionally find its behavior a little bewildering. No doubt it feels the same way about me.

The ideal home appliance should never require a thorough reading of the operations manual—or even a cursory one. The need to call the manufacturer directly should never arise. The controls should be intuitive, and the performance predictable.

While this ideal is perfectly achievable in the case of toasters and even TVs, IEDs are a vastly different animal. The basic problem is that they do too much. Their rich features are too numerous and complex for each to be represented by its own clearly labeled button on an already bulky remote control. Instead, all but the most common and frequently used features are squirreled away, hidden within labyrinthine menus, their locations forgotten almost as soon as they are found.

Of course, these operational difficulties only present themselves to consumers once the machines are operating. Setup and configuration can be the most vexing part of the IED experience. In my experiences with both the TiVo and UltimateTV IEDs, numerous calls to the man-ufacturer and service provider were required just to complete the installation process. In the case of ReplayTV, I managed to complete the process without third-party intervention (if you don't count my 9-year-old assistant), though the five-hour experience left me shaken and exhausted. Your results may vary, but whether it's clearing up the purpose of a mysterious undocumented cable, unraveling a snagged wiring scheme, or troubleshooting a quirky remote control, the setup process seldom runs as smoothly as the manufacturer intends.

When problems do arise, as they inevitably will, consumers may find it a challenge to get the answers they need. In the case of UltimateTV, buyers can find themselves in the middle of a finger-pointing match between the manufacturer (Sony or RCA), the IED service provider (Microsoft), and the satellite provider (DirecTV). For one setup problem I encountered, I spent hours calling all three providers and weeks later I was still without an answer. (Though this is generally a worst-case scenario, your ability to get the support you require will often depend on your own tenacity in dealing with the manufacturers' customer support centers.)

Video IEDs: A Better Mousetrap

Despite the drawbacks of price and complexity, experts are predicting a rapidly expanding market for home IEDs.

Market analysts at Forrester Research estimated that 750,000 U.S. households owned video IEDs at the end of 2000. Within five years, they expected that number to rocket up to 53 million (see Figure 1.1).

FIGURE 1.1
Video IED sales are expected to grow rapidly.

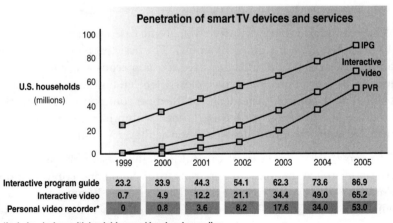

	1999	2000	2001	2002	2003	2004	2005
Interactive program guide	23.2	33.9	44.3	54.1	62.3	73.6	86.9
Interactive video	0.7	4.9	12.2	21.1	34.4	49.0	65.2
Personal video recorder*	0	0.8	3.6	8.2	17.6	34.0	53.0

*Includes devices with hard drives and head-end recording

What will fuel this torrid rate of IED adoption? When he released his findings in June 2000, Forrester principal analyst Josh Bernoff said, "Smarter TV devices like personal video recorders and interactive digital cable boxes will move viewers beyond the passive viewing experience, allowing them to watch TV on their own schedules, interact, and connect to onscreen services."

The enthusiasm for video IEDs isn't dependent on big advances in TV programming, which Bernoff expects to be basically unchanged in 2005—featuring "the same video, the same commercials, and the same cable and satellite distribution." Instead, the major promise of video IEDs and related interactive TV technologies will be to "rejuvenate existing content and bring affluent viewers back to television. And the timing is right—the same technologies will enable viewers to skip 30% of commercials in 2005, causing an unprecedented decline in traditional advertising revenues."

Bernoff expects broadcasters to combat "ad zappers" by creating ever more entertaining and engaging commercials, and by seeking new revenue streams from interactive services, including embedding "commerce opportunities" in programming and offering extensive pay-per-view libraries.

➡ For a glimpse at what broadcasting executives have up their sleeves, see "On Demand Is On Order for AOL Time Warner," p. 114.

Gaming IEDs Get Real

Video game IEDs are also set to go gangbusters. The International Data Corp (IDC) says sales of new game hardware and software will soar, from an estimated $11.4 billion in 2001 to $21.1 billion by 2005.

Sega's decision to exit the video hardware market in 2001 didn't put a dent in forecaster's expectations for the market. Driving the growth for Nintendo's GameCube, Microsoft's Xbox, and Sony's PlayStation 2 will be the significantly enhanced realism of the game software, along with new features such as

- DVD technology
- broadband connectivity for playing games with other gamers over the Internet
- hard drives to store data and speed up the play

Perhaps the single biggest motivator for consumers to buy new game consoles is the lure of online gaming. IDC predicts 40 million households will be drawn into the world of networked game play by 2004 (see Figure 1.2).

FIGURE 1.2
Internet-enabled games are expected to be a major driver for sales of gaming IEDs.

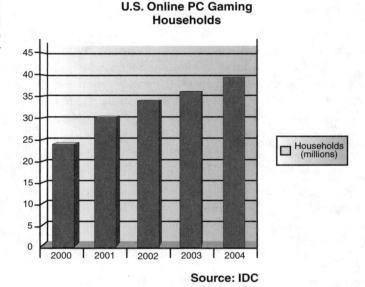

U.S. Online PC Gaming Households

Source: IDC

"The versatility in new consoles can only help to boost sales," said Brian O'Rourke, senior analyst with Cahners In-Stat's Multimedia Service. "Online gaming will grow rapidly over the next three to five years, to the point where it may rival packaged games in revenue. This development will make high-speed Internet access via consoles more important than ever."

Audio IEDs: Finding a Home

Worldwide shipments of devices that play compressed audio, such as MP3 files, added up to 3.3 million units in 2000, according to IDC. IDC says the number will explode up to nearly 26 million units in 2005 (see Figure 1.3).

Research firm Forward Concepts has offered an even more bullish forecast, predicting sales to reach 7 million units in 2001 and driving on up to 42 million units by 2004 (see Figure 1.4).

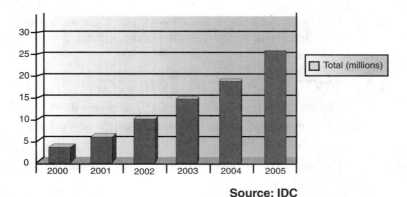

**Worldwide Compressed
Audio Player Shipments**

Source: IDC

FIGURE 1.3
The recent popularity
of MP3 music has
launched compressed
audio players on a
meteoric trajectory.

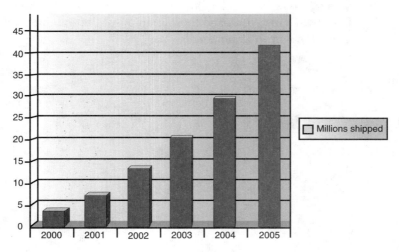

**Worldwide Portable Compressed
Audio Player Forecast**

Source: Forward Concepts

FIGURE 1.4
Portable players will
represent the lion's
share of compressed
audio hardware sales,
but consoles are gain-
ing ground.

While the biggest growth is still in the area of portable players, primarily replacements for bulky CD players, a new and fast-growing category of home audio players has begun to emerge. Combined with
automotive MP3 players and streaming Internet radios, home networked receivers will account for about 39% of compressed-audio

players sold by 2005, according to IDC. Susan Kevorkian, analyst for IDC's Consumer Devices program, says the future looks bright for MP3 players that reside in the living room instead of the hip pocket. "The market for compressed audio players will continue to grow... significantly beyond devices resembling the original, portable (SonicBlue) Rio-like units."

The Living Room of Tomorrow

With numbers like these, it's clear that if you don't already own an intelligent video, gaming, or audio device, there's probably at least one in your not-too-distant future.

The same forces that revolutionized the workplace during the past 25 years are now at work in our homes. The PCs in our dens were only the forerunners of this computer revolution. The real fireworks are taking place in the living room, where computers hidden inside our everyday appliances are poised to transform the way we live.

The trick to getting full enjoyment from these devices is to understand both their capabilities and their limitations. Bottom line: Your days as a couch potato are numbered.

Chapter 2

Intelligent Television—The Boob Tube Wises Up

Overview of Video IEDs

Among the major categories of Intelligent Entertainment Devices (IEDs)—video, music and gaming IEDs—the new crop of "smart VCRs" has probably generated the greatest amount of excitement in the consumer electronics industry. Why are video IEDs getting so much more attention than their musical and games-based cousins?

Intelligent audio products have taken off in the form of portable MP3 players, but costlier stay-at-home versions have been slower to go mainstream. Intelligent game consoles, on the other hand, are already considered a fairly mature business, even though the addition of new digital and online capabilities—and a new competitor in the form of Microsoft—injected some excitement back into the market in 2001.

Meanwhile, video IEDs appear to be poised for spectacular growth. They provide a compelling set of features that consumers want, at prices they're willing to pay.

A VCR on Steroids

Without question, the introduction of the consumer videocassette recorder in the early 1970s completely revolutionized the experience of watching television. Live television shows could be recorded for later viewing. Motion pictures that had seen the end of their run at the box office found new life in the home rental market. For the first time, consumers could really take charge of what they watched and when they watched it.

In addition, the VCR brought to the visual medium a degree of control that had existed only for audio media. It allowed you to rewind, pause, and fast-forward through video programming. The most expensive "prosumer" VCR decks even allowed users to freeze an image and advance or rewind the video one frame at a time.

The new generation of digital video recorders takes the now-comfortable interface of the VCR and overlays it onto a cutting-edge multimedia PC. By substituting hard disks for videotape, video IEDs perform like a VCR on steroids. The same pause, rewind, fast-forward and slow-motion controls are now applied on-the-fly to live broadcast television. The VCR has come of age, and watching television will never be the same.

It's easy for the uninitiated to pooh-pooh the concept of video IEDs, to write them off as a colossal waste of time and money. In reality, the most precious of those two commodities—time—is precisely what these devices give back. You no longer will be tempted to put life on hold to watch a program that interests you. You can determine your viewing timetable, not the networks. You can view commercials only when it suits you. You can decide which parts to skip, and which parts to view again. You, quite literally, call the shots.

What's Still Missing

As good as the first generation of video IEDs are, they are only the forerunners of better designs to come. Following are some of the features that future versions are likely to include:

- The ability to automatically skip commercials altogether—stitching together uninterrupted (and time-condensed) versions of shows that appear on commercial television
- Lower costs
- Easier and more flexible configuration and setup

Skipping Commercials

Although the current generation of IEDs allows you to fast-forward at extremely high speed, skipping commercials is still a clumsy and tedious process.

In fact, ReplayTV brazenly announced in the fourth quarter of 2001 that it would introduce the capability to automatically bypass commercials in its new 4000 Series video IEDs (see Figure 2.1). As expected, TV networks recoiled in horror and promptly dispatched droves of lawyers to stop ReplayTV in its heretical tracks. In a "damn the torpedoes" approach that harks back to the days when ReplayTV's parent SonicBlue was playing David to the music industry's Goliath over MP3 music rights to its Rio portable player, the company went ahead and shipped the product anyway. It remains to be seen where the chips will ultimately fall.

FIGURE 2.1
ReplayTV is the first video IED to offer a device that allows you to skip commercials entirely when watching recorded material.

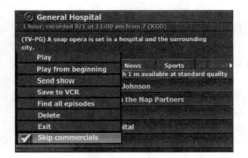

The reasons for craving this capability to banish TV commercials altogether should be obvious, but some might argue that it's only a slight improvement over pressing the 30-second skip button multiple times to effectively accomplish the same thing without incurring the wrath of mighty network executives. What about when you're watching TV while exercising, cooking, or doing any one of a thousand activities that require both hands to be doing something other than wielding a remote control? How about when playing back the recording days, weeks, maybe even years later?

I recently had the experience of sharing the Spielberg classic "ET" with my children for the first time. We carefully dusted off the old videocassette that had been recorded so many years before. The commercials were quaint at first, but the presence of 10-year-old-plus commercials on the tape seemed worse than pointless. They had no benefit or relevance to the advertiser, the network, or to the viewers.

If you still doubt the value of ReplayTV's commercial skip feature, read the rhapsodic words of this happy ReplayTV 4000 owner: "Commercial skip is the killer feature! I don't think I could go back—I love this so much! 30-sec skip is nice too; I like it better than fast forwarding, but commercial skip is like a whole new world in terms of convenience."

➡ **For more information on ReplayTV, see the section in Chapter 3 titled "ReplayTV Rerun," page 49.**

Cost Issues

Forcing users to pay monthly fees simply to avoid crippling the functionality of their equipment seems contrived and somewhat unfair. It's no coincidence that many have sought ways to circumvent those controls and regain full use of the devices they purchased without connecting to the obligatory programming service. The hardware must also come down in cost to see wider adoption. Price erosion has been glacially slow to date.

Simplified Operation

With the exception of UltimateTV, all the current video IED offerings tout the ability to learn the user's tastes and act as a surrogate, selectively recording shows likely to be of interest. However, the rate of success with the current crop of devices is often spotty at best. In practice, this capability can range from amusing to downright insulting. What if your TiVo, for example, instantly develops a penchant for horror films, a taste that no one in your home shares? Searching for programs on the TiVo, ReplayTV, or UltimateTV is also laboriously slow, and not particularly intuitive. Search terms apply only to the title, cast, programming guide description, or genre of a show.

Beyond that, with all the world-class brainpower being devoted to what goes on inside these marvels of modern technology, can't someone help hook them up? Adding a few more inputs and some pass-through capabilities into the IEDs would help. Why not add support for a few more peripheral devices on the remote control (kudos to Panasonic and ReplayTV for having the foresight to add DVD playback controls to the ShowStopper remote). The snarl of cables that results from setting up even a modestly equipped entertainment center (see Figure 2.3) with such typical devices as a video IED, a VCR, and a DVD player—should shame these manufacturers into devising a more elegant solution.

What's Coming Next

Some of these wishlist items are already coming true, although others might never arrive. The good news is that when the next major technological advance occurs, chances are you won't have to consign your current IED to the scrap heap to take advantage of it. Unlike virtually any other consumer appliance shipping today, video IEDs have been designed from the ground up to take full advantage of remote software updates. While the scheme doesn't render obsolescence completely obsolete, it can substantially lengthen a product's useful life.

FIGURE 2.2
This rat's nest of cabling is necessary to connect the author's UltimateTV, iPaq Music Center, VCR, and DVD player to a television set. There must be a better way!

TiVo displayed its confidence in the remote upgrade capabilities of its system by shipping units equipped with hardware features that were inactive at the time of production. As an example, the author's DirecTV/TiVo combo unit featured a second satellite input that was useless for almost a year (see Figure 2.3).

So-called "DirecTivo" units also ship with a mysterious-looking cable that terminates in an infrared transmitter at one end (see Figure 2.4).

Although these hardware devices were so much excess baggage when the units originally shipped, TiVo customers did awake one day to discover that their satellite receivers were suddenly capable of picture-in-picture viewing and simultaneously recording two channels, in addition to providing direct infrared control of their VCRs for archiving digital recordings onto videotape.

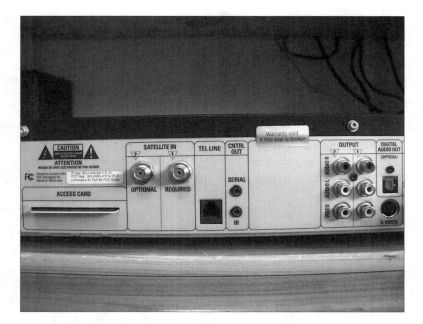

FIGURE 2.3
The second satellite input on the "DirecTivo" combo receiver was finally enabled in a remote software upgrade downloaded by the company in the fall of 2001.

FIGURE 2.4
This odd-looking cable and IR emitter, better known as an IR blaster, came bundled with the DirecTiVo long before the device had learned how to use it to control a VCR.

These are just a few of the short-term enhancements that are in store. What can the video IED platform achieve in the long haul of another 18 months to two years?

- The ability to pinpoint key portions of a video program and construct on-the-fly "highlights reels." (Currently under development at Sharp Electronics, the technology uses pattern recognition to analyze sports video, for example, creating a compilation of scenes that appeared in slow motion during the broadcast, or that were preceded with special graphics by the network.)

- More useful Web surfing capabilities that mirror the PC-based experience to which most people have become accustomed. Broadband connections, support for streaming media, and instant messaging will be among the advancements on tap.

- Larger storage capacity. ReplayTV is currently offering its 4000 series with capacity for up to 320 hours of video recording. Availability of even denser hard drives will continue to boost recording time, while continued price erosion in the disk drive market should make the higher capacity units more affordable as time goes by. (ReplayTV is asking about $2,000 for the 320GB model 4320.)

Sights Set on Set-Tops

The other major technology trend in the video IED's near future will be its continued integration with the set-top box.

EchoStar Communications Corp.'s Dishplayer is the pioneer in this area. Essentially an early version of Microsoft's UltimateTV, DishPlayer combines hard disk recording with WebTV Internet access and a Dish Network satellite receiver. When I unexpectedly encountered one of these devices in the fall of 2000, installed in the unlikely environs of a rustic lakeside cottage in rural Michigan, I was instantly impressed. The successful integration of these high-end features into a relatively small and quite usable home appliance seemed to bode well for the future of video IEDs on the set-top.

TiVo has taken the concept and run with it, offering first its cobranded DirecTV satellite receiver with TiVo functions, and following that up with the announcement of a joint program with AT&T Broadband. (This latter arrangement, however, will not initially combine the

AT&T cable box into the same enclosure with the TiVo.) UltimateTV is available only with DirecTV satellite reception built in.

Cable-box builders Motorola, Scientific Atlanta, and others are busily designing video IED capabilities into their latest generation of set-tops.

Korean electronics giant Samsung might have defined the prototype of this new class of devices. The company fired a shot directly over Microsoft's bow in July 2001 by announcing plans to build a system for cable providers that blends a tuner—featuring IED capabilities licensed from TiVo—with online access and services from AOL Time Warner.

Lean This Way

As its computing capabilities increase exponentially over time, will your IED-powered television eventually replace your PC? It's possible, but the current thinking among video IED designers and market analysts is that the computer in your office or den and the set-top computer in your living room will continue to lead separate lives.

Much talk abounds in the industry about the differences between a "lean forward" and "lean back" experience. PCs will continue to serve "lean forward" needs, which require concentrated interaction with productivity-related software applications—everything from word processing and spreadsheets to desktop publishing. Entertainment, education, and communication will increasingly define "lean back" computing experience, with more of those activities gradually migrating over to video and gaming IEDs.

Getting Hooked (Up) with Intelligent Television

If you talk to most owners of TiVo, ReplayTV, or UltimateTV, you'll learn that these video appliances are not just easy to live with, but the thought of living without them could trigger some serious anxiety.

Of course, this state of bliss can only be achieved when the box is up and running. Unfortunately, that process is not always as smooth as manufacturers intend. The following sections cover just what it takes to get these devices of tomorrow working with the home electronics of today.

Pre-Installation Considerations

First ask yourself this: Do you receive your TV signal via cable, satellite, antenna, or some combination of the three?

This might be a determiner in selecting which IED to purchase. UltimateTV is currently only available for use with DirecTV satellite programming. TiVo comes either with an integrated DirecTV receiver or as a standalone unit that will work with any programming source—antenna, cable or satellite. ReplayTV is only available as a standalone unit, but it is compatible with antenna, cable, or satellite programming sources.

Before your video IED will function, your programming source needs to be installed, activated, and available to the spot where your device will live. For UltimateTV or DirecTiVo, plan to procure two feeds from your satellite dish.

Making a Single Tuner Satisfy the Needs of Multiple TVs

House-top satellite dishes come equipped for one or two lines of video output. One line is required for each tuner in your house.

If you plan to install a dual-tuner device, such as UltimateTV, or a second tuner (for more exotic applications, such as watching a different show in a different room), you'll need a dual-LNB dish.

What if you want a dual-tuner device in your living room, say for watching picture-in-picture or recording one live TV channel while watching another, *and* you want to connect a separate single- or dual-tuner receiver in the bedroom? Because, in this case, you have exceeded your dual-LNB dish's capacity, you'll need to buy yourself a device called a multiswitch (see Figure 2.5).

A multiswitch is essentially a line amplifier, boosting the signal inputs that are received from the satellite LNBs to deliver adequate signal strength to multiple satellite receivers. Each TV in the home still needs its own decoder box to decipher the signal and render it to the TV set, but with a multiswitch, you do not need to have an additional LNB for each set-top box or video IED. Multiswitches generally come in four- or eight-output configurations, and often accommodate antenna or cable inputs as well, allowing you to run both satellite and antenna/CATV input signals over the same coaxial cables. Figure 2.6

NOTE

LNB stands for "Low Noise Block." This is the device in your satellite receiver that amplifies the incredibly weak signal that is being received from the geostationary satellite and turns it into something robust enough for your receiver to decode into TV programming. Incredibly, it accomplishes this without adding a great deal of "noise," or interference, hence the name.

illustrates a typical multiswitch installation for sharing the output of a single satellite dish among multiple satellite receivers.

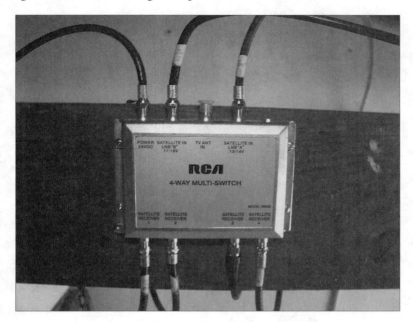

FIGURE 2.5
A typical multiswitch available from RadioShack.

Hooking up a multiswitch is a simple matter of connecting your dish's two output lines to it and adding a 120-volt power source. Voilà, you now have four lines of video output. Professional installation of a multiswitch can run you up to $300 or more. Self installation is not difficult, and it should save you about half this cost (although installation can be tedious if it involves running lots of cable in, around, and under your house).

One low-cost alternative to a multiswitch—or a cheap way to exceed the capacity of your multiswitch, if you've got more TVs than the CNN newscenter—is to split the signal from one of your satellite tuners. This allows you to run a cable to an additional TV that acts as a "slave" unit (that is, both TVs will necessarily be tuned to the same channel at all times). Adding an inexpensive RF remote control transmitter allows you to change channels on the tuner, even from the other end of the house.

FIGURE 2.6
A common layout for distributing satellite signals via multiswitch to multiple DSS receivers.

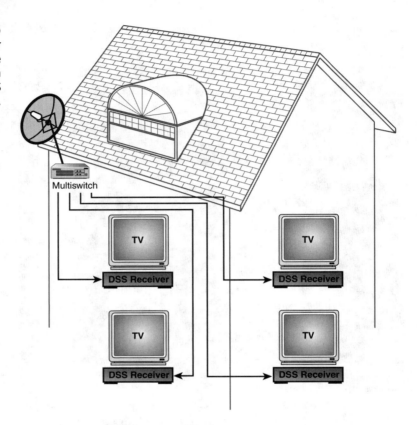

Multiswitch

TV

DSS Receiver

TV

DSS Receiver

TV

DSS Receiver

TV

DSS Receiver

Additional Installation Considerations

Along with a programming source, your video IED requires access to an electrical outlet and a phone jack. The latter is used primarily to download programming information, software updates, and other periodic check-ins with the host service, and for ordering pay-per-view movies and events.

TIP

You don't have a phone jack at your TV location? Consider using your electrical outlet. A "wireless" phone jack extender can be purchased for $30 to $50 that will allow you to run telephone reception through your electrical wiring. The device consists of a pair of units that plug into an electrical socket. One must be connected to a phone jack somewhere in your house. It communicates to the other unit, which plugs into the electrical outlet near your video IED and satellite or cable receiver.

After you have decided where to locate your device and ensured the availability of its life support—programming source, phone access, and electricity—you're finally ready to connect.

Cables: Which Wire Should You Use?

At this stage, the next question to ask yourself is, "S-video, composite or coax?" Listed in order of desirability, each term refers to a different type of wire you can use to connect your video system components (see Figure 2.7).

Coaxial   Composite Video   S-Video

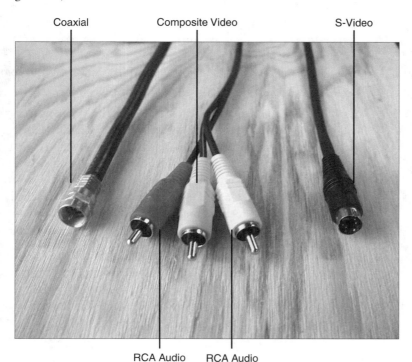

RCA Audio   RCA Audio

FIGURE 2.7
The main types of video connections. Note that coaxial cable carries both audio and video signals, whereas composite and S-video must be paired with RCA (or optical digital) audio cables.

S-video moves the video signals from your video IED to your television in a digital format, offering the best picture quality. The S-video cable is generally a slim black cord terminated at each end with a connector containing several pins that line up with a female input jack on your TV and your VCR. Audio signals must be routed separately using RCA-type analog or optical digital audio cabling.

The next step down from S-video quality is composite video. Designed for audio- and videophiles from the analog world, composite cables are generally bundled into three color-coded strands:

- Red for the right audio channel
- White for the left channel audio
- Yellow for video

These wires come with RCA-type male connectors at either end.

An additional type of video signal, called *component*, is available in some high-end equipment, but might be seen more frequently in coming years as the price of high definition television begins to drop. Whereas composite video blends color and black-and-white display information into a single analog stream, component video breaks out the colors into separate signals, achieving a higher display quality.

S-video is a type of component video, separating the color, or "C" signal, from the black-and-white signal, called "Y." This Y/C arrangement provides better resolution than composite video, but it is still inferior to the three-strand "RGB" component video, which separates the spectrum into red, green, and blue signals. When operating in the quality stratosphere of component RBG video, cables generally terminate with RCA connectors, but a single VGA-type connector or professional-quality BNC-format connectors are also used sometimes.

When component, S-video, or composite connections are not an option, the default choice is basic "coax." Coaxial cables are the same standard black wires through which video programming is usually delivered from the source—cable provider or satellite dish—to your decoder box.

The first step in deciding which type of connection to use is to inspect your TV—and VCR or DVD, if you plan to use one—and find out what your choices are. S-video support tends to be available only on newer, high-end video electronics. As you might assume, it offers the highest video quality. Likewise, composite connectors only started showing up in lower-end TVs in the past few years. Prior to that, they were seen usually only in more expensive "prosumer" models. Composite video offers the middle-of-the-road choice in quality: Less than S-video, but better than coax. Coaxial cables are the default choice. This chunky black workhorse of the wiring world has become synonymous with the rise of cable television and the demise of rabbit ears.

Will you actually be able to see a marked difference in your TV picture quality as a result of which type of cable you choose? Quite possibly. If you're starting from scratch and money is no object, by all means use component video and optical SPDIF audio cabling to the greatest extent possible. Bear in mind, however, that picture quality can depend on a number of factors, including the proximity of other sources of electrical interference around your video equipment. Whatever type of wiring you use in the end, just be sure that all your connections are tight and secure.

Putting It All Together

Now that you have decided on your wiring media, one last challenge remains before turning on your video IED: making the actual connections between the different elements of your entertainment system. As simple as this plugging-in process should be, manufacturers' instructions can still leave you scratching your head. Questions arise, such as, "Does the coax from the dish plug into the receiver, then the ReplayTV, then the television?" and "Where does the VCR go again?" Of course, if you're adding a "home theater" audio system or a video game console, or you want to send one of those 100-plus digital audio channels over to your stereo system, that can open yet another can of worms.

In general, the combination tuner/IED units, such as the DirecTV-equipped TiVo and UltimateTV units, present fewer wiring permutations, thus presenting less of a challenge to connect. The standalone ReplayTV ShowStopper, for instance, offers nine diagrams in the setup manual depicting various connection schemes. However, the prize goes to the ReplayTV ShowStopper TV/Hard Disk Recorder Combination (Model No. PV-SS2710), which combines a 17-inch Panasonic television with an integrated 30-hour ShowStopper IED. Although the combo system should actually be easier to install than the standalone unit—at least there's no need to make additional connections from the IED to the TV—the manual contains 13 separate wiring illustrations. They range from the simplest configuration ("Without a Cable Box") to the most complex ("With a Cable Box, DSS Receiver, A/V Receiver, and VCR").

ReplayTV recognizes the setup issues with its products and has taken the added step of creating an impressive online tutorial using Macromedia Flash animation to illustrate the myriad wiring choices. Using this tutorial, consumers answer questions about their equipment and programming source to arrive at the appropriate configuration diagram and step-by-step connection instructions for their system (see Figure 2.8). You can find the ReplayTV HookUp Buddy by pointing your Web browser to http://www.replaytv.com/contact/hookup.htm.

FIGURE 2.8
ReplayTV's Hookup Buddy interactive online application can simplify the often-grueling job of connecting your new ReplayTV.

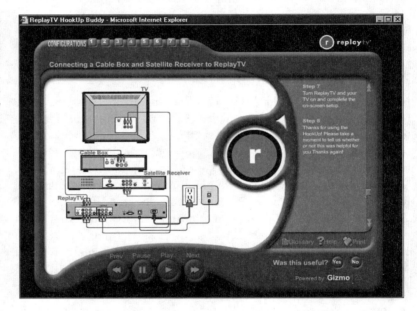

In the end, the answers to your setup issues might involve a combination of following the manufacturer's suggested wiring diagram, using your common sense, and putting in a call or two to the toll-free support line.

The accompanying diagrams show the most common ways of connecting a typical video entertainment system (see Figure 2.9).

➔ For a detailed discussion of advanced setup techniques, check out Chapter 10, "Customizing Your Digital Entertainment Experience," which features a section on "How Does It All Fit Together?" beginning on page 239.

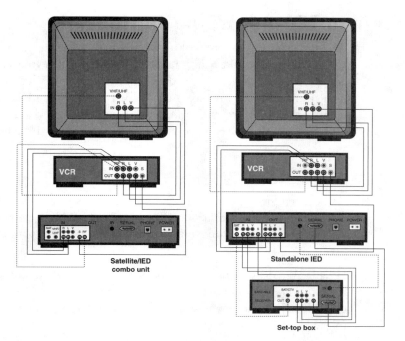

FIGURE 2.9
Setting up your new video IED can get pretty complex in a hurry.

KEEP IT SIMPLE!

Murphy's Law says that if something can go wrong, then it probably will. This becomes especially true when you're hooking up multiple entertainment devices. Perhaps you have hooked up everything exactly as it's supposed to be, but when you expectantly turn on the TV, you're crushed to find only a black or snow-swept screen. Now what?

When in doubt, simplify.

Reverse your steps and calmly (if at all possible) start from scratch. The tried-and-true approach is to build the simplest possible configuration—just connect your satellite or cable "feed" to the receiver box and the TV—confirming that each part is working properly before adding a new variable. Each time another variable is added—the IED, VCR, game box, and so on—stop and check whether the system works before moving to the next step in complexity.

Proceed until you lose the TV signal, and you're again confronted by the Black Screen of Death. At that point, you will have isolated the problem, and you can begin taking corrective measures such as checking connectors for bent pins or loose fittings, substituting cables, and double-checking power sources.

Video IED Recording Options

To appreciate the differences between a true video IED and a simple VCR, you need to take a look at the key benefits this revolutionary new genre of devices offers. The primary ingredients in this visual feast being served up by the likes of TiVo, ReplayTV, and UltimateTV include the ability to shift time and manipulate television programming in ways that have never before been available to the average consumer.

Timeshifting TV

It's been said that the most precious commodity of all—far surpassing gold, diamonds, and other tangible forms of earthly wealth—is time. People are allotted a finite amount, and when they've spent it, it's history.

What value do you place on a device that can actually allow you to recoup time? It is undoubtedly one of the most important features of the video IED genre, and probably the one that has most endeared it to the hearts of consumers.

Consider this: If you took three hours of prime time television programming and carefully pruned away the advertising and promotional "filler" material, you could watch it in about two hours. Multiply that time savings by a year, and you will have reclaimed more than two weeks of your life! Although your results might vary, this is a clear depiction of the value of timeshifting.

Timeshifting is a simple concept that only sounds complex. Because no one has invented a device that can make time run backward, time—for this discussion, television programming that is fed live by a network at a specific time—can only be shifted forward. In other words, *timeshifting* simply means delaying a live program.

Why is that so special? In a sense, it isn't. You can delay programming just as easily with a VCR, recording a live show and playing it back later at your convenience. You can even use that video playback to zap out commercials and promos, realizing the same time savings described earlier. The big difference comes from adding a hard disk drive to the picture. Unlike a VCR, a hard drive-based video IED can record and play back at the same time. This changes *everything*.

Consider the prime time TV example. If the objective is to watch the three hours' worth of shows broadcast from 8 p.m. to 11 p.m. in only two hours, a hard-drive-equipped video IED would allow you to start watching at 9 p.m. and finish at 11 p.m. With a VCR, you could not begin watching until the shows had stopped taping at 11 p.m. You could still finish watching in two hours, but you might not feel as jubilant about your time dividend when you finally hit the lights at 1 a.m.

Random Access

It might not be the most heralded feature of the new video IEDs, but their ability to access any part of a recorded program instantaneously should not be underestimated. In the same way that watching DVDs instead of VHS frees you from having to rewind a tape, watching a recorded program becomes a fundamentally different experience when you can freely skip to and fro, from beginning to end in an instant. This capability, of course, is another bit of magic afforded by storing the content on a disk instead of a linear tape medium. Whether it's the optical disk of a DVD being read by a laser eye, or the magnetic disk inside the hermetically sealed vacuum of a hard drive, no point on that disk is appreciably harder to access than any other. All points of the video are equally within reach and available to you at almost the speed of thought.

Send your VHS tape rewinder to the Smithsonian because it's soon to be just another anachronistic device at which your children will marvel, like a hand-cranked clothes wringer or—gulp—a record player.

Pausing, Zapping, and Deleting

The other form of timeshifting that draws raves from video IED owners is the ability to "pause" live TV. Although the feature appears to work just like the pause feature on a VCR, the actual mechanics are much different. A VCR simply freezes in place—the motors that drive the tape forward and across the playback heads take a breather—while you run off to fix a sandwich, answer the phone, and so on. However, when you hit the pause feature on a video IED remote control, you are actually isolating the video frame that is sent to your television, while your IED continues to race ahead, recording the program to your hard drive and filling up a video *buffer*. When you resume watching, you're seeing video received by your machine minutes before. You can fast-forward through that buffer at any time, zipping past a commercial or

33

two, up to the point where you rejoin the live broadcast feed occurring in real time. Most IED devices include a button that can automatically advance past buffered material to the current live video feed.

Advancing past commercials, or *zapping*, also benefits from your device's hard drive technology. Unlike videotape, where video data is stored sequentially on the linear medium of tape, your IED is spraying the data on a magnetic disk that is spinning at thousands of RPM. This makes it theoretically capable of retrieving any of those bits instantly (in this case, being a second or two). As discussed earlier, this random access capability lets you skip effortlessly and instantaneously from the beginning to the end of a show or any point in between. The only limiting factor is the manufacturer's ability to make these features accessible in a way you can easily understand and control. Ironically, the best method that designers have come up with is to slow the process down and make it less precise in order to mimic videotape, thus providing the illusion of old-fashioned fast-forwarding and rewinding in a linear medium.

Although video IED designers have sacrificed pinpoint accuracy and split-second speed in favor of a more comfortable VCR-like experience, navigating around your programming is still much faster and more satisfying than with videotape. Most of the devices offer a "skip-ahead" feature that jumps forward in 30-second increments, letting viewers zap a stream of commercials with a few flicks of the thumb. Likewise, most of the remote controls offer a quick replay version that instantly backs up and replays the last few minutes of a program. Another button launches into slow motion, rewarding sports fans with the ability to watch the action unfold without missing a move—each frame rendered in perfect digital quality. (That is, of course, if you have your IED set for the highest quality. If you want to get more recording time out of your IED, your mileage—and quality—might vary.)

The ability to instantly delete programs is another specialty of the IED's computer heritage. For a program stored on videotape to become inaccessible, it must be recorded over, or magnetically scrambled (such as by using a professional bulk eraser). On hard disk, the mechanics of erasure are more or less the same—magnetic particles need to be rearranged into new patterns that store different data—or no data at all. However, the user experience is quite different. Although programs recorded on the disk might physically remain there even after a user has "deleted" them, the user has essentially given the device permission to forget where it put something, and to record over it as necessary to carry out future requests. The user experience is much more satisfying: Press the delete button, confirm that you really want the program to go away, and it simply vanishes from the menu of recorded material. It might still be on the hard disk, at least for the time being, but you will never see it again.

Playback and Recording Strategies

This chapter has discussed how the physics of IED recording differ from VCR recording and the benefits that can result. Now consider the impact of the video IED's vastly superior logic on the recording process.

Although a VCR can be programmed to record a particular sequence of video—generally a given channel during a specified period of time—the logic this involves is extremely rudimentary. If your purpose is to record the 8:00 movie, and the movie is postponed 45 minutes because of a baseball game that went into extra innings, will your VCR be able to cope with the change? Chances are, the answer is no. In fact, given the complexity of most VCR timers, if you were successful in programming it correctly for the period of time that the movie *should* have aired, you are to be congratulated.

Given the same set of circumstances, an IED could have prevailed in this scenario. A typical VCR relies on a simple electronic timer to record a particular channel for a set period at a particular time and date. If that sequence coincides with the program you want to watch, lucky you. In contrast, a video IED uses its internal computer to monitor programming information that the networks provide. In many cases, this allows the IED to roll with the programming punches that networks so often throw.

This feature comes in particularly handy in setting up recurring recording events. With features such as TiVo's "Season Pass," consumers can choose to record a particular program every time it airs. Not only will your IED bank a copy of each regularly scheduled episode of *Friends* for you every Thursday, for instance, it will also grab that two-hour weekend special, and possibly even the show that aired a half-hour late following the president's State of the Union Address.

Likewise, your IED's ability to peer into and pour over the *metadata*—essentially databases full of information describing various attributes of individual programs—that the networks provide allows it to search and identify shows to record for you. These personalization features work somewhat differently with each brand of video IED, but the basic premise is the same: By specifying your preferences for a particular actor, title, or entertainment genre, your device will automatically search for similar programs to record for you. Although it's still possible for your IED to misunderstand your tastes and run amuck (see "Simplified Operation" in the "What's Still Missing" section of this chapter), there is a lot of promise in these predictive recording capabilities for truly transforming your TV viewing experience.

Internet Access and Interactivity

As the 20th century turned, it seemed as if the Internet were cropping up everywhere, like some kind of electronic kudzu. Refrigerators and washing machines were not immune to Internet enablement. Web visionaries naturally settled on the home's center of attention—the television set—as the nexus of the much-hyped "wired lifestyle."

As is often the case, Microsoft was ahead of the curve. The company scoped out a fledgling operation that had been working on technology to effectively view Web pages on a standard television screen. In 1997, Microsoft acquired WebTV Networks Inc. for $425 million.

Despite Microsoft's best efforts to grow the WebTV service, it languished. People who wanted to enjoy a full, rich online experience found the TV-based surfing experience too limiting. Generally, plug-ins were not supported, so you could forget about streaming audio or video, using instant messaging, or experiencing Macromedia Flash or JavaScript-enabled content, for instance. Likewise, your ability to view full Web pages as the designer had published them was often impaired, "dumbed down" and truncated to fit in the confines of the television screen. TV resolution also, in general, pales in comparison to that of a computer monitor (in Chapter 4, see the section titled "Displays," page 101).

The real target audience for these devices—people who didn't have PCs—were only mildly interested in having Web pages and e-mail functions interrupt their TV viewing. They found the service too complex and expensive.

Microsoft went back to the drawing board and emerged with a new blueprint for conquering the living room. It kept the TV browser alive, but moved it to the bottom of the feature list. UltimateTV was born.

The first iteration of the UtimateTV design—combining a satellite receiver, video IED, and browser—quietly debuted as the EchoStar Communications Dishplayer set-top box. (For a discussion, see the "What's Coming Next" section of this chapter).

Although Microsoft continues to try to lure TV viewers onto the Web by building out the integration between television and Internet programming, it has yet to hit on a truly compelling model. Yes, a certain portion of the population will want to use the TV for communications through e-mail and instant messaging. And yes, another group will crave interaction with the shows and will be willing to suspend their passive viewing of the program to engage in online games and polls and to browse program-related trivia. For the time being, however, the TV browsing experience is still hampered by slowness (a 56K dial-up modem connection), a clunky interface, and an absence of any really gripping applications.

Microsoft and others (can you say "AOL Time Warner?") are working on solving these issues. Broadband support will be one of the next features to roll out on the UltimateTV, allowing subscribers to trade in their dial-up connections for DSL data lines. (Cable modem support would be mostly superfluous because UltimateTV households rely on satellite as their primary source for TV programming, but don't rule it out for "private-label" set-top versions that Microsoft provides to cable operators.) Although still hampered by the lower resolution of standard TV screens and the need to "dumb down" Web content so that it can be accessed with a remote control, the clunkiness is being addressed and more elegant integration of Web and TV content is occurring. Great minds are certainly at work cooking up new applications to convert society from "lean back" TV viewers to "lean forward" Web surfers, although you would probably do best to take a wait and watch approach.

Meanwhile, the ability to access the Internet via the television remains a feature that looks good on the features list. It helps (at least for the time being) differentiate Microsoft's video IED offering from ReplayTV's and TiVo's. Although a certain percentage of UltimateTV buyers will in fact make use of the service, relatively few will find it habit-forming.

For further information on how to connect and customize your TV-based online experience, see Chapter 3, "Video IEDs: More Than Just Appliances."

Flies in the Soup: Known Bugs and Glitches

Another example of why video IEDs have yet to endear themselves to the majority of TV watchers is that, in many ways, the devices are simply not ready for prime time.

In the world of home appliances, they generally work or they don't. TVs aren't expected to have software bugs. Unlike the desktop PC world, such erratic behavior is not tolerated. When your TV screen flashes its equivalent of the Microsoft Windows "Blue Screen of Death," you don't generally roll up your sleeves and start trying to debug it. You box it up and send it packing back to the company that made it.

Household appliances are simply held to a different standard—a more exacting one—than technology products, and that's been a tough lesson for Microsoft and its Silicon Valley competitors in the video IED arena to learn.

The best-documented bug to afflict UltimateTV users so far has been related to storage (as covered in the Software portion of the "UltimateTV," section of Chapter 3 page 80). Under certain conditions, users in the Spring of 2001 found their hours of program storage capacity inexplicably dwindling away. At almost the same time, TiVo users were confronted by another set of problems. Many found their IEDs spontaneously rebooting at frequent intervals, and even stranger, names of stars such as Madonna and Cher were mysteriously cropping up in users' "Wish List" searches.

In both cases, the manufacturers fixed the problems by issuing software updates that the devices quietly downloaded and installed while making their routine calls for up-to-date TV program lineups. These quickly issued fixes were another demonstration of the impressive self-healing qualities of the video IED's remote upgrade capabilities. (For a discussion, see the "What's Coming Next" section earlier in this chapter.)

TIP

One of the best places to search for—and stay up-to-date on—technical issues concerning video IEDs is the AV Science Ultimate Forum Web site at www.avsforum.com. You will find message forums for UltimateTV, ReplayTV/ShowStopper, and TiVo, some moderated by the manufacturers themselves.

Of course, software can't handle everything. Complaints among TiVo users of video "stuttering," freeze-ups, and eventual system crashes in mid-May of 2001 prompted the company to address, on a case-by-case basis, what was later diagnosed as a spate of hard drive failures.

Chapter 3

Video IEDs: More Than Just Appliances

Choosing the Right Video IED for You

You've decided to take the plunge into intelligent TV entertainment. Now you face the real dilemma: Which video IED do you buy? It's a much different proposition from choosing a VCR, television, or most other home appliances for these reasons:

- With conventional appliances, versions have been around for decades, and dozens of brands and models are available from which to choose. Choice is often based on a combination of price, features, and brand name. In contrast, video IEDs are essentially first-generation devices. There are few models to choose from, relatively little differentiation in terms of features or price, and the brand names are mostly unfamiliar. Even Microsoft, a mighty name in the software business, currently has no brand equity to speak of in the consumer electronics field.

- In the case of video IEDs, consumers are as much choosing a service as they are a product. After a few short years, the monthly subscription fees will have eclipsed the cost of the hardware. (TiVo, which offers a "lifetime" subscription for $249, is the exception.) Like locking into a long-term contract with a mobile phone provider, you must weigh not only the attributes of the physical device, but your confidence that the company offers the best service for your needs, with adequate staying power for the long haul.

- Whom do you trust? Another consideration in choosing an IED is the level of comfort you have with the service provider's ability to protect your privacy. The dark side of the video IED's personalization features is the voluminous dossier that the company will be quietly compiling on your TV-related tastes and activities. Consumer groups are gradually raising the level of alarm over these companies' practice of recording your every move, and they're asking for accountability as to how that data is used, stored, and perhaps sold to other companies that want to market products to you based on your viewing habits. The trade-off here is that collecting this information can—at least theoretically—allow IED service providers to tailor programming to your individual taste. However, the user has to decide whether he trusts the company to keep his private data secure from prying eyes, while using it only in responsible and nonintrusive ways.

- Unlike a toaster or waffle iron, a video IED is a "lifestyle device." A device qualifies for lifestyle status when it creates a significant impact on your daily routine. A generation ago, washing machines were a lifestyle device, freeing millions of women from hours of tedious manual labor. Today, people buy new washing machines simply as replacements for older washing machines, so the net impact on lifestyle is nil. Mobile phones, on the other hand, still have that lifestyle-changing impact, providing the ability to transact business and social obligations from anywhere and at any time.

  The other qualifier for a device to achieve lifestyle status is its cost. A toaster can be had for about $15, representing a marginal opportunity cost because few other things of consequence are available for $15. A video IED, however, represents a significant spending opportunity. By spending money on the new device, you are effectively limiting your freedom in other areas, thus impacting your lifestyle. Lifestyle choices generally are not made lightly—they often require research and a good deal of sober reflection.

Now that you fully realize what you're getting into, how do you choose between ReplayTV, UltimateTV, and TiVo? The following sections look closely at each device so that you can see how they stack up. If none of these devices seem to exactly suit your needs, perhaps you're a candidate for one of the video IED alternatives that will be discussed in Chapter 4, "Playing the Field: Other Video IED Convergence Devices."

ReplayTV

Founded within a month of its rival, TiVo Inc., in the fall of 1997, ReplayTV Inc. considers itself the granddaddy of the video IED business.

After blowing through its seed money, ReplayTV announced its departure from the hardware side of the business in November 2000, ceding sales of the ReplayTV-based ShowStopper product to the consumer arm of Japanese electronics giant Matsushita. Later, SonicBlue, which had already acquired the Rio division of Diamond Multimedia and was aggregating technologies in the IED space, snatched up ReplayTV. For additional details, see Table 3.1.

Table 3.1 – ReplayTV Vital Statistics

Status	Wholly owned subsidiary
Parent company	SonicBlue Inc. (SBLU) 2000 revenues: $536.7M
Business model	Developer of personalized television software and services
Founded	September 1997
CEO, Founder	Anthony Wood
Backers, Past and Present	Paul Allen (Vulcan Ventures), Marc Andreesen (Netscape, Loudcloud), William R. Hearst III (Kleiner Perkins Caufield & Byers), Time Warner, The Walt Disney Co., NBC, Liberty Media Group, Showtime Networks, Intel
Headquarters	Mountain View, California

SonicBlue suffered along with the rest of the tech business sector in 2001, laying off some 600 of its 800-plus employees.

The company surprised many observers—and even some of its partners—in the early fall of 2001 by announcing its return to manufacturing video IEDs (see "ReplayTV Rerun," page 49).

Hardware

The existing ReplayTV/Panasonic ShowStopper product line offers two styles: with TV or without. All models are designed to work with any combination of antenna, cable, and satellite programming sources.

Table 3.2 – The Panasonic ShowStopper Product Family

Model	Hours of Storage	List Price*	Description
PV-HS1000	20	$499.95	ShowStopper Hard Disk Recorder with ReplayTV

Table 3.2 – Continued

Model	Hours of Storage	List Price*	Description
PV-HS2000	30	$699.95	ShowStopper Hard Disk Recorder with ReplayTV
PV-HS3000	60	$799.95	ShowStopper Hard Disk Recorder with ReplayTV
PV-SS2710	30	$799.95	Panasonic PanaBlack TV/ShowStopper Hard Disk Recorder Combination

Current as of December 2001

The standalone ReplayTV models (see Figure 3.1) are basically the same units, differing only in terms of their hard drive storage capacity.

The front panel of the ReplayTV ShowStopper, built by Panasonic, has relatively few functional elements. This is a device for which you had better not lose the remote control; without it, your only operational options will be to turn the machine on or off. In addition to the power button, the unit features status indicators to show whether the device is running or is in standby mode, whether new content is available to watch, and whether a recording session is in progress

The back panel is where the device gets down to business. Inputs are provided for an infrared emitter (the "IR Blaster"), a serial connection to a cable or satellite receiver, an RJ-11 telephone jack, and an A/C power cord. In addition, places are available to plug in an F-type coaxial cable or antenna connector, and two audiovisual inputs (consisting of right- and left-channel RCA-type audio inputs and a composite video or S-video input). Two similar A/V outputs are provided as well.

Inside the ShowStopper is where things become interesting (see Figure 3.2). The unit's hard drive could include a range of available hard disks, depending on the model. The author's, for example, shipped with a Quantum FireBall LCT 10 3.5-inch drive.

FIGURE 3.1
Front and rear views
of the ShowStopper
standalone ReplayTV
from SonicBlue, built
by Panasonic.

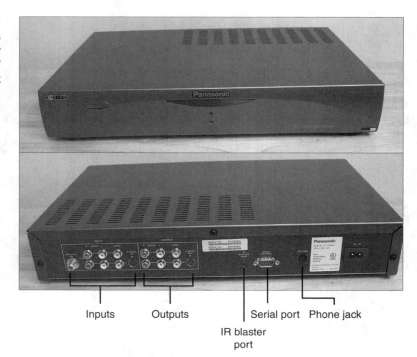

Inputs   Outputs   Serial port   Phone jack

IR blaster
port

For its CPU, the ReplayTV makes use of a Philips SAA7214 chip, which contains a 32-bit MIPS PR3001 RISC CPU core, as well as all the hardware and software that are required to receive and decode MPEG2 transport streams, including descrambling and demultiplexing. The board also contains a Philips SAA7201 chip, an MPEG-2 decoder that combines audio and video decoding, as well as support for enhanced graphics and onscreen displays.

Additional audio handling is provided by a TV sound-processing IC, the Micronas 3430G chip, which is designed for processing multi-channel television sound (MTS) signals conforming to the BTSC (Broadcast Television Systems Committee) standard.

MPEG-2 encoding is performed with a Sony CXD1922. Along with its power-saving features, the Sony chip boasts an advanced "adaptive motion estimation algorithm." Developed by Sony, the software algorithm is supposed to handle the recording and transmission of fast-moving images while allowing minimal image degradation and offering more efficient video compression.

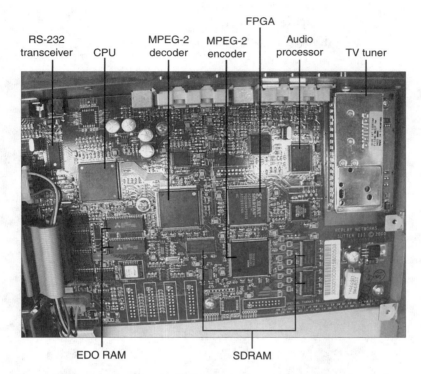

FPGA

RS-232 transceiver   CPU   MPEG-2 decoder   MPEG-2 encoder   Audio processor   TV tuner

EDO RAM   SDRAM

FIGURE 3.2
A close-up of the interior of a ReplayTV ShowStopper stand-alone unit.

The ability to upgrade the ReplayTV's software remotely after the consumer purchases it relies in large part on a field programmable gate array (FPGA), the Xilinx Spartan-II XC2S40.

Memory needs are addressed in a variety of ways from multiple 60-nanosecond 16Mb extended data out (EDO) DRAM chips to Hyundai PC100 SDRAM chips.

Other notable components include the Philips 3139 Series TV tuner and a Sipex SP208CT high-speed RS-232 transceiver chip.

TIP

The ReplayTV circuit board bears the name of the IED's proprietary operating system, Sutter, and to give credit where credit is due, the board has etched into its margin the words *Special thanks to* followed by a few dozen sets of initials.

The "Hidden" Menu

Want to tweak your ReplayTV hardware? Here's a shortcut to a hidden systems menu:

1. Turn on the ReplayTV and tune to a live show.

2. While watching live TV, press 243.

3. Before the channel changes, press Replay Zone.

A systems menu appears, allowing you to toggle on and off an onscreen clock or CPU utilization meter (see Figure 3.3).

FIGURE 3.3
This secret systems menu gives you access to various lesser-known features and information about your ReplayTV device.

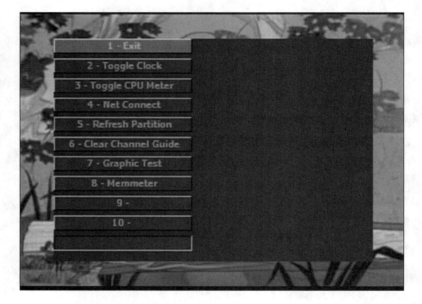

Some of the information items contained in the hidden system menu, such as CPU utilization, are clearly geared more toward the engineers who created the machine than the consumers who buy them. However, some potential goodies for users are included as well.

Live buffering—tucking away video into system memory so that ReplayTV can accommodate your next request to rewind or deliver an instant replay—is a process that constantly takes place while ReplayTV is operating. Some users feel that the process causes high CPU utilization, occasionally making the machine unresponsive to remote control key presses. If your system starts responding sluggishly, you might want to check your CPU utilization.

TIP

One of the few ways to temporarily suspend live buffering is to press Stop while watching a recorded show. This leaves the unit in an "untuned" state, and puts live buffering on hold.

You can also force a service connection, partition the hard drive, or clear channel guide information.

Another feature of the hidden systems screen is a text input area that appears at the bottom of the display, known as *the Claw Foot Portal*, or *CFP field*. Highlight the area and press Select to be presented with a keyboard. The following codes can be entered into the field:

- Enable Disk Spindown to toggle disk spindown when the power is turned off.
- Disable Disk Spindown to turn off Enable Disk Spindown.
- Julie to display the message *Spencer loves Julie*.
- Modesto Girl to turn the red dots in the program guide into hearts. Enter the code again to change them back. (The hearts appear automatically on Valentine's Day.)
- Sportsguard On to enable a global time-padding feature that extends all sports recordings. (Entering Sportsguard Off disables this feature.)
- Tic Tac Toe to display a tic-tac-toe game accessed by pressing 111 and then Replay Zone.

ReplayTV Rerun

Late in the third quarter of 2001, ReplayTV announced that it planned to take another run at the manufacturing side of the hardware business.

Almost one year after the company relinquished making video IED boxes, enlisting Panasonic as its manufacturing partner, the company revealed plans to introduce a high-end series called the ReplayTV 4000. The four-model family will feature a variety of enhanced software features, and substantially increased hard-drive recording capabilities.

The new models are summarized in Table 3.3.

Table 3.3 – The ReplayTV 4000 Family		
Model	**Recording Time**	**List Price***
ReplayTV 4040	40 hours	$699
ReplayTV 4080	80 hours	$999
ReplayTV 4160	160 hours	$1,499
ReplayTV 4320	320 hours	$1,999

**Current as of December 2001

In addition to higher recording times—and correspondingly higher prices—the new models contain numerous added software features, including these:

- AutoSkip: The ability to set the device to automatically omit television commercials as it records shows. This capability, along with video sharing noted in the third bullet, prompted an immediate lawsuit from the movie studios and television networks. As of the time this book went to press, the content creators had failed to stop SonicBlue's rollout plans for the new 4000 series IEDs.

- Room-to-room video sharing: A new Ethernet port will allow users with two ReplayTV 4000 systems to watch recorded programs stored on either unit.

- Video sharing over the Internet: In a move that is sure to raise the ire of programmers, users will be able to transmit recorded shows via the Internet, for playback by other ReplayTV 4000 owners.

- Digital photo slideshows: Supports the ability to copy digital photos from your PC to your ReplayTV 4000 and display them on your TV screen in a slideshow format.

- Screensaver: Taking a cue from competitor UltimateTV, ReplayTV will add a screen saver to avoid TV screen burn-in. Users will also be able to create custom screensavers with their own digital photos.

- Progressive output: 480P progressive output will be added to support high-definition–ready televisions (HDTV). The company says its progressive scanning benefits include improved color purity and detail, as well as reduced color noise and artifacts related to standard National Television Standards Committee (NTSC) displays.

Additional new features will include support for broadband Internet connections, a "show organizer" feature to sort custom channels into categories, a digital audio output port, new front panel control buttons, and a backlit remote control.

Software Highlights

Like the other video IEDs, ReplayTV requires a software operating system to make all of its hardware function properly and give you control over it. In the case of ReplayTV, this operating system is called Sutter. Although ReplayTV does not publicly discuss details of Sutter, amateur forensics experts who have dissected the product say it uses XML extensively, and might be based on VxWorks, the embedded real-time operating system that was developed by Wind River Systems. (ReplayTV has publicly acknowledged that the new 4000 Series is based on VxWorks).

Others speculate that Sutter is based on the Scenix architecture, which is used in the Sony PlayStation. Regardless of its origins, ReplayTV proponents claim the Sutter OS is far more efficient than UltimateTV's OS, based on Microsoft's Windows CE, or Linux, which TiVo uses. Greater OS efficiency allows ReplayTV to reduce processor and memory size.

NOTE

Extensible Markup Language (XML) is a follow-on to the HTML standard for creating Web pages. Whereas HTML relies on a limited number of standardized "tags" or styles to exist within documents, XML is unlimited in this regard, allowing much richer and more versatile construction of Web pages, or in the case of ReplayTV, onscreen displays.

TIP

As ReplayTV makes its nightly phone call to check in with the company, it scans for updates to its operating system. In this fashion, your ReplayTV unit could be running a different software version today than it was yesterday.

If you're interested in checking out which software version your ReplayTV is running, here's a shortcut:

1. Press 411 on your remote control.
2. Press the ReplayTV Zone button.

A diagnostic menu appears, as shown in Figure 3.4.

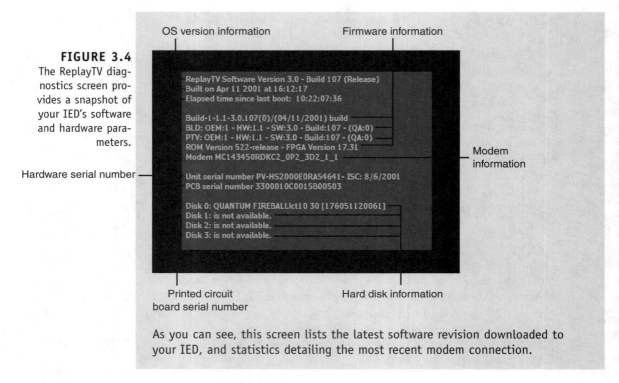

FIGURE 3.4
The ReplayTV diagnostics screen provides a snapshot of your IED's software and hardware parameters.

OS version information   Firmware information

ReplayTV Software Version 3.0 - Build 107 (Release)
Built on Apr 11 2001 at 16:12:17
Elapsed time since last boot: 10:22:07:36

Build-1-1.1-3.0.107(0)/(04/11/2001) build
BLD: OEM:1 - HW:1.1 - SW:3.0 - Build:107 - (QA:0)
PTV: OEM:1 - HW:1.1 - SW:3.0 - Build:107 - (QA:0)
ROM Version 522-release - FPGA Version 17.31
Modem MC143450RDKC2_0P2_3D2_1_1

Modem information

Hardware serial number

Unit serial number PV-HS2000E0RA54641- ISC: 8/6/2001
PCB serial number 3300010C0015B00503

Disk 0: QUANTUM FIREBALLlct10 30 [176051120061]
Disk 1: is not available.
Disk 2: is not available.
Disk 3: is not available.

Printed circuit
board serial number   Hard disk information

As you can see, this screen lists the latest software revision downloaded to your IED, and statistics detailing the most recent modem connection.

The User Interface

A more efficient OS is not ReplayTV's major triumph, however. The company's real strength has been in the area of user interface.

ReplayTV's interface is arguably not as user friendly and intuitive as TiVo's, but the company has succeeded in creating some altogether new ways of watching television that are both innovative and habit forming.

Particularly impressive are ReplayTV's custom channel features, where the search and record functions common to all video IEDs are elegantly harnessed as a tool for creating the equivalent of an on-the-fly cable channel.

Creating Theme Channels

Let your imagination run wild and conjure up your own personal dream channel, suiting your unique tastes. What would it be? The Submarine Channel? The Hurling Channel? Needlepoint? Swimsuit competitions? Or use the title, actor, director or show description search categories to create your custom channel—such as the Sopranos Channel, the Annette Funicello Channel, the Martin Scorsese Channel, the Scrabble Channel. The possibilities are endless, and admittedly, a little frightening.

Following are the steps for creating and accessing your own ReplayTV theme channels.

1. Press Menu on the remote control.

2. Choose Find Shows.

3. Use the arrow and select keys, as shown in Figure 3.5, to spell out a keyword or phrase to use as the search term (*sopranos*, *funicello*, *submarines*, *loch ness monster*, and so on).

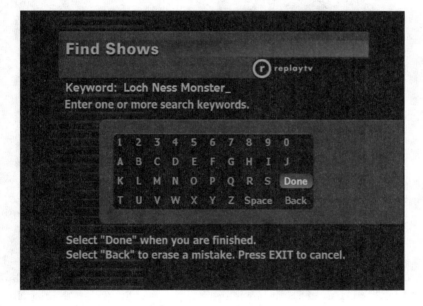

FIGURE 3.5
The hunt-and-peck system for entering search terms will make you wish that ReplayTV supported a wireless keyboard.

When finished, choose Done.

4. Choose the categories, such as actor or director, to be searched. When finished, choose Done.

   ReplayTV immediately begins searching through the next seven days of programming to find matches for your search term. This can take several minutes, but if you're impatient, you can proceed immediately to the next step. (If you choose to move on immediately, you won't get a chance to preview what your search has netted, but it will not affect the outcome and operation of your new custom channel.)

5. Choose Create the *Keyword* Theme Channel from the results that your search has generated (see Figure 3.6.).

FIGURE 3.6
The ReplayTV gives several categories to search, allowing you to narrow the results to just the shows you want.

Although the channel creation features are powerful, they are also powerfully prone to bring back a certain amount of chaff with the wheat. For instance, you might love Robert Deniro, but even a die-hard fan would probably admit that Deniro has appeared in a few stinkers that he (and Deniro) would just as soon forget about. ReplayTV offers no easy way to omit specific instances within the search, such as a movie or program that fits within the search terms but that you simply don't want to record. In addition, it's quite likely you'll end up rerecording many an unwanted movie—say, Deniro's performance in the live-action version of *The Adventures of Rocky and Bullwinkle*—every single time it comes on any channel. Perhaps in the future, Replay will consider including a feature similar to TiVo's, which prevents the same show from being recorded twice in a month (technically, a 28-day period). An even better solution might be to employ TiVo-like "thumbs up/thumbs down" buttons to banish a particular program for life.

Deleting Unsubscribed to Channels

Few things are more annoying than thinking you have a really choice show recorded, only to find that you've missed it. You're in for a lot of this kind of disappointment, especially from your theme-based ReplayTV channels, unless you take the time to delete all the broadcast stations that you don't actually receive, but that are listed in your programming guide anyway.

Stand-alone video IEDs such as ReplayTV can't distinguish between the channels that you get and those you don't, so they might routinely record empty screens and label them as shows unless you get rid of the extra channels.

Conversely, ReplayTV and TiVo can't necessarily identify which Pay Per View channels you receive, or list the content of those channels, forcing users with certain cable systems to add pay channels manually. Note that integrated set-top boxes with video IED capabilities, such as the DirecTV combo units with TiVo or UltimateTV built in, do not suffer from these crises of channel identity. Tighter coupling between the hardware and the programming source means never having to delete the listing of a channel that doesn't appear on your system.

This manual channel deletion can be a tedious and time-consuming process, especially if you are a satellite or digital cable TV subscriber, with potentially hundreds of broadcast channels to which you might not subscribe. Unfortunately, a shortcut is not available. Currently, each channel must be deleted individually using the following process:

1. Press the Menu button and select Setup.

2. Select Add or Remove Channels.

3. When the TV program listings appear, as shown in Figure 3.7, navigate to each channel you don't get or don't want, and press the Select button. You can also press Select again if you want to restore a channel.

NOTE

Note that keeping your actual channel lineup consistent with what your video IED thinks is your lineup is a problem that requires ongoing maintenance. If (and when) Replay adds a channel during its nightly call, the new listing shows up as a "Channel You Receive" item by default. It is up to you to periodically go into the Setup menu and remove these channels if you don't actually get them.

By contrast, it has been noted that TiVo lists new stations as "Not Received," and then notifies you with a screen message indicating that "A lineup change has occurred."

An "X" indicates a removed channel

FIGURE 3.7
Adding and deleting channels that appear on your ReplayTV's electronic programming guide can be a chore.

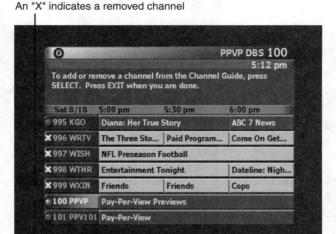

A circle indicates an active channel

4. When you are finished, press Exit.

Creating Show-Based Replay Channels

Often, you want to record all airings of one particular program, rather than all programs that share a common theme. Using the ReplayTV interface, you can also create "show-based" Replay channels directly from the channel guide.

To record all airings of a specific program:

1. Highlight the show you want in the channel guide.

2. Press Select to display the pop-up menu, and then choose Find All Episodes (see Figure 3.8). The ReplayTV will perform a search for matching programs.

3. After ReplayTV compiles a list of all of the selected program's air dates and times, it lists them for you on the screen. If you like what you see, select Create the *Show Name* Theme Channel (where *Show Name* is the title of the program).

NOTE

When your ReplayTV's hard drive starts to fill up—and it will before you know it—the IED will start to get more selective about what it records. In the event of a conflict, show-based channels get priority over theme-based channels.

Like theme-based channels, show-based channels are also subject to recording every episode that comes along. Users can fine-tune the settings by choosing a particular number of episodes to keep, or selecting which days of the week to record. How do you prevent recordings of a particular episode that you've already seen? Unlike TiVo, which is capable of recording only "first-run" shows and omitting repeats, ReplayTV is more single-minded in its pursuit of the most recent episode, regardless of whether it's actually the most recent or a hold-over from last season.

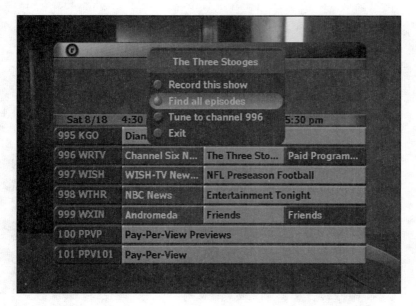

FIGURE 3.8
From the program guide, selecting a show results in a pop-up menu that offers you a variety of viewing options.

However, where there's a will, there's a way, and some determined users have figured out a workaround. If you're absolutely resolved not to record that upcoming repeat of your favorite show, you can try this procedure:

1. Select the show-based channel, and then select Find All Episodes.

2. Highlight the first listing and disable recording. (This affects all episodes.)

3. Turn on recording for just the first episode in the list (assuming this is an episode that you really *don't* want to record).

4. Select the next listing and set that episode to record using Record All Episodes.

5. Turn off recording for the first episode. That should result in disabling record for that episode only.

TIP

If you just want to continuously record the most recent episode of a show, highlight the show in the channel guide and press Record twice. This is a great feature, for instance, for recording the nightly news, but it can be tricky when used with shows that might be airing new episodes on one channel, while older programs from the series are being run in syndication on other channels, and so on.

Watching Custom Channels

To start watching your custom channels, just press the Replay Guide and select a program from the categories you have created (see Figure 3.9).

FIGURE 3.9
The Replay Guide screen not only lists the shows it has recorded for you, but tells you how much storage space has been allotted to each Theme channel.

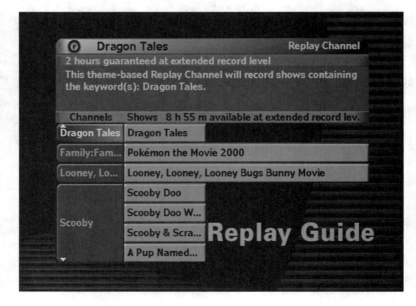

Remember that your device will be constantly looking for new shows to record that fit your theme, and it will be periodically erasing older shows to make room for the new ones. If it happens to record something you really want to hang on to for a while, be sure to use the Preserve option to make the show immune to auto-deletion.

Programming ReplayTV from the Road

Other software features of the ReplayTV that stand out from the competition include the MyReplayTV.com Web service. The major features include these:

- Check and manage the contents of your IED's hard drive via the Replay Guide tab on the Web site (see Figure 3.10).

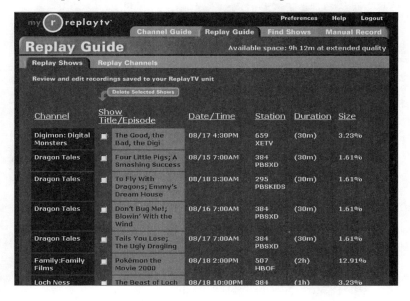

FIGURE 3.10
The MyReplayTV.com service allows you to not only set up recordings from the road, but also to manage your recorded shows and delete those you no longer want.

- Search for programs to record, and set up new Theme- and Show-based ReplayTV Channels using the Find Shows tab. (You can see the tab in Figure 3.10.)
- Check TV listings using the online Channel Guide.
- Set up a manual recording session (see Figure 3.11).

To activate these online features, go to www.myreplaytv.com using your PC's Web browser and register with your product "key" (a 21-digit number obtained using the procedure referenced in the Tip that follows). Now you can log on from any location around the world, and have access to most of the same capabilities you would have if you were sitting in front of your ShowStopper at home.

FIGURE 3.11
To make sure that you get the end of a program that might have a variable ending time, such as a sports event, you can program the recording using MyReplayTV.com's Manual Record function.

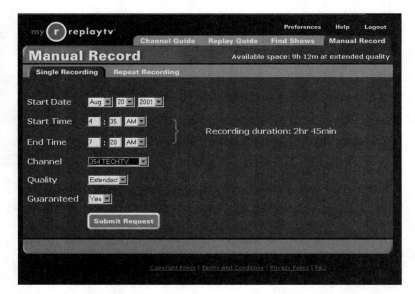

TIP

If you want to sign on to the MyReplayTV service and need to locate your product key, follow these steps:

1. Press Menu on your unit's remote control.

2. Select Setup, and then select Register.

3. Jot down the 21-digit "key," as shown in Figure 3.12.

FIGURE 3.12
The Register ReplayTV screen where you can find the product key.

Needless to say, the concept is great. How many times have you been away from home—at work or on vacation or a business trip—only to suddenly think of an upcoming show you want to record and have no way to do so? With this service, all you need is Web access. It does have one major drawback that the company says it's working to address: As of this writing, record commands issued via the MyReplayTV Web site are only retrieved by your IED unit once a day. For all intents and purposes, you need to log on and set your IED to record 24 hours in advance of the program's air time. This severely limits the utility of MyReplayTV's Web-enabled remote recording capability. As of late summer 2001, the company was planning to increase the frequency of the system to twice daily communication between the consumer's IED unit and the MyReplayTV server.

You might find yourself competing with your ReplayTV more frequently to use the phone line, but at least you will be more likely to have your last-minute recording commands fulfilled.

> **TIP**
>
> As of this writing, the MyReplayTV.com Web remote control features are not supported on the Panasonic TV/ShowStopper Hard Disk Recorder Combination. Panasonic officials say the combo unit uses an earlier software revision than the standalone ReplayTV boxes do.

Other features currently unique to the standalone units include the following:

- The ability to view the contents of Pay Per View channels from the program guide.
- Translucent program guide screens that allow you to view live television behind the programming grid.
- Scrolling titles, which display show titles that are too long to fit within the program guide grid.
- Manual recording, which allows you to manually enter times and channels for a recording session, regardless of what the programming guide lists for that time period.

It appears unlikely that the combo units will ever be upgraded to a version of the operating system that supports the myreplaytv.com features. Even if SonicBlue decides to allocate some developers to port additional versions of the ReplayTV OS to run on the combo devices, it will probably always be at least one software revision behind the standalone versions of the ReplayTV system.

An Evolving Platform

If you find that certain functions in ReplayTV would be useful but aren't yet present, be patient. As services like ReplayTV collect more information about problems and suggestions their customers have, they periodically issue downloadable OS updates that fix bugs and sometimes offer new features. Some additional features not found on the original ReplayTV units that were added in the Fall 2000 revision of the ReplayTV software include these:

- Cosmetic changes to the user interface, the most obvious of which is a full-screen Main Menu.

- Integrated onscreen setup for controlling your cable box or satellite receiver through the ReplayTV remote control.

- Manual Record, which according to the company, "is great for recording shows that do not fit into normal programming blocks, like delayed sports events, music videos, and 24-hour news streams." You can also use Manual Record to record specific segments of shows, such as the first 15 minutes of the news.

- A Show Extender feature that lets you add extra record time at the beginning or end of a scheduled recording. This is handy for when you suspect that a program will run over, or, as ReplayTV puts it, "if the broadcaster's schedule does not match perfectly with the Channel Guide."

  This is a diplomatic way of saying that if you rely on recording from the channel guide information only, you might frequently get programming you didn't bargain for.

- Adjustable Recording Days allow you to specify which days to record when you set your IED to capture all episodes of a particular program. This could come in handy if, for example, you only wanted to record a daily show on Tuesdays and Thursdays, perhaps to coincide with a particular segment that doesn't air every day.

- "Pause Screens" that displayed "tips, trivia, and special promotions" after a show had been paused for 20 seconds.

  ReplayTV issued a press release in September 2000 announcing that Coca Cola had signed on to advertise in the spots, but the sponsored pause displays were soon abandoned and have ceased to appear.

Dumb ReplayTV Trick (Easter Eggs)

In real life, Easter eggs are objects that are made to be hidden, and once discovered, to delight the finder. In the world of software, Easter eggs refer to secret features, messages, or graphics that programmers frequently embed in their software. Often, an Easter egg consists of a list of development team members, but occasionally it contains a more elaborate or amusing surprise.

Here's how to find an Easter egg on your ReplayTV:

1. Activate the hidden systems menu (refer to Figure 3.1) by pressing 243 and then pressing the Replay Zone button while watching live TV.

2. Scroll down to the input box placed below the 10th item on the menu, and press Select. An onscreen keyboard appears.

3. Enter Me Like Cookies by selecting the letters and space keys using the onscreen keyboard. Then press Select on the remote. A "funny" remark will appear.

4. By repeatedly pressing the Select button, you are treated to more than 30 messages. Some are humorous, and some are just odd.

TiVo

Technically older than ReplayTV by a month, TiVo has managed to remain independent (at least as of this writing). That could change. Some have speculated that AOL Time Warner could do worse than buying the remaining 82% of TiVo that it doesn't already own, perhaps rolling that into the AOLTV/DirecTV set-top box offering that was scheduled to ship in the final quarter of 2001.

TiVo cut 80 employees from its staff of about 350 in April 2001, part of a restructuring that founder, CEO, and President Michael Ramsey said was meant to position the company for the long haul. (For additional details, see Table 3.4, "TiVo Vital Statistics.") At the same time, TiVo tried to increase its revenues by raising the cost of a lifetime subscription to its service from $199 to $249. Fees for the monthly subscription plan, however, stayed the same.

Despite a tough year for all technology and electronics companies—particularly ones that are dependent on skittish consumers who are worried about an uncertain economy—many analysts have remained relatively upbeat about TiVo's prospects, based largely on the affinity that people continue to show for the TiVo product. It's easy to love.

TIVO: SHOWING THE LOVE

How much do people love their TiVo? A snippet from the popular *TiVo Underground* board on www.avsforum.com gives us a hint.

Board member "Loner" has drawn a great deal of interest by relating his good luck in finding a 20-hour Philips-manufactured TiVo IED at a Target store in Akron, Ohio on close-out for only $139. He then took his receipt to a nearby Best Buy store, which agreed to match the price, and bought another. When he informs the forum community that he plans to give the second TiVo away as a wedding gift, he draws this response from "nymjk":

Wait a minute!!!

You're giving a TiVo as a wedding present????

I mean, heck, I love TiVo, I really do. But I sure hope you are good friends with the bride because once the groom gets his hands on a TiVo, his new bride will be ONE LONELY GAL.

Table 3.4 – TiVo Vital Statistics*

Status	Independent public company (TIVO) 2000 revenues: $3.6 million
Business model	Developer of personalized television software and services
Founded	August 1997
Co-founder, President, and CEO	Michael Ramsay
Backers, Past and Present	Philips Electronics, Sony, AOL Time Warner, DirecTV, Discovery Networks, Comcast, Cox Communications, Paul Allen (Vulcan Ventures)
Headquarters	Alviso, California

Reaching Out to the Consumer

What best distinguishes the TiVo offering from the competition is neither the hardware nor the software, although both are well executed. It's the company's single-minded focus on ease of use and customer comfort.

It begins with the TiVo logo, a smiling bipedal television sporting an extraterrestrial set of antennae. Like a friendly visitor from another planet, it radiates goodwill. At the initial bootup, consumers are greeted by an animation featuring the happy little creature, frolicking across the screen (see Figure 3.13). The whole message of this window-dressing is, "Forget the fact that you've just plugged in a powerful proprietary PowerPC-based Linux computer in your living room and given it control of your family's television. You can do this. It's fun. In fact, it's child's play."

FIGURE 3.13
TiVo's mascot evokes a feeling of playfulness to make consumers feel more comfortable with the device.

Clearly, the message works.

TiVo has carried through with this mission of coddling the consumer by providing its own documentation to supplement that of the manufacturer (alternatively Sony, Philips, or Thomson/RCA). Although the ReplayTV units you receive might ship with only a bare-bones black-and-white Panasonic operations manual translated into multiple languages—and practically incomprehensible in any of them—TiVo comes with a slick user guide featuring clear language and colorful illustrations.

Another example of TiVo's consumer focus is the clever and comfortable remote control. TiVo has been awarded at least four patents for its remote control's design and housing. Although you might initially be confused about the unique "thumbs up/thumbs down" buttons and cause TiVo to register your vote for a "thumbs up" or a "thumbs down" vote about recording more of such programs, operating the unconventional and uncluttered device quickly becomes second nature. In contrast, both the UltimateTV and ReplayTV remotes are bristling with buttons—most of which never get used in the course of daily TV viewing.

Figure 3.14 shows the differences between the TiVo remote control and those that ship with UltimateTV and ReplayTV.

FIGURE 3.14
The TiVo remote (front center) has fewer buttons and a more intuitive design than remotes that ship with the (rear, left-to-right) UltimateTV, ShowStopper combo IED/TV, and ShowStopper stand-alone.

Keep in mind that all TiVo remote controls are not created equal. Although the Philips DirecTV/TiVo combo box—and a similar one made by Hughes Electronics—both feature the classic hourglass-shaped TiVo remote control, a Sony-manufactured TiVo uses a slightly different design. Although the layout is different, the function buttons are nearly identical.

Hardware

Unlike ReplayTV's abortive initial attempt at building and selling its own branded hardware—resulting in $1,499 boxes that languished on retail shelves—TiVo planned from the get-go to organize itself as a design and development firm and service provider. This decision left the brute-force manufacturing side to world-class players such as Sony, Philips, and Thomson.

In contrast to the Panasonic ShowStopper ReplyTV design, the typical TiVo allows you to use the device even when the remote is hidden away somewhere in the sofa cushions (although this does not apply to all TiVo devices). Common TiVo front-panel controls include a TiVo button (which takes the user to the TiVo's main IED function screen), a guide button (which also toggles the live TV display), as well as buttons for Select, Menu, Standby and more. Indicator lights let the user know whether the machine is powered up, when it's receiving IR codes, and when it's recording or connecting to the ReplayTV service via modem.

The rear of the TiVo is similarly well equipped. It has connectors for an RJ-11 telephone jack, A/C power cord, two satellite inputs, one cable or antenna input, and two connectors that are not yet supported by the TiVo operating system: an IR blaster port and a serial port for connecting to a cable receiver.

TiVo provides signal outputs in the form of two sets of right- and left-channel RCA audio connectors, two composite video outputs, one S-video connector, an optical SPDIF digital port, and an F-type connector for older TVs that don't support composite or S-video connections.

The locations of TiVo's front- and rear-panel features are shown in Figure 3.15.

TiVo has shown itself to be resourceful and versatile in the area of attracting world-class consumer electronics companies as its manufacturing partners, giving credibility to its product line and adding to its perceived stamina in the marketplace (see Tables 3.5 and 3.6).

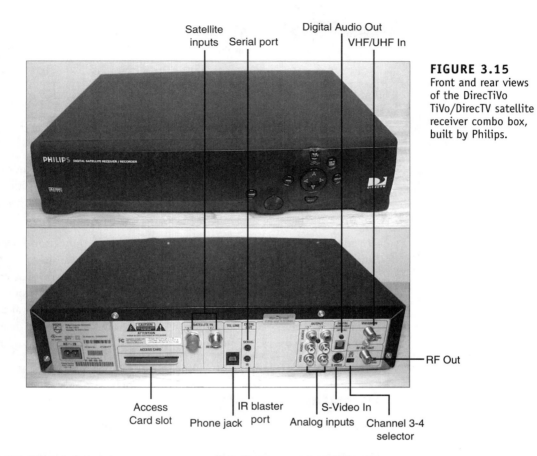

Satellite inputs   Serial port   Digital Audio Out   VHF/UHF In

Access Card slot   Phone jack   IR blaster port   Analog inputs   S-Video In   Channel 3-4 selector

RF Out

FIGURE 3.15
Front and rear views of the DirecTiVo TiVo/DirecTV satellite receiver combo box, built by Philips.

Table 3.5 – Standalone TiVo IEDs			
Manufacturer/Model	**Hours of Storage**	**Works With***	**List Price****
Philips HDR212	20	A, C, S	$199
Philips HDR312	30	A, C, S	$299
Philips HDR612	60	A, C, S	$599
Sony SVR2000	30	A, C, S	$399
Thomson PVR10UK***	40	A, C, S	$430

A=Antenna, C=Cable/Digital Cable, S=Satellite (DirecTV, Dish Network, and so on)

**Current as of December 2001*

***United Kingdom only*

Table 3.6 – DirecTV Receivers with TiVo

Manufacturer/Model	Hours of Storage	Works With	List Price*
Hughes GXEBOT	35	DirecTV only	$399
Philips DSR6000	35	DirecTV only	$299
Sony SAT-T60	35	DirecTV only	$399

*Current as of December 2001

Be sure to check street prices for the units listed in the preceding two tables. The $399 Hughes GXEBOT has been seen selling online for as little as $189. Sales and rebates can have major impact on pricing of these devices.

Inside the TiVo resides the proprietary TiVo application-specific integrated circuit (ASIC), which provides the lion's share of the device's video and interface "personality." The ASIC works in conjunction with an IBM PowerPC 403GCX embedded RISC processor running at 66MHz, along with an IBM CS22 MPEG decoder and an STi5505 OMEGA-DVD chip, which handles DVD back-end decoding and host processing functions.

Other notable components include the onboard Conexant V.90 modem and abundant memory chips, including Hyundai 16-bit DRAMs and 16-bit, 143Mhz SDRAMs.

A close-up view of the interior of a Philips-built DirecTiVo appears in Figure 3.16.

Software

TiVo's Linux-based operating system offers essentially the same basic software features that are found in the ReplayTV and UltimateTV IEDs. Product differentiation, in this case, really comes down to the implementation—packaging and accessibility—of those features. TiVo's execution is arguably the best in the market, combining elegant simplicity in design with a powerful set of underlying capabilities. Best of all for TiVo's faithful hack-minded underground, the Linux system is essentially an open book for developers, practically inviting audience participation in the reverse engineering and enhancement of the device.

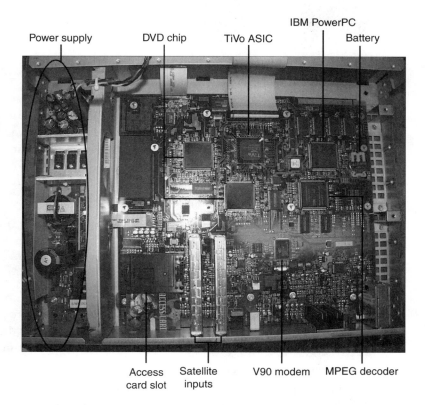

FIGURE 3.16
The DirecTiVo motherboard revealed.

Power supply   DVD chip   TiVo ASIC   IBM PowerPC   Battery

Access card slot   Satellite inputs   V90 modem   MPEG decoder

> **TIP**
>
> If you're unsure of whether you have the latest version of the TiVo OS, you can check out which version you're currently using.
>
> Press Menu, and then select Messages & Setup. Select System Information.
>
> Using this screen, you can not only find out which version of the OS you have, but also the make and model of your device and your TiVo account number.

The Operating System

Like ReplayTV, the operating system that ships with the boxed product continues to receive periodic updates that contain new features and fixes you will want to take advantage of. Some of the more recent updates occurred in Summer 2001 for users of the DirecTiVo combo box, followed by a Fall 2001 update for users of standalone TiVo boxes. Some of the additional features that were added in the 2.5x updates of the TiVo software include these:

- Capability to record two programs at once (DirecTiVo).

  TiVo activated the second satellite tuner in DirecTiVo receivers, allowing you to record two programs on different channels—even while watching a third, already-recorded program. This feature does a great deal to close the gap between TiVo and UltimateTV, but it is limited to DirecTV satellite service subscribers with a dual-LNB dish and a DirecTiVo combo box.

- Saved disk space (standalone TiVo only).

  A new option for saving disk space—reducing the video quality so that your recordings can take up less storage capacity— allows you to fit more programs in Now Playing.

- Capability to skip to "tick marks."

  While fast forwarding or rewinding, press the Advance button to instantly jump to the next "tick mark." Tick marks represent 15- to 30-minute increments, depending on the length of the program. It's a faster way to navigate around a long program.

- Enhanced WishLists.

  TiVo has improved the speed and ease of browsing WishLists, the lists of programs that are returned by programming searches. Also added was the ability to search for similar words in Keyword and Title WishList searches, such as a search for both *horse* and *horseback*, or *49er* and *49ers*.

- Improved parental controls.

  New controls and options allow you to, among other things, turn off the automatic relock feature. Apparently, a few too many TiVo users temporarily disabled parental controls for the babysitter or an overnight guest, forgetting that they relock after four hours. TiVo also added more options for setting ratings limits on TV content.

- Shorter phone calls (DirecTiVo).

  By using the satellite to deliver TiVo Service information, such as TiVolution Magazine and Showcases, TiVo was able to reduce the length of the system's nightly telephone sessions.

These new features build upon the previous 2.0 software updates, which incorporated the following highlights:

- Faster performance when using the program guide or making selections from menus.

- New remote control shortcuts, allowing you to reach the Now Playing menu faster (by pressing the TiVo button twice), and enabling easier deletions of programs using the Clear button.

- Title WishLists, allowing programming searches by title.

- A "Keep at Most 5" command that limits repeat recordings (such as Season Passes and auto-recording WishLists) to a maximum of five episodes at a time.

- Additional parental controls, such as requiring a password to delete programs that violate parental limits "so that your kids (or your roommate!) can't delete them."

The ability to record an extra few minutes before or after a program was another of the many useful additions not found in the first version of the TiVo operating system.

Although none of the features incorporated into the 2.0 or 2.5 software updates offers overwhelming improvements to the overall user experience, it does show that TiVo programmers are actively working on the product, filing off the rough edges and tuning the interface in direct response to customer feedback.

The User Interface

TiVo has the edge in the interface department. The company seems to have thought through how consumers really use the device, and it shows the results of that forethought in the way the system appears to have an uncanny knack for surfacing handy features at opportune times.

Example: You sit down and turn on the IED. Using the channel guide, you find a show you would really like to see. Unfortunately, you have already missed half the program. What can you do? Unless you got lucky and the IED was previously set to that channel—or you're willing to settle for watching just the second half—you need to go through the tedious process of creating a search for the show by title, looking for another opportunity to record it. With TiVo, the answer to the dilemma is obvious and intuitive:

1. When you press the Record button, a pop-up menu appears.
2. Select More Recording Choices (see Figure 3.17).

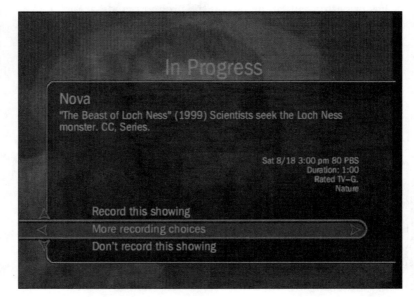

3. Press the right arrow button and scroll down and select View Upcoming Episodes.
4. TiVo displays a list of alternative times when you can record the show (see Figure 3.18).

Of course, this is handy for recording, say, an old movie that airs frequently, but no video IED currently on the market can help you if you miss out on the season premiere of your favorite show. If your device was tuned to a different channel at the time it aired, you will have to wait (and hope) until the network shows it again in a few months.

In general, the learning curve seems significantly shorter when learning how to use TiVo than it does for ReplayTV or UltimateTV.

Conversely, some might find the TiVo too simplistic. Fewer buttons on the remote translates into fewer features that are available at the touch of a finger. As a result, more of the advanced features are hidden away behind layers of onscreen menus. In the end, the best way to choose which video IED will be right for you is to visit multiple electronics stores (right now it's highly unlikely that you'll find a single store that carries all three brands of video IEDs). This allows you to experience each machine's interface first-hand and find the one that best suits you.

FIGURE 3.18
TiVo's user interface takes into account that you might decide to record something that is already in progress, and gives you some intuitive options.

TiVo's Hidden Backdoor

Another facet of TiVo that has turned many of its more technically oriented owners into lifelong fans is the ability to customize the system through the use of undocumented "backdoor codes." These codes are easily accessed, and in many cases, they are quite powerful. They are so powerful, in fact, that some of the codes have the ability to completely (and perhaps permanently) disable the system if used incorrectly. Because the manufacturer only grudgingly admits the very existence of these codes, and no official documentation exists for them, their true functions in some cases are still unknown. It is only through the trial and error experiences of intrepid TiVo users that they have come to light at all, being passed from one TiVo owner to the next in e-mail messages and user forum postings.

> **TIP**
>
> As with ReplayTV, TiVo devices have included certain Easter eggs for those with the free time to find them. One such "trick" is called the Shagwell Easter egg and can be found by doing the following:
>
> 1. Turn on your TV's closed captioning.
> 2. Press the TiVo button to go to TiVo Central.
> 3. Choose Pick Programs to Record.
> 4. Select Search by Title and choose All Programs.
> 5. Type Shagwell.
> 6. Press the Thumbs Up key.
>
> Recognize anyone? (Apparently the TiVo 2.0 team included some die-hard Austin Powers fans.)

For TiVos that are still running pre-2.0 versions of the software, the "backdoor mode" is accessed through the following steps:

1. Press the TiVo button on the remote to access TiVo Central.
2. Choose Pick Programs to Record.
3. Choose Search By Title.
4. Choose All Programs.
5. Using the remote control and the onscreen keyboard, type in the search term 0v1t (TiVo spelled backwards, substituting zero for the letter *O* and the numeral one instead for the letter *I*).
6. Press the Thumbs-Up key.

For TiVos that are equipped with version 2.0 of the TiVo operating system, use the same procedure, but substitute the search term *2 0 TCD* (note the single space between the 2 and the zero, and another space between the zero and *TCD*). To enter backdoor mode for systems that are running version 2.5 of the software, use the search term *B D 2 5* (putting a single between each character).

When you successfully complete the sequence, you are rewarded with a message indicating that backdoor mode is activated. To exit backdoor mode, reboot the TiVo.

You can get additional codes by searching the www.tivocommunity.com user forum for "backdoor codes." Before attempting to use any of these codes, be aware that you might be risking the future functionality of your TiVo, so proceed with caution.

CEC Codes

One category of backdoor codes for TiVo uses the Clear, Enter, Clear (C-E-C) button sequence, followed by an additional key that defines the function. A few of these codes include the following:

- C-E-C Thumbs-Up

  This gives you access to TiVo's log files on your TV screen. Page up and page down to move through the log information, which chronicles everything you've been doing on your TiVo. Use the right arrow to move through the log files. Press the left arrow key to exit to the normal TiVo menus.

- C-E-C-0 (in version 2.0 only)

  This turns off the display of "Scheduled Suggestions" in the ToDo List. It also removes the black bar from behind the clock (see S-P-S-9-S).

- C-E-C-5

  This toggles on and off the "overshoot correction" employed during fast forwarding.

- C-E-C-Fast Forward

  This reboots the TiVo (and thus turns off backdoor mode).

CCEE Codes

The following codes utilize the sequence Clear, Clear, Enter, Enter (C-C-E-E), followed by an additional key that defines the function. You must enter these commands while displaying the System Information screen, as described earlier in this chapter.

- C-C-E-E-2

  This toggles on and off the Debug mode, which sends debugging output to the /var/log/tvdebuglog file on the TiVo's hard drive. This setting remains on even after rebooting, so the procedure must be repeated to turn it off. It might not be advisable to leave this logging function running for extended periods of time.

- C-C-E-E-8

    This takes you to the Channels You Watch page, but with no channels selected. This can be used as a shortcut for clearing your channel list.

Thumbs Up/Down Codes

A few known codes utilize a series of Thumbs Up and Thumbs Down (TU/TD) key presses to activate the function. Because these codes are still being found and are not well understood, they should be considered experimental.

- TD-TD-TU-Instant Replay

    When activated while displaying the ToDo List, this turns on Scheduled Suggestions. When performed from the Now Playing list, it displays the hidden recordings, such as paid programming.

- TD-TU-TD-Instant Replay

    When performed from the Now Playing display, it calls up a new menu called Clips on Disk, which offers access to the same hidden recordings broken up into clips. Note that if you don't have clips stored on your hard drive, this code reboots the TiVo.

Other Codes

Some additional codes are available that do not require the TiVo to have backdoor mode enabled. One set of codes uses the sequence of pressing Select, Play, Select, followed by a fourth button that determines the requested function; then press Select again to set the code.

For instance, the sequence Select, Play, Select, 9, Select (abbreviated as S-P-S-9-S) toggles a digital clock display in the bottom-right corner of the screen. To turn it off, repeat the procedure. The clock remains visible until you exit the live or recorded TV display by going to a TiVo menu, and then return to the show.

Additional codes using this procedure include the following:

- S-P-S-Instant Replay-S

    This toggles a status display in the bottom-right corner, displaying information on what the TiVo is currently doing. It's not too useful, really. Like the clock display, you must repeat the procedure to turn it off, and then exit to a TiVo menu and return to the program to make it disappear.

- S-P-S-Pause-S

  Toggles the "fast disappear" of the progress bar at the bottom of the screen.

- S-P-S-3-0-S

  This feature appears to be enabled in versions 1.3, and 2.5 of the software, but not versions 2.0 or 2.01. It toggles the 30-second skip mode on and off. This command turns the Skip to End button (also known as the Advance button) into a 30-second skip button. This can be extremely handy for zipping past commercials without zipping right past part of the show you're trying to watch.

Other "non-backdoor" codes include the following:

- TiVo 0

  Plays the TiVo character startup movie.

- TiVo 1

  Shortcut to the Now Playing list. (In version 2.5, it goes to the Season Pass Manager.)

- TiVo 2

  Shortcut to the ToDo list.

- TiVo 3

  Shortcut to WishLists (in version 2.0 and above).

- TiVo 4

  Shortcut to the Search by Title screen.

- TiVo 5

  Shortcut to view live TV in version 2.0. Shortcut to the Browse by Channel screen in versions 1.3 and 2.5.

- TiVo 6

  Shortcut to the Browse by Time screen.

- TiVo 7

  Shortcut to the Manual Record screen.

- TiVo 8

  Shortcut to the TiVo's Suggestions screen.

- TiVo 9

  Shortcut to the Network Showcases screen (renamed simply Showcases in version 2.5).

- TiVo TiVo

  Shortcut to the Now Playing List (versions 2.0 and above).

Conclusions

It's easy to discover why TiVo has such a loyal customer base. It is an extremely well thought out consumer device, with a responsive and capable team of engineers and developers behind it.

What's still missing? Users would like to see numerous other features, and it's likely that many of these software bells and whistles will appear by the next software revision in 2002.

Will TiVo add the full commercial bypass features that ReplayTV has in its 4000 series machines? It's unlikely. In fact, TiVo's chief technical officer has flatly denied any plans to do so, ever. The company would rather make friends than enemies among the Hollywood power brokers—at least for the time being. However, if ReplayTV is not ultimately prevented from enabling the bypass feature through legal challenges, and it later turns into a big hit with consumers, TiVo's allegiances could change.

Will TiVo add WebTV-like e-mail and Web-browsing capabilities? It doesn't seem to be a priority for either the developers or the consumers. However, that doesn't mean that it might not be appealing to some of TiVo's potential partners. (Why not a YahooTV set-top box to compete with AOL and MSN in the future?)

Regardless of what changes come about, TiVo has already established itself as one of the more viable video IED options on the market.

UltimateTV

Microsoft is the Johnny Come Lately of the video IED business, introducing its UltimateTV months behind schedule in early 2001. However, with its substantial mass—dwarfing tiny TiVo and ReplayTV—Microsoft ought to be able to quickly make up for lost time (see Table 3.7 for additional details on the company).

Recruiting Sony as its initial manufacturing partner should help fill in any credibility gaps that Microsoft might encounter in the consumer electronics space.

Table 3.7 – Microsoft Vital Statistics	
Status	Independent public company (MSFT) 2001 revenues: $25.29 billion
Business model	Developer of microcomputer software and related services
Founded	August 1975
Founder, Chairman and Chief Software Architect	William H. (Bill) Gates III
UltimateTV business partners	Sony, DirecTV, Thomson (RCA)
Headquarters	Redmond, Washington

Hardware

When it comes down to a straight comparison of features, Microsoft's UltimateTV lives up to its name. Its out-of-the-box ability to watch and record two live TV channels simultaneously set it firmly apart from any other offering (at the time of this launch), as did its integrated Web surfing and e-mail capabilities.

➡ **For a discussion of the relative merits of UltimateTV's Web surfing features, see "Internet Access and Interactivity," p. 36.**

Although UltimateTV seems in many respects a step behind its competitors on the software front (see the following discussion on "Software" in this chapter, p. 86), the hardware needs no apology. Owing perhaps to Microsoft's previous experience building the EchoStar DishPlayer, the UltimateTV has the look and feel of a solidly constructed and well thought out piece of equipment. Although it might have lost some of its competitive luster when TiVo finally enabled its second satellite tuner, UltimateTV definitely has a bright future and a growing base of satisfied customers.

Currently, only two UltimateTV devices are available through retail channels. Both are listed in Table 3.8.

Table 3.8 – DirecTV Receivers with UltimateTV			
Manufacturer/Model	Hours of Storage	Works With	List Price*
Thomson/RCA DWD490RE	35	DirecTV only	$299
Sony SAT-W60	35	DirecTV only	$450

*Current as of December 2001

ULTIMATETV KEYBOARD SHORTCUTS

As the newest video IED to enter the market, users simply haven't had adequate time to uncover many of UltimateTV's secrets, its shortcuts, Easter Eggs and miscellaneous peccadilloes. However, UltimateTV's DishPlayer heritage has resulted in a few carryovers chronicled in the pages of DishPlayer user groups, such as those at www.dbstalk.com and www.echostaruser.org.

For example, in addition to typing e-mail and video search terms, you can use your UltimateTV keyboard as a giant remote control for your IED. Following are some keyboard shortcuts derived from the DishPlayer:

- To advance the programming guide by 12 hours, press and hold CMD and press the right arrow.
- To jump back 12 hours, hold down CMD and press the left arrow.
- To jump to the top or bottom of a page, press Scroll Up or Scroll Down.
- To bring up a Picture In Picture (PIP) window, or to remove it, press CMD and W.
- To move the PIP window left or right, press CMD and M.

UltimateTV's roster of exterior hardware features is impressive—at least until you realize what they do—and in some cases *don't* do.

The front panel offers status indicators for power, service connection, messages, and new recordings (called My Shows in UltimateTV parlance).

Taking a cue from TiVo rather than ReplayTV, the UltimateTV offers a full set of front panel controls to allow operation without the remote or keyboard. These include buttons for Power, Guide, Home (UltimateTV's version of TiVo Central) and Select, along with directional arrow buttons for onscreen navigation. The front of the device also sports two smartcard readers. One is for the DirecTV access card. The other's use has not been specified, but it is expected to eventually support gift cards and other transaction-based smartcard services.

It's in the area of inputs that some consumers have found disappointment. You will find inputs for RCA audio, composite video, and a microphone jack in the front panel area, whereas the back panel includes enticing inputs for additional audio and video devices (analog and S-video). Unfortunately, none of these is designed for use outside of UltimateTV's e-mail functions.

Want to connect a DVD or VCR player to UltimateTV? Think again. The composite video and S-video ports were intended to let you capture and send multimedia e-mails, not to let you simplify connections to your TV. UltimateTV setup guides show VCRs and DVD players connected directly to the TV or running through an A/V receiver, not to the UltimateTV, which lacks a pass-through feature to route signals from these external devices to the television set. As if to add insult to injury, UltimateTV currently does not support the video and audio e-mail features either, so the multiple inputs are essentially useless.

In the same vein, the parallel printer port is not yet enabled, and the device's two USB ports only support connections to keyboards. If you have a wireless keyboard that came with your Sony-built unit, the USB ports are particularly pointless for the time being. The only good news here is that future revisions of the software could potentially enable these dormant features, giving the UltimateTV some interesting new functionality.

The back panel does include some other useful inputs, however, such as a place to plug in an IR blaster for VCR control. (This allows you to record UltimateTV programs onto videotape. Note that this requires routing UltimateTV output to the VCR as well as to your TV during the setup process.) You will also find an RJ-11 telephone jack, an A/C power cord, two F-type satellite inputs, and an F-type antenna (UHF/VHF) input.

In terms of outputs, the UltimateTV presents a full range, from multiple audio (RCA and optical SPDIF digital) jacks to composite, S-video, and F-type video.

The exterior features of the UltimateTV are detailed in Figure 3.19.

FIGURE 3.19
Front and rear views
of a Sony-made
UltimateTV device.

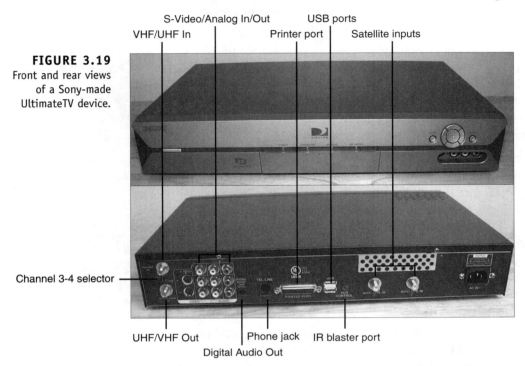

Internally, UltimateTV relies on a 250MHz version of the 32-bit RM5231 CPU chip that is manufactured by PMC-Sierra's MIPS Microprocessor Division (formerly Quantum Effect Devices), which is the same 64-bit RISC processor found in Sony's popular Aibo2 robotic dog.

The real guts of the system, however, is the Solo2, designed by the WebTV team in 1999. Named after WebTV founder Steve Perlman's German Shepherd, Solo, the chip was Perlman's final effort after he sold WebTV to Microsoft for $503 million in 1997. Perlman left Microsoft soon after to found a new video IED-related startup called Reardon Steel.

Meanwhile, Microsoft contracted with Toshiba Corporation to manufacture the Solo2. Working in conjunction with a second chip that was mysteriously—and some might say ironically—labeled WebTV FUD v.2.0 (Microsoft has long been accused of disseminating

"FUD," a popular acronym for fear, uncertaintly, and doubt), the chips combine to provide UltimateTV's Internet browsing, interactive television, and video recording features. August 2000 reports indicated the Solo2 chip contained about 2.2 million transistors, and hinted that Microsoft was already working on a more powerful version said to contain about 9 million transistors (roughly the same as an Intel Pentium 2).

For memory, UltimateTV appears to rely on four Micron 32MB SDRAM chips. A Conexant Bt835 VideoStream III Decoder supports the machine's NTSC, PAL and SECAM, and S-video video decoding and display capabilities. A bus-mastering OPTi FireLink 82C861 chip serves as the system's USB hub controller. UltimateTV's dual "smart card" capabilities are provided by a Philips TDA8004T smart card interface chip.

For a glimpse inside the UltimateTV, check out Figure 3.20.

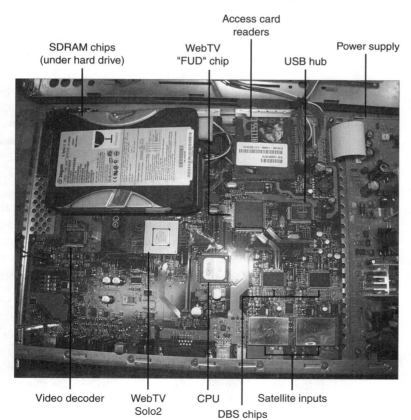

FIGURE 3.20
UltimateTV's internal layout is surprisingly uncluttered.

Software

Whereas TiVo's use of ultra-stable, ultra-unobtrusive Linux is one of the product's major strengths, UltimateTV's reliance on Microsoft's homegrown Windows CE is considered by some to be the product's Achilles Heel.

One example of Windows CE's potential pitfalls occurred in April and May 2001, when Microsoft was forced to release a patch for a problem that inadvertently shrunk viewers' available recording time. When UltimateTV subscribers paused a program during recording and then tried to delete it, the show would disappear from the My Shows listing without actually being deleted from the system. The detritus of these undeleted shows continued to take up space on the IED's hard drive, leaving subscribers unable to record additional shows, while also unable to view the shows that were clogging their hard drives.

Was Windows CE the cause of the programming mishap? It might well have complicated and delayed the creation of the fix. The primary knock against Windows CE in the UltimateTV appliance is related to the speed of processing user commands.

Aside from the OS uncertainty, check out any online forum discussion of UltimateTV, and you'll find one prevalent complaint: too slow. Many people find they have a certain period of adjustment to endure before they become accustomed to the pace of channel and program guide changes on the UltimateTV. The unit just seems to take its own sweet time in responding to your request, leading many first-time users to assume their remote control isn't working, and repeat the command several times. When the commands start taking effect, only fractions of a second later—although it can seem like hours when you're impatient—the delayed reaction might make the device seem as if it's behaving erratically. In fact, it's just carrying out orders, but not as crisply as its ReplayTV and TiVo counterparts.

The other major criticism of the UltimateTV—or UTV as it's often abbreviated by owners—is the subtle absence of certain "fit and finish" features that TiVo and ReplayTV users have come to expect. Some of these little things include the ability to record only the latest episode (while automatically erasing older episodes), the ability to turn off the system sounds that correspond to remote control commands, the ability to "protect" or "guarantee" a particular recording and ensure that it won't be overwritten by a subsequent recording command.

These features are routine on competing Replay and TiVo models. As "Synchro" from Northern Virginia opined in his posting on the AVS Forum, why didn't Microsoft "stand on the shoulders of giants, and at least match most of the features other PVRs have had for years?"

Perhaps the answer is that those competitors did not reach "giant" status overnight; several revisions of their software were required to refine the basic feature set that seems to satisfy the majority of customers. Microsoft will undoubtedly get there, but it might take many more months, a year, or more. After all, it took them three iterations of Windows CE for handheld devices to hit on one that didn't draw staunch criticism in comparison to the Palm OS.

Regardless, whether the issue of slowness can be fixed through a software download, or if it's some inherent and incurable latency in the Windows CE operating system or even the hardware, remains to be seen.

Many vocal owners defended their beloved UTVs despite admitting to its faults. The dual-tuner capability alone probably has gone a long way toward endearing the UTV to its consumer base. Being able to tape two live shows while watching a third previously recorded program might have done more to save marriages and keep families together in the latter half of 2001 than the efforts of doctors Joyce Brothers and Ruth Westheimer combined.

For those who remain critical of UltimateTV's less-than-ultimate speed and feature set, Microsoft's UltimateTV Digital Recorder Forum moderator "jleavens" offers this solace: "Give your UltimateTV a chance. PVRs are... the first consumer electronics that can only get better over time without buying a new unit."

Making UltimateTV Better

As if to prove the point, Microsoft rolled out a Fall 2001 software upgrade, specifically featuring two requested capabilities: Keep Until (the ability to save a recorded show until you erase it) and Custom Recording (the ability to set a specific start time and end time for a recording session).

The purpose of the Keep Until feature is self explanatory: Nothing is more frustrating than recording the big show you've been waiting for, and then finding that your smarty-pants machine decided of its own accord to dump it in favor of recording another show. (According to Murphy's Law, this other show is bound to be something you already saw or something you never really wanted in the first place.)

The custom recording capability offers more creative uses. Why not record just the last, most exciting quarter of that playoff game? Or perhaps you just want to see the first few minutes of the nightly news to get the top stories, or you're only interested in the weather or sports segment that comes on at a certain time. You're no longer locked in to recording entire programs, as listed in the program guide.

To access the Keep Until feature, perform the following steps:

1. Go to My Shows.
2. Select the show you want to keep.
3. Choose Keep Until.
4. Choose how long to keep the recording.
5. Choose Done.

To access Custom Record features, follow these steps:

1. Go to My Shows.
2. Scroll to the bottom.
3. Choose Schedule Recording.
4. Choose Using Custom Settings.
5. Choose the day to begin recording.
6. Choose the start and stop times for your recording, and then choose Continue.
7. Enter the channel using the numbers on your remote control, and then choose Continue.
8. If everything is correct, choose Continue, and then choose Done.

A few, less conspicuous features have also been rolled into some recent UltimateTV upgrades. The new security features, Channel Settings and Block Channels, allow subscribers to customize how channels appear in the Channel Guide, and to set limits on which channels can be viewed.

The Channel Settings feature gives you the ability to disable channels so that they do not appear in the Advanced Programming Guide. To access the feature, follow these steps:

1. From TV Home, select Settings.

2. Choose Channels.

3. Remove the check mark from any channels you want to remove from the Channel Guide. You also have the option to check All or None. Be careful here! The occasional slowness of the UltimateTV to respond to remote control input has led some impatient subscribers to inadvertently delete all channels from the Channel Guide, and forced them to painstakingly rebuild their channel preferences. If the screen doesn't respond to your key press, wait a moment before continuing.

4. Choose Done.

The Blocked Channel feature is designed to let you block certain channels from being accessed via the remote control or the keyboard. Follow these steps to block TV channels:

1. From the TV Home screen, select Settings.

2. Choose Locks & Limits.

3. Select the channels to which you want to lock access.

4. Create a password if this is your first time to access this feature.

5. When you successfully create a password, you will be reminded to write it down (always sage advice).

6. Choose Done.

Diagnostics and Other Housekeeping

Interested in what's going on inside your UltimateTV? Here's a shortcut for checking it out, for running diagnostics, and for performing other housekeeping items:

1. Turn off the UltimateTV. Wait for the green power indicator light to stop blinking and go out completely.

2. Press 411 on the remote control.

3. Turn the UltimateTV back on. You will see the lights on the unit flash, and then it will display the Technical Information screen (see Figure 3.21).

FIGURE 3.21
UltimateTV's 411 screen provides access to the unit's vital statistics.

The initial screen displays information on:

- The current DTV client software version
- Boot software version
- SSID, chip, and SysConfig information
- Modem information
- Hard drive model number
- Available memory

At the bottom of the Information screen are selections allowing you to view satellite information, force a service connection, or power down the unit. The Satellite Information tab brings up a screen containing even more information (see Figure 3.22).

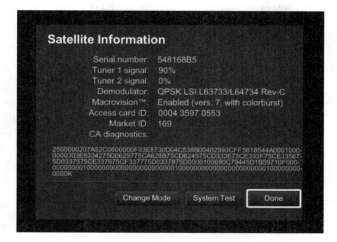

FIGURE 3.22
UltimateTV's initial Satellite Information screen is a portal to system diagnostics and satellite reception options.

In addition to information on satellite signal strength and the software version of the demodulator, at the bottom of the screen, you will find additional tabs for changing modes and running a system test.

The system test can help diagnose problems you might be having with your reception, program guide information, or other aspects of the UltimateTV's hardware and service. It runs some brief diagnostics on the phone connection, the satellite reception, the unit's two satellite inputs, and the access card, ideally returning the message OK for each device.

From the diagnostics screen, you are offered a choice to further investigate your system. Selecting System Information yields details on the hardware's manufacturer and model number, along with the device's subtype (DTV 1.0) and serial, SSID, and control numbers to aid UltimateTV's record-keeping as to which machine this is and to whom it belongs. An Upgrades button then appears at the bottom of the screen. Selecting it renders the date of your last system software upgrade, and whether a new one is scheduled. Selecting More Information leads you to an additional System Information screen, this one offering a list of services that is supported on your machine (DirecTV Multi-Sat, Dolby Digital Bitstream Out, WebTV Internet Service, UltimateTV, and so on), and a readout of your total recording capacity, in hours.

The Satellite Information screen's Change Mode selection provides a choice of changing the operational mode of your satellite receiver from Normal to Special. Special mode suppresses all introductory pages, even after a software upgrade.

UltimateTV's Ultimate Future

Although UltimateTV's relatively recent debut and its use of a closed, proprietary operating system initially thwarted grassroots efforts to "customize" the device beyond the manufacturer's specifications, a determined effort by the video IED underground has apparently yielded some significant fruit.

When it first became available, hackers had their fingers crossed that the UltimateTV would be as easily upgradable as its predecessor, the venerable DishPlayer. Expanding the storage capacity of a DishPlayer is a breeze, involving little more than extracting the old hard drive and plugging in a new one. If you managed to remove and replace all the correct wires and screws without electrocuting yourself on the unshielded power supply, you were treated to instant gratification. Just compare this procedure to the horribly involved and painstaking process of upgrading a TiVo or ReplayTV! (See the description of how to hack a TiVo in Chapter 11, in the section "Tweaking Your Video IED," page 258.)

Unfortunately, upgrading the UltimateTV proved not so easy. The device steadfastly refused to recognize the new drives. The hardcore hackers scurried back to their drawing boards to begin carefully reverse engineering the product and peering into its arcane files and formats.

Then in late December 2001, a holiday present appeared in the form of a post in the UltimateTV community on the AVS Forum. A user reported that he had successfully upgraded his hard drive to 100GB. The secret was so simple that UltimateTV hackers across the country began viciously kicking themselves: All they had to do was use a Western Digital hard drive.

Numerous confirmations have now been posted, along with more detailed instructions, for replacing the original UltimateTV hard drive (a 40GB Seagate "U" Series 5 drive in the RCA unit) with a Western Digital 80GB, 100GB, or 120GB drive. The usual risks apply (kiss your warranty goodbye, and be careful what you touch), but one happy upgrader description of the 20-minute upgrade process says it all: "SUCCESS! That was so easy it's ridiculous… 120GB of lovin'!"

Discoveries such as this can have a profound impact on the future of a particular IED platform. After all, once word of this feat is widely publicized (which is sure to have happened before this tome ends up on your bookshelf), anyone with a mind toward upgrading their video IED would have to think long and hard about buying a TiVo or ReplayTV instead of an UltimateTV. Why fiddle with downloading software utilities, installing and uninstalling and mounting and unmounting hard drives in a PC, and then transferring them in and out of your IED, when Microsoft has unintentionally done all the work for you?

Then again, when Microsoft learns of the hack, what's to prevent them from introducing a bug in the next software revision that nullifies the upgrade?

Only time will tell. In the meantime, happy hacking! Microsoft might soon come to realize that this unannounced, probably inadvertent feature might be the secret weapon that clobbers the competition.

Chapter 4

Playing the Field: Other Video IED Convergence Devices

Can My PC Be My IED?

While the dedicated video IED appliances—Replay, TiVo, and UltimateTV—have much to offer, some may want to consider turning their PC into an IED. There are some benefits:

- While a PC—even a cheapie—costs considerably more than an appliance-style video IED, chances are you already own a PC that can probably be modified to serve as a video IED.

- The dedicated video IEDs are proprietary "closed box" systems. Open the case, and say goodbye to your warranty. While there is an active community of those who routinely "hack" into their IEDs to expand their storage capacity and even to extract and distribute the digital copies of their videos (see Chapter 11, "Hacking Your IED"), the practice is risky from both cost and (potentially) legal standpoints. A PC, on the other hand, is an open book. Files encoded to the PC, however bulky and unwieldy, can be freely stored, copied, edited, and shared.

Of course, there are a few disadvantages to buying or building your own PC-based equivalent of a video IED appliance:

- Quality may be an issue, but it depends on who you talk to, and how much you spend. Satellite/IED combos are able to capture and deliver live TV streams in an all-digital format, while your PC is most likely going to be working from an analog signal and translating it into a digital format.

- Cost: While you may already own a PC, handling real-time video is one of the most demanding applications around. Have you ever wondered why this capability of behaving like a TiVo doesn't ship as standard equipment on every Dell, Gateway, and Compaq that goes out the door? Well, mainly because it requires a specialized TV tuner card, a massive and extremely fast hard drive, the beefiest CPU you can lay your hands on, and so on. By the time you add up all the upgrades you might need to turn your PC into a ReplayTV-equivalent, you've blown right past the cost of a dedicated IED.

- Most PC-based software and online programming guides currently can't equal the ease of use and superb integration that a ReplayTV or TiVo device offers. Even advanced new entries like the nVidia Personal Cinema (see the section, "nVidia," later in this chapter for details) lack features such as the ability to selectively record a program by selecting its listing on the interactive program guide.

For these reasons, dressing your PC up to look like a TiVo may look better on paper than it does in your living room. There is one consideration, however, that could level the playing field between a dedicated video IED appliance and a video-enabled PC: The latter does not require a monthly service fee.

If you're intent on creating your own video dream machine from scratch, the following sections offer some resources that should help get you going.

Thinking Inside the Box: PC Hardware Requirements

The first thing you'll need to start with when building a PC that can serve as a video IED is a computer that can handle the demanding task of becoming your personal video server. Like every technology purchasing decision, your fist step is to ask yourself what you hope to accomplish, then "spec out" the right hardware and software to do the trick. Whether you're planning to convert an existing PC to become your video IED, or you're looking to get a fresh start with a brand new box, you'll want to give some thought to the basic system needs in terms of processor, memory, hard disk, display, tuner card, and software.

Processor and Memory

When people think about how "powerful" their computers are, very often the components that first come to mind are the processor and memory.

How much horsepower do you really need under the hood of your custom video PC? There are ample examples that suggest you shouldn't need massive megahertz to watch TV on your PC. For one thing, there are plenty of set-top boxes running Intel 486 processors, a type that waved goodbye to the mainstream PC desktop market in the mid 1990s. In fact, ReplayTV and UltimateTV both use inexpensive, relatively low power MIPS-based CPUs to execute operating system commands and other general housekeeping duties. TiVo actually debuted with a PowerPC processor that runs at a measly 50MHz.

How can this be? Well, these dedicated video IED computers are designed so that the CPU is not really doing the heavy lifting in terms of video processing. In the case of TiVo, for example, the video signal does not flow through the PowerPC 403GCX processor at all. Instead, video processing is handled by a proprietary ASIC (application specific integrated circuit) that TiVo calls Media Switch.

While a relatively wimpy central processor might be good enough for a custom-designed video IED, grafting a TV tuner card onto an off-the-shelf PC may yield very different results. In general, simple TV viewing shouldn't exactly require a 2GHz Pentium 4. However, higher functions such as recording video and time shifting are likely to require a heftier CPU (central processing unit).

Timeshifting, for example, involves encoding a live TV signal while simultaneously decoding a stream of recorded video—no easy task. I suggest at least a 600MHz processor with 128MB of SDRAM, DDR SDRAM, or RDRAM memory—depending on your motherboard type—for acceptable time shifting performance.

If you've looked at TV tuner cards on store shelves, you've no doubt noticed that they do mention minimum system requirements. However, comparing actual system requirements from tuner card manufacturers doesn't provide much help in choosing a processor and memory configuration that will provide the best results. It is unfortunate—though predictable—that most manufacturers tend to trumpet their ability to work with an underpowered system, thinking this will give them access to a broader market. By sending the message that "you don't need to upgrade to use this product," they can potentially increase their sales in the short term, but they harm the consumer and the market as a whole by spreading dissatisfaction when an underpowered PC can't offer adequate performance to justify a purchase.

Hauppauge, maker of the Win TV line of tuners, requires only a minimal 300MHz Pentium II processor to run its Win TV-PVR card—but read the fine print: A 300MHz card only enables "TV pause with half screen playback." For full screen playback, you'll have to come up with at a 450MHz PII. Similarly, Matrox Graphics—maker of the Marvel G450 eTV tuner card—advertises system requirements of a minimum 300MHz CPU (400MHz for DVD playback capability) with 64MB of

RAM. However, for timeshifting and video capture features, it ups the ante to 600MHz and at least 128 megabytes of RAM.

ATI, maker of the popular All-In-Wonder product family, recommends for use with its RADEON 8500DV card an Intel Pentium II, III, or 4; a Celeron; or an AMD K6 or Athlon chip. That gives users a fair degree of latitude.

In general, video capture and manipulation—particularly timeshifting— are the ultimate stress test for a desktop PC. You can't go wrong by investing in the fastest processor you can manage, and a full rack of DRAM modules to go along with it.

Hard Disk

Next to raw CPU computing power and system memory, the most important feature for juggling video on your PC is storage space. You simply can't have enough.

Consider this: Typical NTSC (National Television Systems Committee) video, the U.S. TV signal standard, delivers programming at the rate of about 26MB per second. Even if you get rid of extraneous carrier information, it translates to about 1.5GB of hard disk space per minute of video! At that rate, an hour-long program will have eaten 93.5GB of hard drive space. Considering that most computers ship with hard drives in the 30–60GB range, it's easy to see why data compression plays such an important role in handling TV signals on a PC.

Even compressing down to the DV (Digital Video) standard used by digital consumer devices, such as a DV camcorder, requires 3.6 MBps, or about 12.9GB for an hour of video. MPEG-2 compressed video will fill up your hard drive at the rate of between 3 and 10Mbps (that's mega*bits* per second—not mega*bytes as in the previous example*). Of course, the amount of disk space needed to store a given amount of video depends largely on your quality preferences: Better quality video requires a lower compression rate and takes up more space on your hard drive. One hour of typical MPEG-2 video recorded at 8Mbps will eat up about 3.6GB on your drive. MPEG-1 compression drops the data rate (and the quality) down considerably, to 1.5Mbps. At that rate, an hour-long program will consume about 720MB.

To get a rough idea of how much video can be stored on a typical hard drive, see Table 4.1. In addition to some popular compression settings, I have included for comparison uncompressed NTSC video, and rough estimates for the recording quality settings used by TiVo and ReplayTV video IEDs.

Table 4.1 – How Many Hours of Video Can You Fit on Your Hard Drive?

Format	Transfer Rate (Mbps)	Maximum Video Storage on a 20GB Disk (in Hours)	Maximum Video Storage on a 40GB Disk (in Hours)	Maximum Video Storage on a 60GB Disk (in Hours)	Maximum Video Storage on a 80GB Disk (in Hours)
NTSC	208.0	0.21	0.43	0.64	0.85
MPEG-2 ("High")	10.0	4.44	8.89	13.33	17.78
MPEG-2 ("Medium")	8.0	5.56	11.11	16.67	22.22
TiVo "Best" + ReplayTV "High"	7.7	5.81	11.62	17.43	23.24
TiVo "High" + ReplayTV "Medium"	4.8	9.32	18.63	27.95	37.27
MPEG-2	3.8	11.76	23.53	35.29	47.06
TiVo "Medium"	3.6	12.28	24.55	36.83	49.11
TiVo "Good" + ReplayTV "Standard"	2.2	19.84	39.68	59.52	79.37
MPEG-1	1.5	29.63	59.26	88.89	118.52

ReplayTV and TiVo bit rates are estimated. All storage requirements are approximate, and do not take into account storage needs of other software applications and disk formatting data.

Dell Computer sums up the hard drive issue well in its technical literature on digital video editing: In a nutshell, Dell's video-centric customers are advised to consider "buying the largest hard drive possible within your budget."

Displays

When you're choosing a PC monitor for viewing the TV programming captured by your tuner card, the same general rule of thumb applies as when choosing a television set (or a CPU or a hard drive, for that matter): the bigger the better. Unfortunately, you'll usually pay more per square inch for a computer monitor than you will for a television. From a consumer standpoint, this may seem counterintuitive: After all, why should a "dumb" PC monitor—merely a display device—cost more than a comparably sized television set, which can not only display video but also includes speakers and a tuner? The reason is that the cathode ray tubes (CRTs) used for computer displays require much higher resolution than their TV counterparts. In simple terms, they are capable of providing a much richer display in the same screen area.

This greater resolution is an advantage in most applications, but one notable exception occurs when computer monitors are used to view TV programming. The higher screen definition on your computer monitor serves as a magnifying glass for the "artifacts" or flaws that are inherent in TV transmission signals. Television sets based on the U.S. standard (NTSC) offer typical display resolution of 640 pixels per line on each of 480 visible scan lines, with a visual quality just blurry enough to gloss over these artifacts. By comparison, a typical 17-inch computer monitor with resolution of 1,280 by 1,024 won't miss a glitch. As the resolution of the image increases on your PC screen, so does the conspicuous appearance of the flaws in your TV signal.

One suggestion: Don't plan on sitting up close, as you normally would when working at your PC. Sit back and relax. Just like with a big screen TV, putting some distance between you and the display will make the imperfections less noticeable.

Your other option is to purchase a graphics card with TV-Out capability so you can output information normally sent to your PC monitor to a television screen. Many, though not all, newer graphics cards do offer some form of TV-Out functionality.

TV Tuner Cards

Graphics cards with integrated TV tuners are becoming increasingly popular, particularly in Europe. According to market research firm

In-Stat, tuner-equipped cards already account for 40% of the total market for PC graphics cards. In Europe, about one half of all graphics cards sold have TV tuning features.

Most TV tuner cards for PCs rely on a simple tuner chip to take the signal input from a coaxial source—your antenna, cable box, or satellite dish—and, with the help of additional decoders and processors, convert it into audio and video data that your PC can handle. In fact, many, if not most, commercial TV cards use the exact same chip: the Philips TDA9800T VIF-PLL demodulator. Typically, you'll find this integrated circuit on the add-in card, shielded from electromagnetic interference (EMI) inside a small metal box.

This metal box contains the Philips
TDA9800T VIF-PLL demodulator chip.

FIGURE 4.1
The layout of the ATI All-In-Wonder Rage 8500 board, shown here, is typical of PC tuner cards.

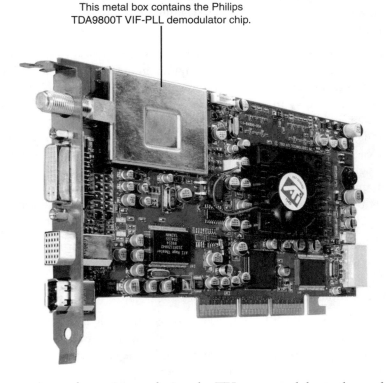

As an alternative to placing the TV tuner module on the card, several manufacturers also offer an external unit, usually connected to the PC via a Universal Serial Bus (USB) connection. One possible advantage to the external unit is that the tuner chip is housed "outside the box,"

not inside the PC's chassis where its signal can be degraded by electro-magnetic interference, or EMI (see discussion of nVidia's Personal Cinema product, below).

Hauppauge

One of the most popular video capture and TV tuner solutions for your PC, the Hauppauge WinTV product family, is available in a dizzying array of shapes and styles, ranging from an internal interface card to external USB-connected devices. Likewise, different versions offer a wide variety of encoding and playback quality for both audio and video signals, multiple input/output configurations and various TV and even radio tuning capabilities. Current pricing for WinTV products range from $49.99 for a basic WinTV-GO PCI TV Tuner Card to $424.99 for the high-end WinTV-HD HDTV Receiver PCI Card.

For those trying to build a reasonably priced video IED out of their PC, Hauppauge's answer is the WinTV-PVR. The $249 package offers MPEG-2 capture settings at rates from 2Mbps up to 12Mbps. In addition to the obligatory 125-channel cable-ready TV tuner, the card comes with an IR remote control (though this, unfortunately, lacks a record button) and an FM stereo radio receiver. The accompanying software supports many advanced IED features, such as timeshifting; however, it lacks an integrated program guide—a major disadvantage.

ATI

A close competitor of Hauppauge is ATI Technologies of Thornhill, Ontario. The company's current line-up includes the ATI-TV Wonder and TV Wonder VE tuner cards, the external TV Wonder USB Edition, and the All-In-Wonder family of combo cards.

While the $99 TV Wonder USB Edition, shown in Figure 4.2, offers easier installation—no need to crack open the chassis—ATI acknowledges that variations in power output from your PC's USB port can affect TV image quality. In addition, there is a compatibility problem with motherboards that use an AMD OHCI USB Controller chip. These systems intermittently fail to detect the TV Wonder device, although this problem does not appear to be isolated to ATI. The AMD controller also has been reported to sporadically lose touch with certain USB keyboards and mice.

FIGURE 4.2
The TV Wonder USB
Edition offers easy
installation via an
open Universal Serial
Bus port.

The only ATI products that approach the recording quality of a dedicated TiVo/ReplayTV/UltimateTV appliance are the company's $199 All-In-Wonder add-in card products, which are capable of supporting MPEG-2 video compression. These cards come equipped with video IED software features, including timeshifting and Gemstar-TV Guide's GUIDE Plus+ interactive program guide. A choice of graphics processors is available: either the Rage 128 or the Radeon chip. Onboard graphics memory is configured as follows: 16MB or 32MB of SDRAM on the All-In-Wonder 128; 32MB of SDRAM on the All-In-Wonder 128 Pro; 32MB of DDR SDRAM on the All-In-Wonder Radeon; 32MB of SDR SDRAM on the All-In-Wonder Radeon PCI; and a choice of 32MB or 64MB of DDR on the All-In-Wonder Radeon 8500DV.

The All-In-Wonder Radeon 8500DV adds new features to the ATI line, including an RF (radio frequency) remote control that works from anywhere in the house, dual IEEE 1394 "FireWire" video input ports, and higher resolution capabilities, up to a maximum display size of 2048 by 1536.

Matrox

In a similar class with the ATI 8500DV is the Matrox Marvel G450 eTV card. The Matrox card comes with 32MB of DDR memory, and uses a Samsung S5D0127X chip for video and closed caption text decoding, working alongside the standard Philips TV tuner chip. The card's maximum output resolution is 2048 by 1536, just like the

Radeon 8500DV, though for optimum clarity and sharpness, viewers may want to ratchet the resolution down to around 1024 by 768 or lower. The eTV card is unique in its use of Matrox's proprietary "DualHead" output feature which allows simultaneous viewing on a PC monitor and a TV (see Figure 4.3).

FIGURE 4.3
The Matrox Marvel G450 eTV card features "DualHead" technology to display simultaneously on a PC monitor and a television.

Matrox's PC-DVR software enables IED features such as timeshifting and picture-in-picture, but the product comes with only an onscreen "virtual" remote control—a poor excuse for the real thing—and it lacks an interactive program guide.

nVidia

Another new entry worth noting is the Personal Cinema product that nVidia announced in late summer 2001 and released later that fall. This device is a direct competitor of the WinTV and All-In-Wonder product lines, with a few interesting twists.

Although the nVidia product doesn't match WinTV's nifty ability to monitor closed captioning text and trigger automatic recording when it encounters key words designated by the user, it does claim to offer improved video and audio quality as a result of housing its tuner in a "breakout box" rather than on the interface card inside the PC. nVidia engineers say the electrical interference inside the box creates signal "noise" that can only be avoided by locating the tuner assembly outside the computer enclosure. Versions of the nVidia Personal Cinema product were slated to go on sale for as little as $150.

Video IED Software for Your PC

In most cases, the TV tuners listed in the previous section ship with bundled software that contains at least a few of the rudimentary functions needed for your PC to record, timeshift, and view video programming from a broadcast source.

Table 4.2 – Video Capture/TV Tuner Software

Product	Platform	MPEG 1	MPEG 2	Program Guide	Remote Control	Zoom
PowerVCR II 3.0 Deluxe	Windows	✓	✓	✓		
CinePlayer DVR Plus	Windows	✓	✓		✓	
WinDVR	Windows	✓	✓	✓		
SnapStream PVS	Windows	✓				
ShowShifter	Windows			✓	✓	
MGI·TV	Windows		✓	✓	✓	✓
iuVCR	Windows 2000					
VCR	Linux					
CapTV	Windows					

In fact, there are a dozen or more commercially available software packages designed to put your tuner card to work. All support video recording to some degree, and most now offer some timeshifting features. All of them aim to approximate the viewing experience of a dedicated video IED. Table 4.2 provides a summary of these programs, their major features, and where you can download them. Next, we'll break out a few of the applications and discuss them in greater detail.

Time-shifting	Free Demo File	Added Features	Price for Full Version	Web Site
✓	✓	Multi-channel preview, enhanced DV camera support	$129.00	www.gocyberlink.com
✓	✓	ISO-compliant MPEG encoding	$79.95	www.ravisentdirect.com
✓	✓	Part of video suite that includes WinDVD	$99.95	www.intervideo.com
	✓	Supports handheld devices, networks, CD-R burning	$49.99	www.snapstream.com
✓	✓	DVD, MP3 playback	$49.95	www.showshifter.com
✓		DVD, CD playback	N/A	www.mgisoft.com
	✓	Native Win2K and ActiveMovie support	$25.00	www.iulab.com
	✓	Support for Web-based remote recording	Free	www.stack.nl/~brama/vcr
		Supports multiple capture devices	Free	www.micromediaenterprises.com

ShowShifter

Home Media Networks, based in Edinburgh, Scotland, is the creator of ShowShifter. Some users in ShowShifter's online forums have criticized the software for using non-standard interface designs rather than familiar Windows control screens, inducing an initial "interface shock" when first encountered (see Figure 4.4). However, HMN's chief executive Colin Tinto has publicly stated that—at least in Showshifter's case—the move away from Windows is deliberate. The reason is to make onscreen details clearly legible, even when the remote-control-equipped user is comfortably esconced on a sofa several yards away.

FIGURE 4.4
Although some users have claimed "interface shock," the company says the use of a nonstandard interface is a conscious effort to allow people to view and manipulate the software from across the room.

ShowShifter has shown itself to be in active development, with regular bug fixes and feature additions taking place. In addition, ShowShifter's user community has made a contribution in the form of plug-ins and companion programs. These include the following:

- Web Scheduler—Lets users view, schedule, and add new timed recordings over the Web.
- Depg—Retrieves electronic program guide (EPG) data from GuideScraper (North America).
- Digishift—Adds support for EPG features on Digiguide (UK and Ireland).

- ACTiSYS IR200L Remote Control—Allows use of a remote control to control ShowShifter.

- Music Mixer—Compiles playlists for MP3 files and provides graphics to accompany playback.

- Blue Skin—Changes ShowShifter's look by altering the background colors.

SnapStream PVS

SnapStream PVS shipped a new version in November 2001 with support for an interactive electronic program guide (EPG) from TitanTV.

One of the more unique features of SnapStream is its support for PocketPC handheld computers via the company's PocketPVS software. The program synchronizes recordings between your desktop and palmtop PCs, allowing you to watch shows either at home or on the road (see Figure 4.5).

FIGURE 4.5
SnapStream PocketPVS software enables you to record programs on your PC and transfer them to your PocketPC-based personal digital assistant, such as a Compaq iPaq.

Depending on the choice of quality settings, recordings for the PocketPC platform tend to consume about 1MB for each minute of video. Thus a two-hour recording will require about 120MB of storage, which can be a bit much for handheld devices with limited memory resources. PocketPVS Module v1.5 is available for $29.99, or bundled with SnapStream PVS for $79.98.

VCR

On July 30th, 2001, programmer Bram Avontuur released Version 1.08 of his Linux-based video recorder software, called simply VCR. One focus of the program is to allow remote recording commands to be set via the Internet, in a fashion similar to ReplayTV's www.myreplaytv.com features. As Avontuur states, "Now, you can finally record your favorite program from a remote place, because Murphy's law dictates that you remember to record it when you're as far away from your home as possible." The remote capability is supported by a separate piece of freeware called webvcr. The "Web/database interface" is available from webvcr.sourceforge.net (see Figure 4.6).

FIGURE 4.6
The open source WebVCR allows users of Linux-based PCs to set up video recording parameters remotely via the World Wide Web.

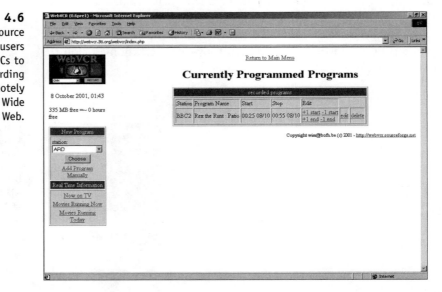

WebVCR was created as a Linux-based "open source" project, in which a group of freelance developers collaborate to produce the code. The resulting software is placed in the public domain, available as a free download.

CinePlayer DVR Plus

Ravisent, the Malvern, Pennsylvania company behind CinePlayer DVR, is planning to implement support for Windows 2000 and Windows XP operating systems in the upcoming version 2.6 release of the software. Plans also call for adding instant replay functionality to

CinePlayer's existing timeshifting features, as well as GuidePlus+ EPG support.

CinePlayer DVR Plus, formerly known as WinVCR, is functionally identical to the less expensive CinePlayer DVR except for the addition of support for MPEG2 encoding (see Figure 4.7).

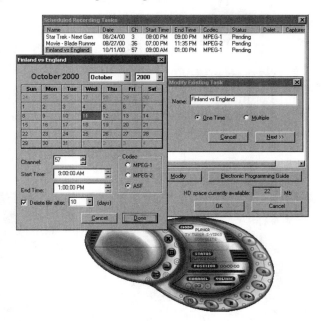

FIGURE 4.7
CinePlayer combines standard Windows screens, as shown here in the scheduling features, with nonstandard interface elements, such as the free-form control panel.

The 2.51 revision of CinePlayer DVR adds support for additional color formats, while fixing glitches such as the software's pesky "recording past midnight" error.

WinDVR

WinDVR is another full-featured video recorder application for the Windows platform, replete with timeshifting, EPG, and MPEG-2 support. The package comes free with nVidia's Personal Cinema TV tuner product, or as a standalone application selling for $99.

WinDVR is part of InterVideo's WinCinema suite of video and audio processing software. Other WinCinema components include WinRip (MP3 encoder and player), WinCoder (encoder for MPEG-1 and -2 video), WinProducer (video editor), WinDTV (HD and SD TV decoder), and WinDVD (DVD player software).

It bears mentioning that WinDVR contains some innovative features, including one called Time Stretching. The premise is to enable users to adjust the playback speed of recorded video from half-speed to double-speed while maintaining natural audio quality. As the developer, InterVideo of Fremont, California, explains it, "Short on time, but want to finish the movie tonight? Use Time Stretching to play that two-hour movie in one hour! "

Buying Off the Rack: The Sony Digital Studio PC

For those who want the flexibility and control of a Windows PC configured to act like a video IED, but don't want to get their fingernails dirty, Sony makes the elegant and pricey Digital Studio PCV-590G. The top-of-the-line tailor-made video workstation was introduced on October 11, 2001 (see Figure 4.8).

FIGURE 4.8
Sony may be correct in describing the newest member of its VAIO Digital Studio Series, the PCV-590G, as a "giant step forward in the evolution of the ultimate entertainment device."

With a price tag of $2499, the PCV-590G leaves little to be desired. Major features include

- Pentium 4 2.0GHz processor with 512MB of PC-800 DRAM
- Built-in MPEG-2 TV tuner
- Asus AGP-V7100 graphics card (based on nVidia's GeForce2 MX chip) with 32MB of SDRAM
- 100GB Ultra ATA/100 hard disk storage
- HPNA V.90 modem
- 10-BaseT/100-BaseTX Ethernet

- DVD-RW CD-ROM drives
- Memory Stick play and record capability
- MPEG-2 real time encoder/decoder card
- Internet Electronic Program Guide
- Giga Pocket Personal Video Recorder software

Without a doubt, the Sony PCV-590G is a lot of machine, giving you TiVo-like capabilities with the added luxury of being able to copy your MPEG-2 video files to a recordable DVD disc. But are you sure you're willing to shell out the equivalent of somewhere between 6 and 12 TiVos for the privilege of being able to burn your videos onto removable media? For most consumers, that's a bit of a stretch. However, if you're already in the market for a high-end PC and a dedicated video IED, the Sony Digital Studio may be just the ticket.

What's Coming Next?

The future of "personalized" television viewing and programming is practically anyone's guess at this point. Despite consumers' love affair with video IEDs, Wall Street has not been sharing in the warm feelings. TiVo, ReplayTV, and UltimateTV are all hedging their bets on the consumer market by cozying up to satellite and cable programmers, vying for the rights to provide IED capabilities in their next generation of set-top boxes.

How will programmers and service operators contend with the ability of consumers to zap away commercials, undercutting the fundamental economics of free (or at least subsidized) television? One step will be for the networks to stop the denial and change television to reflect the way viewers increasingly want to consume the medium: On demand.

Speaking at a cable industry convention in June of 2001, AOL Time Warner chief executive officer Gerald Levin said, "I believe all television will be distributed either in real-time or in on-demand format. When I say 'all television,' I mean everything—every show, every piece of music."

ON DEMAND IS ON ORDER FOR AOL TIME WARNER

Shortly after his prophetic pronouncement at the cable conclave, Levin put his money where his mouth was. In August 2001, he announced the formation of an interactive video unit to be headed by the former chief of Time Warner Cable, Joseph Collins.

The new division's charter? As Levin explained to the *New York Times*, "This is very personal for me. Joe and I have worked for 30 years toward the same dream of video on demand."

One day later, five major movie studios announced their plans to collaborate on a wide scale video-on-demand venture. Coincidentally, AOL Time Warner's movie unit, Warner Bros., led the charge, along with Metro-Goldwyn-Mayer, Viacom's Paramount Pictures, Sony Pictures Entertainment, and Vivendi Universal's Universal Studios. (On the same day, shares of the Blockbuster video rental chain fell about 9%.)

The other shoe dropped a few weeks later, when Walt Disney Studios and News Corp. announced formation of their own video-on-demand joint venture, called Movies.com.

It's a daunting prospect: Having an enormous library of media available at your whim, without the need to constantly monitor broadcast schedules to glean the relatively few shows you're actually interested in. Within the next two years, we can expect to see such services materialize, though only time will tell if they can be delivered in a fashion that is convenient and financially attractive to both consumers and industry.

Chapter 5

Intelligent Game Consoles—
Gaming Goes Global

Overview of Gaming IEDs

When it comes to pulse-pounding, sweaty-palmed exhilaration, few home entertainment experiences compare to video games. Although a good movie can sometimes draw us into the story and make us identify with the main character to the point that we feel projected into the onscreen action, a great video game can add the element of interactivity, occasionally blurring the line between reality and fantasy. When we hit the racetrack wall and disintegrate into a ball of fire, or our opponent's weapon fells us in the middle of some heroic act, we literally feel the physical and emotional impact. Likewise, when we make the checkered flag flutter down or vanquish some particularly unsavory enemy, the flush of victory we feel is often quite real.

What elevates a video game from the mundane to the sublime is the ability of the game designer to suspend our disbelief and sense of reality, effectively immersing us in a world of their imagining. It might be no coincidence that the story line of many roll-playing games is oddly similar to the game designers' own professional experience: a constant quest for power, and a hell-bent race to acquire the arcane tools and technologies needed to harness that power.

Is the PC Passé?

If the lifelong quest of a game developer is more power to bring his visions to life, why is there such neglect for the PC as a gaming platform? Some estimates show that only about 20% of the multibillion-dollar game software market is comprised of titles for the personal computer. The overwhelming majority of new video games are being created for dedicated game consoles, and the gap is widening as more developers are attracted to the promise of new game devices that appeared on the market in late 2001.

These new devices—specifically Microsoft's Xbox and Nintendo's GameCube—seem to combine some of the best features of a game console and a PC: superb graphics tuned for games with high-power data processing, expanded storage capacity, and support for high-speed Internet access. Does this mean that PC gaming will go away? Obviously not. Even if there were conclusive proof that games run faster, look better, and are flat out more fun on a console than a PC, it would not sway the many millions of hard-core PC gamers or the developers that cater to them. Fortunately for their peace of mind, no such proof exists, and many new titles will continue to come out for PC players.

The debate over which gaming platform is superior has raged unabated since the Commodore 64 got people wondering whether they should buy another Atari-type console or splurge for an all-purpose machine that played games and ran computer programs, too.

Separating PCs from Consoles

Many of the basic dynamics have not changed since this initial PC versus console showdown that took place 20 years ago. In a nutshell:

- PCs cost considerably more than dedicated game consoles. In fact, a PC that is fully configured for high-end gaming can easily cost 10 times as much as a dedicated console.

- The higher price for PCs is justified because they can do much more than play games. In addition, many people already own a PC.

- Consoles are designed to operate like a consumer appliance; that is, they require no technical knowledge to configure, they turn on instantly, and they are generally ready to play games right away without a multitude of bootup screens and user selections. Incompatibility issues and system crashes are relatively rare.

- Consoles increasingly provide access to a greater array of the most popular video games.

These considerations aside, deciding which machine provides a better gaming experience is a highly subjective and rather individualistic process. Game consoles—and particularly new ones like the GameCube shown in Figure 5.1—have the advantage of being "one-trick ponies." They are optimized to do one thing and do it well. Game designers need not worry about what one developer calls the "hellish compatibility sweeps of today's PC environment." Whereas PCs must be all things to all people, conforming to diverse hardware setups of various graphics and audio cards, motherboards, and even processors, game boxes are blessedly circumspect in what they set out to do. As a result, PC developers face a huge burden of ensuring that their software runs on a system that can be configured and modified in thousands of different ways. Conversely, game box developers are working in a small, tightly controlled environment where all client machines are configured identically. Ironically, this can give them much greater artistic expression because they are wasting no unnecessary effort on compatibility issues.

FIGURE 5.1
Because they are single-purpose machines that are capable of running only one application at a time, dedicated game devices such as the Nintendo GameCube can present a more manageable software platform for game developers.

However, one of the reasons that many gamers make PCs their platform of choice is precisely because of the open architecture and unlimited upgradability. Want a faster CPU, a more powerful graphics card, a bigger hard disk, a more versatile audio processor? It's all available, for a price. Bear in mind, though, that PC game developers tend to target their games at a midrange PC specification. You might have the highest of high-end PCs on your desk, but that doesn't mean the game software will take full advantage of all that powerful hardware.

In the final analysis, deciding between a PC or a game console is a personal choice. And let's face it—millions of people have both. This book is written primarily to help you assess and enjoy the capabilities of new entertainment appliances that contain computers, not computers that can be configured as entertainment devices. If you are interested specifically in optimizing your PC to provide a better gaming experience, you can read numerous books and visit numerous Web sites to help you do that. Before you decide to follow a PC-based path to your own personal gaming Nirvana, ask yourself a few questions:

• Is the game that I'm most interested in playing available exclusively for the PC or for a console?

• Would I prefer to play games sitting in front of a computer screen, enjoying maximum resolution and visual quality, or am I more into lounging on a sofa with friends in front of the TV?

- Do I prefer rich, sophisticated strategy and simulation games, in which the PC excels, or do I crave arcade-style games and fighting/action titles that seem to proliferate for the console?

These and other factors will add up to help you make a clear choice for the game platform that suits you best.

The Winds of War: Console Versus Console

Microsoft. Sony. Nintendo. They add up to nearly a trillion dollars worth of marketing and manufacturing muscle—and they all want to dominate the video game space. The stakes could not be higher.

Imagine if this struggle for game console supremacy were actually taking place inside a fighting action video game, such as Tecmo's best-selling Dead or Alive series. Nintendo would be the aged and wily warlord character, Sony the powerful warrior and sensei, and Microsoft the fearsome and brutal streetfighter/novice. Each brings unique qualities and combat styles to make the fight for game box domination a colorful, if bloody, spectacle.

In this particular battle, Sony is already the high scorer, with runaway sales of its PlayStation 2 placing it well ahead of the competition in both units and software titles (see Figure 5.2). The consensus among professional game industry analysts is that Sony is a shoo-in for taking a commanding lead in console sales, at least through the first half of 2002. More impressive, though, is that it will accomplish most of this growth prior to shipping its promised hard drive or network connections, items that Microsoft Xbox offered at the outset.

Nintendo's GameCube presents some interesting challenges. Although this platform is destined to be a hands-down favorite among the younger game players who continue to line up for the adventures of Mario and family—and who can never get enough of all things Pokémon—it might be a hard sell with older gamers. Fewer titles at launch and the lack of DVD playback features in U.S. versions of the machine could hamper sales of this compact console, despite its lower price. Nintendo hopes that the GameCube's ties to the wildly successful GameBoy series of portable players will prove to be the console's ace in the hole. In fact, Nintendo of America vice president George Harrison has publicly stated that the company intends to use

GameCube's ability to link Game Boy Advance, shown in Figure 5.3, via an optional cable attachment as a "Trojan horse" to place more GameCubes in American living rooms.

FIGURE 5.2
Market forecasters predict that Sony's lead will continue to mushroom during the next several years, with Microsoft bumping Nintendo into the No. 3 slot.

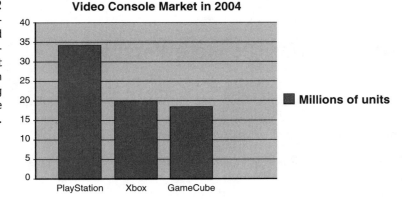

Source: International Data Group

FIGURE 5.3
Nintendo's GameBoy Advance will add a new dimension to the GameCube, possibly enticing players of the portable device to purchase Nintendo consoles.

Meanwhile, Microsoft plans to take a similar approach to its belated entry in the video IED market. As with its UltimateTV gambit, Microsoft will try to outflank its adversaries with pure hardware power: the fastest processor, the most video memory, the biggest hard drive, and the only broadband connectivity offered as standard equipment. Will it be enough to overwhelm the entrenched and much more experienced competition in this cut-throat business? Perhaps not, but being the volume leader in game box sales might not be the software giant's primary objective. Some conspiracy theorists believe that Microsoft's true aim is to hook game developers on its DirectX graphics tools in an indirect effort to re-ignite the flagging PC market with new Windows-based game software.

And what of older generation, so called "legacy" consoles such as Sony PlayStation, Nintendo 64, or Sega Dreamcast? With the possible exception of the PlayStation—lately rechristened as the "PSOne" and equipped with a new LCD screen for portable play—these are essentially orphaned products. Although these legacy consoles might still provide a viable choice for people who don't mind sacrificing cutting-edge performance and access to the hottest, most technically advanced game titles, they don't merit a detailed analysis here. Because their life as an active product and development platform is grinding to an end, they are ultimately destined to join the Atari, Magnavox Odyssey, ColecoVision, Fairchild Channel F, and others in the Valhalla of dead video game consoles.

What's in a Game?

Since the first video game console traded in its diodes for a real processor chip in the late 1970s, these machines have earned the title of Intelligent Entertainment Devices. They employ many of the same types of components that are found in personal computers, but with the exception of their cutting-edge graphics, they are typically a generation or two behind their desktop cousins. With the debut of the Xbox and GameCube in 2001, that disparity might have narrowed, but a generation gap will likely always exist between PCs and game consoles. Furthermore, whereas PC designs are refreshed every few months to add the latest and greatest CPU, graphics, and storage capabilities, game consoles are expected to have a shelf life of five years or more between design cycles. As a result, the cutting-edge cachet of new consoles quickly passes as they begin their inevitable slide toward obsolescence.

What's inside a typical console? The parts list generally looks like this:

- CPU
- RAM
- Operating system software

- Graphics processor with TV output
- Audio processor with RCA-type output
- Storage medium for games (DVD, CD-ROM, or cartridge)
- Power supply
- User control interface

Additionally, the latest generation of consoles adds broadband or dial-up modem support, and in Microsoft and Sony's case at least, a hard disk drive. Let's take a look at what these new hardware devices can do to enhance the gaming experience.

Hard Drives

Microsoft's Xbox was the first game console to include an 8GB hard disk drive within the unit. Sony was scheduled to introduce a 40GB hard drive unit for its PlayStation 2 in North America in early 2002. Designed to fit into an expansion bay on the back of the PS2, the internal hard drive was already shipping in Japan in the fall of 2001, priced at about $144. Nintendo has remained mum on any plans to offer an optional hard drive for GameCube, although the system sports some unexplained connectors that could suit this purpose.

Pure console gamers have little experience with hard drives, and many have expressed in online chat rooms and bulletin boards some mixed feelings as to whether these storage devices can provide any tangible benefit. Microsoft, naturally, sees the addition of a hard disk as a major breakthrough in gaming.

Just prior to the Xbox launch in North America, I met with Microsoft games marketing director John O'Rourke, who among other qualities, might have been hired specifically for his infectious enthusiasm.

"The hard drive can be used in many ways, including bringing down graphical texture information," O'Rourke says.

One of the major benefits of an onboard hard drive, according to O'Rourke, is the freedom from "loading" screens that intrude on the game experience.

In the sci-fi first-person shooter (FPS) game Halo, created by Microsoft subsidiary Bungee Studios, developers set out to specifically take advantage of the Xbox's hard drive features. "You can have these incredibly large levels and you don't run into these loading screens every 3 minutes because the information can be fed off of the hard drive. In addition, when you've got 64MB of potential video memory, you can create environments that are huge, levels that are bigger than many whole games of the past."

O'Rourke says that the automatic and imperceptible loading of new levels and data-intensive backgrounds provides a more intense game experience. Let's face it—no one needs extra distractions while tramping through a mysterious ring-shaped world, trying to concentrate on saving the remnants of mankind while blowing away members of a vicious alien race called the Covenant.

"When you're playing a video game, your goal is to sort of get immersed in that game and escape, and have a chance to live and dominate in that world for a while," O'Rourke says. "Every time you run into a loading screen, it sort of takes you out of that world and reminds you that you're back on the couch. If you don't run into those, you can have hours and hours immersed in that game and really get the true entertainment experience."

The hard drive also plays a role in such features as allowing the machine to play appropriate background sounds, dialogue, real-time commentary, and music composed on the fly in response to actual gameplay. In addition, the expanded storage allows users to store seemingly unlimited numbers of saved games and game levels—tasks that would otherwise fall prey to the limitations of smaller-capacity portable memory cards.

A perfect example of the advantage that a built-in hard drive offers comes from Madden 2002, available for the Xbox, GameCube, and PlayStation 2. To save both game profiles and league data in the GameCube version of Madden 2002, you would need two $20 memory modules—and that's just for use with one game. With the Xbox version, you don't need memory cards unless you intend to use that data with someone else's Xbox.

Modems

When Sega introduced the Dreamcast in September of 1999, it was a sensation. Developed in conjunction with Microsoft, it offered unparalleled 3D graphics among game consoles and a wondrous new peripheral: a 56K modem. The addition helped Sega position the product as the world's first truly Internet-capable video game console. Users could surf that astonishing new medium known as the World Wide Web (at least it was still new to many potential buyers of the Dreamcast), in addition to exchanging e-mail and playing a few online games offered by the console company's inhouse online service.

Dreamcast was a hit, selling a half-million units in the first two weeks, and surpassing the million mark in a little over a month. But perhaps the most far-reaching impact of the Dreamcast would be its tantalizing glimpse into the arena of online gameplay.

Fast forward now to the fall of 2001. Modems have become standard equipment—or at least a standard option—for new console platforms. Xbox ships with broadband connectivity via a built-in Ethernet port, whereas GameCube offers a Conexant V90 56K modem as an accessory, to be bolstered in early 2002 by a broadband-capable version. Sony promised to release an Ethernet/modem adapter for the PlayStation 2 in late 2001, though that has slipped into 2002, allowing for broadband and dial-up Internet connections, and giving users access to e-mail, instant messaging, and Web browsing.

Of course, the pièce de résistance for connected game consoles is their ability to interact with other game consoles. This relatively new phenomenon sweeping the game community represents a sea change in how video games are played and the impact they have in many persons' lives.

As constituents of a growing number of organizations, such as the 170,000 member Online Gaming League (www.worldogl.com) will attest, wired collaborative game play is here to stay. Founded in 1997, the OGL claims to be the world's largest action game competition Web site, having served more than half a million gamers since its inception (see Figure 5.4). Like members of a bowling league, players form teams and schedule regular meetings to compete against other teams—only instead of throwing strikes and gutterballs, they might be clashing virtual swords or firing interstellar laser blasts at one another.

In fact, sites such as this are but one aspect of the multifaceted world of massively multiplayer games. The action is everywhere. A brief peak at www.gamespy.com on a quiet Sunday morning in November revealed 61,374 gamers online.

FIGURE 5.4
Typical ladder listings on sites such as the Online Gaming League show growing interest in multiplayer online games.

Sony Online Entertainment has invested heavily in the online gaming arena, boasting 100,000 players per day showing up for Jeopardy! Online, based on the TV game show, and more than 375,000 registered users for EverQuest, a Medieval fantasy role-playing game (RPG) that is arguably the most successful massively multiplayer title to date. With players plunking down from $10 to $40 for the PC software, and another $9.98 per month to join in online melees that can accommodate some 90,000 simultaneous players, the category is rapidly becoming a major cash cow.

What's the attraction? After extensively researching the games marketplace, Microsoft determined that the seemingly solitary act of interacting with a PC or console game is actually an inherently social experience.

"Playing against and competing with other people—or cooperating with them—is why (gamers) play video games. It is social, it's not a solitary environment," Microsoft's O'Rourke explains. "What really excites them is the chance to come in and be the best on a particular platform, have tournaments, have ladders, have competitions."

"Imagine it's a basketball game, and rather than it being just offense versus defense, it's me and four of my best friends playing you and four of your best friends. And I'm in Seattle and you're in San Francisco, and we're all in our own separate houses playing real-time basketball. I'm moving around and I'm calling the plays, and it works because of the power of the Xbox, because we've got the fast connection and because we've got voice."

That fast broadband connection and voice support are, in fact, key to Microsoft's yet-to-be-announced online service strategy for Xbox. As of this publication, Microsoft has not divulged specifics of the business model for Xbox Online, which is tentatively scheduled for debut sometime in the first half of 2002.

In the meantime, Xbox's Ethernet port can be used to link together as many as four separate Xbox units, with each capable of supporting four players.

How would this network look and feel in action? "Halo has the capability to connect four different Xboxes and have 16 people playing either cooperatively or competitively against each other," O'Rourke says. "So if you're thinking about a bunch of 20-year-olds in their dorm, they could potentially be having a Halo party. I can tell you this is one of the most common recreational activities around Xbox (business unit in Redmond, Washington) halls these past few weeks. It's been tough on productivity when you have an amazing game like Halo around and the chance for people to compete with each other" (see Figure 5.5).

Some might be turned off by multiplayer gaming and prefer a more controlled environment where they can always be the hero without enduring the meddling of fellow humans. For them, Microsoft sees another role for the online connection: the ability to download new data to keep games fresh and engaging for the easily jaded teens and young adults that the Xbox has targeted. This could also lead to a benefit that PC gamers have long been used to but has been impossible, up until now, on game consoles: patching.

Few games ship completely without errors, or "bugs," but with a hard drive and a connection to the Internet, it becomes possible for developers to deliver fixes right to users' living rooms even after the game has shipped.

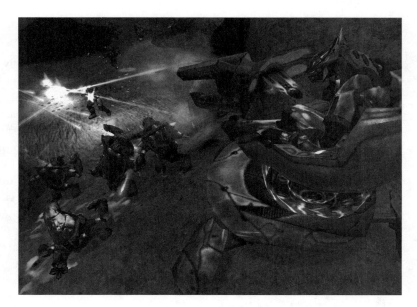

FIGURE 5.5
Even without broad-
band capability,
Microsoft Games' Halo
sci-fi shooter game lets
up to 16 players mix
it up.

O'Rourke becomes glassy-eyed as he describes what the Xbox's combi-nation of 8GB hard disk space and an always-on broadband connection could do to enhance future gameplay. Citing a what-if scenario involv-ing the new Microsoft-developed Xbox title, NFL Fever, "Imagine a world when you've got this thing connected to broadband and you can download real-time statistics. Who's been traded? Who's on which team? Who's injured and who's not injured? You can actually download weather patterns, too. If you're coming in to the next Monday night football game and you want to know what the weather's going to be like, you could roll that into your game and play it like the real Monday night game is going to be. That's something you've never been able to do in a video game in the past because (your console's) never been con-nected."

Nintendo has been more tight-lipped about its online strategy for GameCube, but industry sources have reported that a major planning effort is underway to build out online communities where players can trade data and play games.

In a rare public statement about the game platform's future online capabilities, Genyo Takeda, Nintendo's corporate director and general manager of integrated research and development, made this comment in August of 2000 about GameCube. "It will combine Nintendo's world-class design and beloved franchise characters with the expansion of the world of gaming by an online network."

Sony has also been less than forthcoming when it comes to divulging the full scope of its online plans for PlayStation 2. A clue was provided in October 2001 at a Sega consumer conference during the Tokyo Game Show, where Sega COO Tetsuo Kayama outlined a strategic alliance with Sony Computer Entertainment to bring Internet TV capabilities to the PS2 in Japan. As of this publication, Sony representatives had revealed that streaming audio and video would be supported by the modem-equipped PlayStation 2, in conjunction with the pending availability of a hard drive accessory. The online services for PlayStation 2 in the U.S. market will be provided by Sony Computer Entertainment of America (SCEA) partners such as America Online, Macromedia, and Real Networks, supporting such games as Activision's Tony Hawk's Pro Skater 3 and Sony's SOCOM: US Navy Seals.

What's Still Missing

If only we could combine the best features of all three game platforms into one device, creating a true crème de la consoles. It would include Xbox's superior hardware features, PlayStation's overwhelming software library, and GameCube's connection to portable devices and action characters that are so cherished by children and children-at-heart the world over.

Of course, this imaginary hybrid—XCubeStation? GamePlayBox?— would also feature a low price and the ability to surf the Web and send and receive e-mail while simultaneously playing DVDs.

Alas, it is not to be. Gamers without unlimited access to funds will continue to need to choose wisely between these three contenders to the game console crown.

As for these makers of gaming IEDs, filling out their respective product lines while converging on the sweet spot of hardware and software completeness will keep the three companies busy for the foreseeable future. Whether Microsoft meets with enough initial success to continue the Xbox line into perpetuity will remain an open question at least until late in 2002, and perhaps beyond.

The perennial quest for better graphics, greater connectivity, higher utility through the addition of DVD movie playback and Web surfing features, and ever more engrossing software titles, is laudable. Yet game consoles still have failed to achieve (or even pursue) the full mission of intelligent entertainment.

In both the audio and video IED categories, we have seen the creation of devices that harness the computers inside the box in an attempt to better understand their human masters. With TiVo in particular, we have witnessed the beginnings of an effort to study and learn from the choices we make, and to respond by offering us more of what we want. In the audio space, OpenGlobe-powered devices such as the Compaq iPaq embody this same goal of using the intelligence inside the appliance to discern our tastes and present us with a panoply of relevant choices. In the music center's case, the idea is to make us offers to complement our musical collection with direct online access to additional recordings, events, and merchandise from the artists we love.

Where is the intelligent entertainment equivalent to TiVo and OpenGlobe services among these new gaming IEDs? Just as GameBoy Advance is Nintendo's Trojan horse for additional hardware sales, Xbox and UltimateTV will eventually become Microsoft's Trojan horse for additional services in the home.

The time it will take for the software giant to whip these hardware devices into shape and begin to realize their true IED potential is difficult to judge. UltimateTV has been in the marketplace for a year, yet its interface seems to have progressed at glacial speed. Microsoft has announced ambitious plans for the IED (see Chapter 12, "Where's the Service?"), but those enhancements may not materialize until mid-2002.

A fine line must be walked between providing desired and complementary services to consumers, or alienating them with poorly targeted and exploitative come-ons for things that aren't wanted. The former quickly degenerates into the latter when the offer is presented in a time and manner that serve to irritate rather than entice. Although no one seems to have hit the nail squarely on the head in this regard, there is more to be learned from OpenGlobe than from UltimateTV at this stage.

All IED manufacturers are struggling to strike the right balance between service and abuse. I can definitely see a future in which Nintendo steps in as soon as I have finally freed Mario from his ghostly captors, and subtly offers to sell me instant access to additional levels of Luigi's mansion. Or Sony, taking note that I inevitably choose the 1976 Oakland Raiders as the home team in Madden NFL 2002, might politely inquire whether I am interested in buying an authentic jersey worn by quarterback Kenny "The Snake" Stabler.

Until the game platform providers set out to make this a reality, we will be left with a handful of consoles that simply provide adrenaline-pumping entertainment. Come to think of it, maybe that's all we really want them to do after all.

Chapter 6

Choosing the Right Gaming IED for You

Overview

Gaming IEDs can be compared on several levels—performance, features, software and price being some of the primary categories. However, in the final analysis, a combination of these attributes will determine which machine is the ideal choice for your home.

This chapter breaks down these categories and discusses some of the metrics used to assess each of the three console gaming platforms.

Performance

As most of you know by now, an electronic video game console is yet another form of intelligent electronic device (IED)—in other words, a computer designed to function as a consumer appliance. Although gaming IEDs offer only a limited set of computer functions, they require a tremendous amount of horsepower to perform those functions.

Electronic gaming is a highly specialized and thoroughly demanding computer application, whether the application is running on a dedicated IED or a general-purpose PC. It's no coincidence that PC gamers often become obsessed with their hardware, constantly upgrading it, refining it, sometimes resorting to overclocking, refrigerating the CPU, and other extreme modifications in their effort to wring the highest possible performance out of their machines. The results of these ministrations can be quite gratifying when the speed, agility, and audiovisual quality of gameplay noticeably improve.

Game consoles, however, are not as easily tweaked. Traditionally designed as closed, proprietary appliances, game consoles come with a custom, tamper-resistant operating system, nonstandard components, and extremely limited upgradability. As a result, these devices tend to debut with eye-popping new capabilities, only to wither into obsolescence within a few years.

Whereas a new PC can be viewed as a work in progress—perhaps even a blank canvas upon which the user can improve at will—game consoles have always had more or less fixed performance levels that will not change over the life of the product. In this way, it is easier to make an apples-to-apples comparison of gaming IEDs based on how they perform common tasks, such as rendering graphics, reproducing audio, and so on.

Central processing units (CPUs) that are used in dedicated gaming IEDs seem typically underpowered. Even the Xbox's 733MHz Pentium III processor, boasting a significantly higher clock speed than either Nintendo's or Sony's IED CPUs, is still essentially last year's chip as far as PC buyers are concerned. Actual performance, though, is not measured purely in clock speed.

Although the gaming IED's CPU certainly has an important job to do—in fact, several jobs—it is the game system's graphic processing unit (GPU) that typically handles the real dirty work (see Figure 6.1).

FIGURE 6.1
GameCube's GPU, code-named "Flipper," is a 51 million transistor chip from ATI's ArtX team (Photo courtesy of AnandTech.com).

The GPU is a specialized piece of silicon that, upon instructions sent by the CPU, creates the mesmerizing and rapid-fire three-dimensional graphics that quicken your pulse and keep you glued to the TV screen for hours on end. In this respect, the relationship between CPU and GPU in a game box is similar to that of the CPU and video processor in a video IED (see the "Hardware: Processor and Memory" section of Chapter 4, page 97). As in that example, a relatively weak CPU is sufficient to handle the system's housekeeping functions, although the real horsepower is devoted to a specialized processor that is dedicated to the visual computations in these most visual of computers.

The GPU's primary job—graphics rendering—is often measured in terms of polygons, the most basic geometric building blocks from which visual game data is constructed. As you learned in math class, a polygon is a multisided geometric figure, such as a triangle, square, or hexagon. The potential shapes and sizes of polygons are limitless, but perhaps more important for gaming aficionados is the variety of ways that polygons can be rendered on the screen.

The world is three dimensional, and your brain is highly adapted to discerning the depth and distances of objects and the play of light and shadow upon them. Your brain processes this information so instantaneously and automatically that your body often reacts long before you are conscious of the cause and effect sequence that has just taken place. For instance, when another car swerves into your lane, your body might take evasive action while your brain is still playing catch-up. There simply isn't time to wait for cold reasoning to occur. Your body must act immediately, processing the sensory input and subsequently issuing orders to your arms to turn the wheel and your legs to stomp on the brake.

Action-oriented video games intentionally try to manipulate your sensory system to evoke the same kind of response. When done correctly, these games can even kick your hormones into gear, flooding your system with adrenaline. When this happens, look out: You have another potential best-selling game title on your hands!

To fool your senses and deliver that adrenaline rush, game designers must use every programming trick and all the system resources at their disposal, to create images that stir up a real physical and emotional response in the viewer. Audio can enhance and heighten the experience, but it's no substitute for superb visual quality. The key to that visual experience lies in the polygons, which are defined by their depth, shading, color, number, and speed. In general, the best game hardware is that which is capable of showing the maximum number of polygons, in the greatest amount of clarity and detail, in the shortest amount of time.

One of the fascinating things about displaying 3D objects on a computer screen is that it's essentially impossible. After all, how can any object be accurately rendered in three dimensions when viewed using a flat, two-dimensional display device? In reality, the effect is achieved by performing the complex calculations of precisely what space the object would occupy if it actually did have three dimensions, and then gradually hiding or displaying the depth of the object as the perspective changes. The viewing plane is still only two dimensional, but the quality of the rendering can effectively simulate the ability to see an object's depth and to convey a sense of its mass.

For these reasons, 3D graphics rendering hardware is frequently measured in polygons per second. All polygons are not created equal, however. Although some game console and 3D graphics accelerator manufacturers only quote "raw" polygon rendering speeds, it is important to also compare the rates at which devices can render complex polygons—that is, polygons that are shaded (or lighted), textured, curved, and otherwise detailed. After all, a game that is composed of plain old polygons, without proper lighting and texturing, would look more like *Pong* than *Dead or Alive 3*.

Among the factors that can help determine these display speeds is the bit rate of the processor—for instance, a 64-bit chip versus a 128-bit chip—and the amount of available memory for temporary storage, or *caching*, of graphics data.

Software

Regardless of metrics that measure properties such as the number of lit, curved, and textured polygons produced in a given second, graphics quality tends to be rather subjective. The machine's brute force ability to render polygons is only half the battle. The rest is up to the game designer's artistry in harnessing that horsepower and turning it into an emotionally engaging visual experience.

Software for dedicated gaming IEDs falls into two categories: the operating system, or *kernel*, and the game software. Although the kernel is important to the game developer, it is of no direct relevance whatsoever to the game player. The gamer cares about which software titles are available for the IED and how they perform on that platform. Quite simply, the game platform with the most extensive software library wins—providing that enough of the games are the *right* games.

For this reason, Sony, Nintendo, and Microsoft are battling not just for the hearts and minds of the gaming community: They must first win over the development community.

Nintendo's chairman Hiroshi Yamauchi demonstrated his grasp of the issue in a November 2000 interview with Wit Capital. "I've been told that Sony won over Nintendo by surrounding itself with software companies, and I will admit that situation was there in the past," he told the investment house. "However, times have changed, and it's no longer a race to see how many useless companies you can get on your side."

To counter the Sony threat, Nintendo has worked hard to simplify its game development environment. Sony PlayStation has been widely criticized by game creators as a particularly difficult development platform. Yamauchi also had harsh words for Microsoft's alleged practice of buying the loyalty of game makers with excessive cash outlays for agreements to develop new titles for Xbox.

"There are many people in the industry that know nothing about games. In particular, a large American company is trying to do the same thing by engulfing software houses with money, but I don't believe that will go well." As Yamauchi himself concluded, only time will tell, but all three console makers fully understand that success is impossible without wholehearted support from game developers.

Features

Gaming IED manufacturers are as susceptible as any to the insidious *Swiss Army Syndrome* (SAS). SAS describes the prevalent tendency to add feature after feature to a product in hopes of achieving a critical mass of capabilities that will almost magically open a consumer's wallet. Also called *feature creep*, SAS has come to define Microsoft's approach to product design, both in software and in hardware. Witness Xbox's ability to act as both a DVD and an audio CD player. It can even create MP3 tracks from audio CDs. Likewise, Sony PS2 doubles as a DVD player, and in the future it might likewise serve as a set-top box and a home networking gateway.

It might benefit both Sony and Nintendo to study the example set by personal digital assistant makers Palm Computing and Handspring in pioneering new ways to compete with Microsoft. In November 2001, Handspring founder and CEO Jeff Hawkins revealed how, during his tenure at Palm Computing, he intentionally withheld new features when he introduced the Palm V handheld device. In fact, he deliberately prevented any new functionality from being added to the new handheld so that it would be impossible for journalists to create feature comparison charts, which he was convinced would favor Microsoft's feature-heavy PocketPC platform. By focusing attention on the Palm V's sleek and slim design, he was able to successfully compete against Microsoft's Swiss Army-style approach.

Microsoft has "infinite amounts of money and people, and you can't compete against them. I wasn't even wanting to," Hawkins explained during his keynote address at Comdex Fall 2001. "I said, 'Let's do something they don't do. They don't build hardware. I build hardware, and they don't. Let's build a beautiful piece of hardware. Let's not try to add new features, because we'll never catch them on the software side.' So we started down the path to building the Palm V, and this was specifically to prove the point that we could compete against Microsoft by not trying to do what they do, but doing something different."

"Palm V was all about style and elegance… I figured if we added new features, the reviewers would come out and say, 'Palm adds three new features, Microsoft adds 30 new features.' We'd lose. But if I had no new features, they couldn't do the features comparison chart! There was nothing they could do! So all they could talk about was how thin and beautiful it was. And that was a very successful strategy."

Price

Along with performance, software, and features comes the consideration of price. Aside from DVD playback—a feature notably absent in Nintendo's current and future versions of GameCube for the North American market—game consoles serve no utilitarian purpose in the home. They are completely discretionary and designed for leisure. Furthermore, a large segment of gaming IED purchasers are parents buying for a dependent child. Under these circumstances, price definitely matters, as Microsoft in particular might learn the hard way. Even at $299 per unit, Morgan Stanley analyst Mary Meeker estimates that Microsoft could lose $1 billion on Xbox by fiscal 2004 before finally breaking even on the game hardware business.

Nintendo's Yamauchi, who set the launch price of GameCube at $100 less than PS2 and Xbox, said in a February 2002 interview that the days when it was acceptable to take a bath on game hardware sales might be over. "Up until fairly recently, it was safe to lose money on hardware sales, since you more than made up for it in the software sold. It's impossible to get a system out the door that way anymore. So when you release a system today, you don't necessarily have to profit from it, but you can't afford to lose money on every single console you sell."

Although these are words that might very well haunt Microsoft in the years ahead, it is worth pointing out that Microsoft cut few corners in terms of adding useful hardware extras into the Xbox, which cannot be said of the GameCube. The question is whether or not a DVD player, built-in hard drive, Ethernet port, and a more powerful design are worth an extra $100 to consumers.

That Certain *Je Ne Sais Quoi*

In the next section, as you learn how each gaming IED stacks up in those specific categories, it might seem as if there are some clear winners and losers. Bear in mind, however, that these devices are purely luxury items, and as such, their sole purpose is to give pleasure. By all means, before you make up your mind, go down to your local toy store kiosk and take each one for a spin. Perhaps rent a unit from your neighborhood video store, along with a few of the games that hold the greatest interest for you and your family, and find out first-hand which consoles disappoint or delight you. That will be the surest way to make a purchase that you're unlikely to regret.

After all, as Xbox sales and marketing director John O'Rourke puts it, "When (people) buy a video game system, it's not just for a couple of months, but it is for years. They want that game to be fresh. They want that game experience to be something that they're going to enjoy the first year, the second year, and the fifth year."

Nintendo GameCube

"Leave luck to heaven." The proverb is one of many interpretations of the word Nintendo, the name chosen in 1889 when a wealthy Kyoto artisan named Fusajiro Yamauchi decided to open a playing card factory. Since that time, the company has passed from family member to family member, dabbling in businesses that ranged from instant rice to taxicabs to brothels, but always returning to its game-playing roots (see Table 6.1).

Table 6.1 – Nintendo Vital Statistics	
Status	Independent public company (NTDOY)
Business model	Developer of electronic game hardware and software
Founded	1889

Table 6.1 – Continued	
CEO	Hiroshi Yamauchi, great-grandson of founder Fusajiro Yamauchi
Headquarters	Kyoto, Japan
Employees	Approximately 1,000*

*Estimate

In more than 110 years of developing and marketing original games and toys, Nintendo has amassed a huge store of expertise and an extremely valuable lineup of virtual talent. In 1959, Fusajiro's great-grandson Hiroshi Yamauchi signed Nintendo's first license agreement. His choice of partners was prophetic. While manufacturing playing cards under license to the Walt Disney Company, Hiroshi Yamauchi might have begun to understand the power of the printed images that appeared on those cards—the likenesses of Mickey Mouse, Donald Duck, and other world-famous characters.

Whether his epiphany came in 1959 or much later, Yamauchi certainly came to recognize the importance and inestimable value of those characters. Yamauchi eventually directed Nintendo's creative department to develop similar character franchises that are now among the company's most precious assets: Mario and Luigi, Pokémon, Donkey Kong, and Zelda are but a few of Nintendo's cavalcade of characters that are known and loved worldwide.

Nintendo's mercurial leader deftly explained his vision for the GameCube in a recent interview with the Japanese financial newspaper *Nihon Keizai Shimbun*. Following the back-to-back announcements of new game consoles from Nintendo and Microsoft during the Electronic Entertainment Expo (E3) in May 2001, Yamauchi was asked to contrast the two rival platforms.

"The ideas behind Xbox and GameCube are fundamentally different," Yamauchi said. "Xbox has a built-in hard drive and is being touted as an extension of a PC. Microsoft is going after performance only, and does not understand that the game is played with software.

"The GameCube is the most advanced machine for playing games, and it is totally different from the Microsoft product. It is just like trying to compare a sumo wrestler and pro wrestler: They play by totally different rules. We do not consider Microsoft to be our competitor."

Asked why Nintendo had chosen to sell the GameCube for $100 less than Xbox or Playstation, he replied, "People do not play with the game machine itself. They play with the software, and they are forced to purchase a game machine in order to use the software. Therefore, the price of the machine should be as cheap as possible."

Although Nintendo's chairman might come off as glib regarding potential competition from Microsoft, no one doubts that the venerable company is losing plenty of sleep over Microsoft's initial success. The truth is that there really isn't a single "right" approach to the game console market. "Different strokes for different folks" makes for a more interesting and diverse offering—and a win for consumers.

GameCube has clearly staked out the low end of the market—the price-sensitive portion that is largely represented by young parents buying for their younger children. Xbox has gone to the other end of the age and income spectrum. To a large degree, they are aimed at older teens and young adults. Xbox costs more, but it gives more back for the price. Sony hopes to occupy the middle ground, with a library of games that covers both extremes of the electronic gaming market. Although Sony currently rules the roost in sales volume, it would not be surprising to see Nintendo and Microsoft's gains in 2002 come mostly at Sony's expense. Sony's aging PlayStation architecture and lukewarm commitment to higher performance and broadband connectivity will hurt it with the hardcore, older gamers, although its price—equal to Microsoft's but without many of the technological bells and whistles—might be a turn-off to the younger and more price-sensitive side of the market.

Hardware

At this point in its history, Nintendo has truly returned to its roots. The launch of GameCube in the United States in November 2001 was a testament to its commitment to being nothing more or less than a game company.

GameCube's design reflects that simplicity. Gone are any add-ons or doo-dads that do not directly enhance gameplay. Unlike competitors Sony and Microsoft, which clearly have ulterior motives in addition to selling as many game machines as possible, Nintendo has set out to do one thing, and to do it extremely well. The early returns indicate that the buying public endorses the strategy. Within days of releasing

GameCube to U.S. stores, Nintendo had sold out its initial allotment of the machines and immediately ordered that an additional 200,000 units be shipped to U.S. stores, bringing the total units hitting North American shores to 1.3 million.

Enclosure

The outside of the GameCube is attractive, impressively compact, and strictly functional. Initially available only in black and purple (a colleague groaned that it would never suit her décor), its classic cube shape is punctuated by a back-mounted handle. As the smallest and lightest of the three gaming IEDs, Nintendo means for it to travel, from room to room and from home to home (see Figure 6.2).

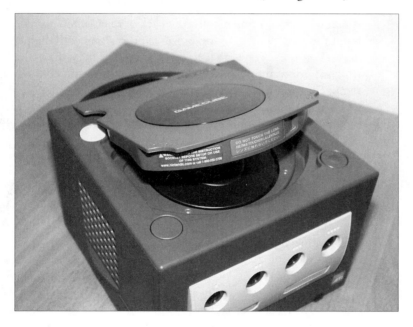

FIGURE 6.2
The GameCube's exterior is a study in elegant simplicity.

Although the GameCube design does not resemble the other black, rectangular appendages that are currently attached to your TV—video IED, VCR, DVD player—this has never been a requirement of game machines. However, that might have changed with the advent of Playstation 2, which was the first gaming IED to actually look at home with other living room video components. Microsoft's Xbox has also opted for the sleek, black look. For its part, Nintendo's decision to opt for livelier colors and a more fanciful shape is consistent with its market position: appealing to younger gamers.

141

TIP

Technically, the GameCube is not a cube: The enclosure is 4.3 inches high, 5.9 inches wide and has a depth of 6.3 inches, making it a little shorter and squatter than a perfect cube.

The top of the cube features its control interface, a hinged lid for the unit's proprietary GameCube optical disk, and buttons for Power, Open, and Reset. A crescent-shaped amber LED glows to tell you the machine is powered up. The front of the unit presents ports for four controllers, and two symmetrical hinged doors accept Nintendo's 4Mb flash memory cards for storing games and characters.

Along with its carrying handle, the back of the GameCube contains the input for its 12-volt, 3.5-amp power supply, along with digital and analog A/V outputs. The other notable surface of the cube is the bottom, which sports a number of unobtrusive hinged plastic doors that, when removed, alternately reveal access to the machine's "Hi-Speed" parallel port and two serial ports. (The probable purpose of these expansion ports is discussed in the section titled "Input/Output," page 144, later in this chapter.)

Processing Power

To power its newest game machine, Nintendo turned to IBM's PowerPC architecture for a custom 485MHz processor with 64K of level 1 cache and 256K of level 2 cache (see Figure 6.3). Named Gekko, the chip was created using IBM's advanced copper wire interconnect technology and .18 micron fabrication process. All this allows the chip to process data as quickly and efficiently as possible, with external data bus speeds offering peak bandwidth of up to 1.3GB per second. IBM's copper technology is also touted as supporting faster throughput, lower power consumption, and cooler temperatures than comparable aluminum-based Pentium chips.

FIGURE 6.3
The GameCube's motherboard prominently features the Flipper GPU and the IBM PowerPC-based Gekko CPU (Photo courtesy of AnandTech.com).

Gekko's principal role is to run game scripts and provide the artificial intelligence that lends game characters their personalities, whereas a dedicated GPU handles the core graphics processing and input/output functions. Nintendo delegated the graphics grunt work to a custom chip from ATI called Flipper. (It is probably no coincidence that the GameCube was developed using the code name Dolphin.) The 162MHz graphics processor also uses a .18 micron process, and features a 2MB embedded frame buffer and an additional 1MB of texture cache. The architecture offers peak bandwidth of 10.4GB per second for texture data, and 2.6GBps for transferring data to and from main memory.

An additional 81MHz custom Macronix chip handles the system's audio processing, producing 64 simultaneous audio channels, or voices, with a respectable sampling frequency of 48KHz—that's not quite CD quality, but it's still pleasing to the ears.

Of course, the true legal tender of 3D gaming performance is polygons. How does the GameCube system stack up? The company claims the ability to process somewhere in a range of 6 to 12 million "real world" polygons per second. This number seems abysmally low compared to the numbers touted by Microsoft and Sony, but Nintendo has been careful to stipulate that the polygon rate it is quoting reflects "complex" polygons that are fully textured and lit, displayed under actual gameplay conditions. (The subtext is that the competitors' polygon data is theoretical and rather pointless.)

Comparisons aside, the results of GameCube's graphics horsepower can be readily seen in the device's mastery of complex texture mapping, which includes a variety of effects—from fog to multiple light sources rendered in hardware—without causing undue strain on system performance.

Memory

For its main system memory, Nintendo has provided GameCube with 24MB of advanced 1T-SRAM (single-transistor static RAM), complemented by an additional 16MB of 81MHz DRAM.

➡ **Further details on how GameCube's memory is allocated and its impact on performance are discussed in the Xbox section of this chapter under the heading "Memory," page 158.**

Despite some prelaunch confusion that GameCube's optional memory cards might contain 4 mega*bytes* of memory rather than 4 mega*bits*, buyers learned to their chagrin that it was, in fact, the lesser capacity. Although the cards only hold about an eighth of the hoped-for storage space—approximately .5MB—there is hope for heftier cards to come, made possible by a planned Secure Digital (SD) flash card adapter. At the time of GameCube's November 2001 launch, the company indicated plans to support the stamp-sized, 64MB SD Memory Card recording media from Matsushita Electric Industrial Co.

TIP

The $15 Memory Card 59, named for the 59 memory blocks that the card contains, can hold about 15 saved *Luigi's Mansion* games, or about five games stored while playing *Wave Race: Blue Storm*.

In addition to the primary function of allowing players to save games, characters, and levels, the GameCube's memory cards could provide a portal for possible feature and memory expansion in the future.

Input/Output

Along with I/O connections for four game controllers and audiovisual display—including full digital A/V output that is suitable for HDTV-enabled computer monitors and televisions—the underside of the GameCube features three special-purpose connectors, labeled Hi-Speed Port, Serial Port 1, and Serial Port 2. Although Nintendo has refused to fuel speculation about plans for either the Hi-Speed Port or the Serial Port 2, the purpose of the third connector has been made abundantly clear: Nintendo intends to offer a choice of modems for GameCube, both of which will snap into the form-fitting Serial Port 1 device bay. Conexant will manufacture both the modem for broadband links and a 56K version for dial-up connections. These ports can be seen in Figure 6.4.

FIGURE 6.4
The underside of the GameCube hides access to future expansion possibilities.

Like its competitors in the gaming IED market, Nintendo had yet to articulate its online strategy at the time it launched its next-generation platform. However, Nintendo's corporate director and general manager of integrated research and development, Genyo Takeda, stated that the modems would allow GameCube owners to connect to both the Internet and fellow gamers, "creating a rich and dynamic entertainment experience."

Nintendo has launched an internal business unit to develop its online service and community offerings, reportedly under the leadership of former technical director, Jim Merrick.

Storage

Perhaps the most revolutionary step that Nintendo took in the GameCube design was to discard the cartridge-based software media it used in all of its previous game consoles and replace it with a proprietary optical disk.

Looking like a shrunken CD, shown in Figure 6.5, the disk measures about 3 inches in diameter, and is capable of storing approximately 1.5GB of data—the equivalent of two conventional CDs (but approximately 3GBs less than the capacity of a DVD—depending on the format). The storage system was developed in close collaboration with Matsushita, the parent of global consumer brand Panasonic. Although the optical drives are based on a derivative of the DVD format, Nintendo decided shortly before launch not to offer a DVD-capable unit in the United States, although a Panasonic-branded combo GameCube/DVD player is still slated for introduction in the Japanese market. Industry sources said software piracy concerns foiled the U.S. version of the combo product.

TIP

One user-friendly feature that Nintendo added to the GameCube is a fail-safe capability that pauses gameplay if the optical disk drive door is opened, then neatly resumes play when the access door is closed again.

Try ejecting the disk from a PS2 while playing a game and you'll see that generally, the results are much less graceful.

The fail-safe feature is a nice touch—particularly for a console that expects to be a strong seller among youngsters, who might not always be able to resist the temptation to punch the Open button—even in the middle of playing Super Monkey Ball.

Controller

Although some gearheads care deeply about what's inside the box and what makes a particular IED tick, most gamers really care about two things: the game software and the controller.

FIGURE 6.5
A proprietary GameCube disk appears tiny next to a conventional CD-ROM disk.

By and large, the GameCube controller has been relatively well received by the hardcore game review community. Whether these people—mostly adults—are truly representative of Nintendo's target audience is somewhat dubious. In fact, a frequent complaint from reviewers is that GameCube's controller is too small—an attribute that could be a plus if your core audience is mostly made up of kids (see Figure 6.6).

Most gamers will find the main controls familiar, and placed where they should be. Some users have complained about the location of the Start/Pause button, saying that its placement in the center of the controller—equidistant from either hand grip—is inconvenient to reach when in the middle of gameplay. However, it should be noted that this button isn't generally used when a player is in the throes of battle, so the point is essentially moot.

FIGURE 6.6
The GameCube controller is small, lightweight, and functional.

The relative merits of a particular game controller are strictly a matter of personal preference. They either fit your hand and your playing style or they don't, although most people are surprisingly adaptable when they want to be.

The new GameCube controller features built-in force feedback, or *rumble*, capabilities. No additional batteries are required, as was the case with Nintendo 64's add-on Rumble Pack. The only downside is that the shaking is often poorly timed and out of synch with the game visuals. For instance, in Luigi's Mansion, pounding an object with Luigi's fist produces a vibration of the controller, but it doesn't occur until after Luigi is finished with the maneuver. If the game designer's goal was to make the user feel more connected to the onscreen action, then the aim was not achieved.

Another new feature that is being introduced with GameCube is the ability to use a Game Boy Advance portable game console as an additional controller. This requires users to purchase an optional Game Boy Advance Link Cable. (For more information on the relationship between GameCube and Game Boy Advance, see Chapter 5's section, "The Winds of War: Console Versus Console," page 119.)

TIP

If you find yourself enjoying your GameCube, but still pining away for your old PlayStation controller, there's hope. An $18 device from May Flash allows you to connect your old PlayStation controller to your GameCube. Called the Cube JoyBox, it's extremely simple to install:

1. Make sure the GameCube is turned off.

2. Insert the plug from the Cube JoyBox adapter into the GameCube controller jack.

3. Insert any PlayStation controller into the Cube JoyBox.

4. Turn GameCube back on and you're (literally) ready to "rumble."

The Web site for May Flash products is located at www.mayflash.com.

Bored with basic black, or "indigo," as Nintendo likes to call purple? You can purchase additional $35 GameCube controllers from the company in "spice" (orange) and "clear indigo," a translucent purple.

Software

For a company that places such emphasis on software over hardware, Nintendo did a poor job of supporting its initial GameCube release with compatible titles.

Placing great—perhaps inordinate—importance on having the most exclusive software titles of any gaming IED provider, Nintendo had only two exclusive English language games available at the time of the U.S. launch: *Luigi's Mansion* and *Wave Race: Blue Storm*. Additional exclusive titles such as *Super Smash Bros. Melee*, *Star Wars Rogue Leader: Rogue Squadron II*, and *Pikmin* were unavailable at launch, but began shipping before the end of 2001. The following are among the nonexclusive GameCube titles—meaning those that are also available for other platforms—that were on sale at the time of the launch:

- *FIFA 2002*
- *Tony Hawk's Pro Skater 3*
- *Crazy Taxi*
- *Dave Mirra Freestyle BMX2*
- *Batman Vengeance*
- *Super Monkey Ball*

- *Tarzan Untamed*
- *All-Star Baseball 2002*
- *Madden 2002*
- *NHL Hitz 20-02*

All the games sold for about $50 at launch. Although there was enough variety to round out the offering, none of the games was a category-busting hit, with the exception of Tony Hawk's Pro Skater. The most widely anticipated of the first-round game offerings were the Game Boy exclusives, particularly *Luigi's Mansion* (see Figure 6.7). In the latest installment of the Mario Bros. franchise, the lesser known of the famed plumber brothers wins a haunted mansion, which he must rid of pesky poltergeists using a hopped-up vacuum cleaner. Although the game is engaging and the graphics are top notch, you probably won't find it a habit-forming pursuit that keeps you or your children riveted for hours on end—and that is precisely the type of experience that Nintendo and its rivals must strive for to thrive in so highly competitive a market.

FIGURE 6.7
This screenshot from Luigi's Mansion conveys the graphics details that Nintendo has achieved with GameCube.

Tips, Tricks, and Modifications

Due to the month-plus lag between GameCube's Japanese launch and its subsequent debut in the United States, many imaginative cheats and modifications had already been documented before the machines made it to American retail shelves.

Perhaps the most daring hack in the early days of GameCube availability was the one attributed to Donnie Yoo and Raymond Souza of Gamestation in La Crescenta, California.

The pair was able to convert a unit designed for the Japanese market to a U.S. version, allowing them to play games created for the American audience, and even displaying English text.

The hardware exploit involves soldering closed a tiny circuit—known as R6—on the GameCube motherboard. After the circuit has been closed, the GameCube can no longer play Japanese versions of games—unless the intrepid IED tweaker decides to install a switch that is capable of toggling the R6 circuit back and forth.

Full instructions for carrying out the somewhat delicate procedure are available at the comprehensive gaming site www.ign.com. Those who are understandably skittish about the real possibility of wrecking their GameCube (needless to say, this is *not* covered under the warranty) might opt to have the unit modified by a professional, such as an online retailer like www.ncsx.com, which offers the service for $38 plus shipping.

On the software side, determined players have unearthed a number of ways to cheat, or to uncover hidden features of various games. In particular, *Luigi's Mansion* seems to have an inordinate number of secret passages and other undocumented features.

> **TIP**
>
> A few of the more interesting cheats for *Luigi's Mansion* include the following:
>
> **Teleporting to the main entrance of the mansion from the gym**
>
> This requires using a Game Boy Advance connected to act as your GameCube controller (see the description of the optional Game Boy Advance Link Cable earlier in this chapter). While Luigi is facing the mirror located in the rear of the gym, press the A button on the Game Boy Advance.
>
> **Changing to a new mansion**
>
> Complete the game and save it. (This requires an optional memory card. See the description earlier in this chapter.) An option is then unlocked allowing you to start a new game in a different mansion.
>
> **In-game resetting**
>
> While the game is running, hold down B and X on the controller, and then press Start for about two seconds.

Wave Race: Blue Storm for Nintendo GameCube also offers a wealth of hidden treats for the unrelenting game cheat forager.

> **TIP**
>
> A few of the more interesting cheats and tips for *Wave Race: Blue Storm* include the following:
>
> **Quick start**
>
> Press A immediately before "Go" is announced and get an immediate green light.
>
> **Weather**
>
> Successfully complete the Expert Championship in first, second, or third place to unlock the weather conditions in Time Trial mode. Finishing in first place grants you weather access under the Expert difficulty setting. Second place unlocks it for the Hard difficulty level, and third place grants access for Normal difficulty.
>
> **Alternate costumes**
>
> Highlight a racer while the character selection screen is being displayed, and then press the Z button.
>
> **Victory Gate track**
>
> Successfully complete the game in Championship mode under the Expert difficulty setting to be admitted to the Victory Gate track.
>
> **Cool Ocean track**
>
> Successfully complete the game in Championship mode under the normal difficulty setting for admission to the Cool Ocean track.
>
> **Control loading screen**
>
> Press the Left analog stick while a track loads to control the water.
>
> **Tournament mode**
>
> While the options menu is being displayed, press the X, Z, and Start buttons simultaneously to unlock the "Password" selection. Passwords for various time tournaments can now be entered.

Microsoft Xbox

The video gaming world changed forever when Microsoft decided to crash the party.

Even though Sega was originally an American-owned company that sounded Japanese (American entrepreneur David Rosen changed the name of his Tokyo-based company from Rosen Enterprises to Service Games—or Sega, for short—in 1965), the video game console industry has been essentially a Japanese cartel since Atari hit the skids in the mid-1980s. A series of lawsuits launched by the U.S. gaming pioneer against Sega, Nintendo, and others did little or nothing to slow the rising tide of Japanese domination in the field. Following the introduction of the PlayStation in 1995, it became a showdown between Sega, Nintendo, and Sony. When Microsoft showed its intention of entering the fray, third-place Sega folded its tent and announced plans to vacate the hardware space altogether.

Why has the software giant decided to pour billions of dollars into creating a new hardware platform? To quote Microsoft Chairman Bill Gates, Xbox is "a key part of our strategy to drive the digital entertainment revolution and deliver the future of interactive entertainment to the home." But there's more to it. Among the key factors influencing Microsoft's decision to enter the game console business:

- PC sales are declining, reducing Microsoft's core software markets.

- Game programs are among the fastest growing of all software categories, with the lion's share of development being devoted to proprietary console games rather than PC-based games. To participate in this activity—and ideally, to someday make game developers as dependent on Microsoft as PC application software developers are today—Microsoft had to get a Windows-based game platform on the market.

- Third-party hardware companies, to whom Microsoft reportedly first tried to sell the Xbox concept as a reference design, declined to take on the job of manufacturing and marketing the product under their own brands. Microsoft was forced to conclude that, if it wanted the job done right, it would have to do it itself.

To those who doubt that Microsoft will have the stamina to stay the course and establish itself as a major player in the games market, look to Microsoft's commitment to the pen-based and handheld computer categories (see Table 6.2). It took several major attempts and more than a decade, but Microsoft finally won a significant share of the market. During the same period, the market matured into something with

153

adequate scale to make the investment meaningful. In its ability to take a long-term approach to a problem and ultimately achieve the goals it sets, regardless of the obstacles, Microsoft demonstrates a strategic approach that is almost, well, Japanese.

Table 6.2 – Microsoft Vital Statistics	
Status	Independent public company (MSFT)
Business model	Software company attempting to invigorate new hardware categories to counter shrinking PC software market
Founded	1975
Chairman and Chief Software Architect	William H. (Bill) Gates III
Headquarters	Redmond, Washington
Employees	47,600*

Source: Microsoft Annual Report (June 2001)

Hardware

If you were to buy a gaming IED based solely on its hardware specs, you would waste little time in choosing Microsoft's Xbox over the competition. Its faster processor, standard hard drive, and Ethernet port, bolstered by larger memory capacity, add up to a clearly superior offering from a strictly hardware standpoint.

Unfortunately for Microsoft, that is not really what most gamers base their decision on. As Nintendo's president Yamauchi so aptly stated in his February 2002 interview with *Business World*, "Gamers play games, not hardware!"

However, Xbox is not targeting just any gamer. "We think that as the newcomer to the category, we really do have the chance to make (inroads with) what we call 'passion players'—the 16- to 26-year-old males that play over 10 hours a week and that love playing video games. It's the chance to really inspire them and deliver the type of gameplay they've always wanted," Xbox Director of Games Sales and Marketing John O'Reilly said shortly before the Xbox launch. Microsoft is betting—and betting big—that this demographic of older, more committed game players will heed the siren call of Xbox's superior performance.

The early returns indicate that Microsoft's gamble could pay off. Xbox units disappeared off retail shelves at a fast pace, despite the $300 price tag. In fact, many—if not most—Xbox buyers paid far more. Although some large discount chain stores allowed buyers to purchase the Xbox unit by itself, the practice of requiring consumers to shell out for mandatory game bundles was widespread in stores and online.

Why would anyone in their right mind splurge up to $540 for Electronic Boutique's Xbox "Blitzen Bundle," with four games and an extra controller? If a picture was ever worth a thousand words, the display generated by the supercharged Xbox running an exclusive title such as *NFL Fever 2002* or *Dead or Alive 3* (unfortunately, neither of the titles are included in your Blitzen Bundle) is just such a picture. The visual quality is simply arresting, but it doesn't stop with the visuals. The Xbox's PC-derived innards are able to bring the characters to life in a way that has never been possible in the video console category (see Figure 6.8).

FIGURE 6.8
This detail from Tecmo's *Dead or Alive 3* demonstrates the cinematic quality of Xbox graphics.

Regardless of whether Xbox can ultimately unseat Sony or Nintendo for the console crown, there's no denying that Microsoft has irrevocably changed the rules of engagement among game IED makers.

The following sections take a closer look at Xbox's unique attributes.

Enclosure

While Nintendo engineers were busily streamlining and shrinking their designs to fit into the petite purple GameCube case, Microsoft unapologetically decided to present the world with a bulky black box (see Figure 6.9). Xbox is the largest game console around, weighing in just shy of 9 pounds and a full three inches longer than the approximately five-pound PlayStation 2.

FIGURE 6.9
Xbox's front panel reveals all the system controls.

Its louvered plastic body is festooned with a large X and bears the signature green Xbox "jewel." The unit's pebbly matte finish is not simply black: As the Xbox marketing machine proclaims, the console is rendered in a "rich shade of black." It would seem that while Microsoft was redefining everything else, it went ahead and redefined black as well. (For the record, Webster's still defines the non-color as "being of the darkest achromatic visual value: producing or reflecting comparatively little light and having no predominant hue.")

On its front panel, Xbox features the front-loading DVD tray, Power and Eject buttons, and four controller ports based on a proprietary USB implementation. The back panel houses connectors for the power cord, A/V cable, and an Ethernet port.

Processing Power

Fastest, largest, most advanced—all the superlatives seem to apply to the Xbox's internals (see Figure 6.10). For its central processing unit, Microsoft chose a modified 733MHz Intel Pentium III processor with a maximum bus transfer rate of 6.4GBps. Both the clock speed and bandwidth compare favorably to GameCube's 485MHz Power PC chip with 2.6GBps and PlayStation's 295MHz processor with 3.2GBps.

FIGURE 6.10
A look under the hood of the Xbox shows a layout that—except for the unshielded power supply on the left side—could almost be mistaken for a PC. (Photo courtesy of AnandTech.com.)

In a pure clock speed assessment, Xbox's Nvidia-built GPU also makes Sony and Nintendo seem anemic. The 233MHz custom-designed Nvidia graphics engine would appear to leave GameCube's 162MHz Gekko and Sony's 147MHz graphics processor in the dust. Nor does Microsoft fall down when it comes to performance claims. The Nvidia chip produces polygons to spare, at the rate of 116.5 million per second, according to Microsoft, compared to Sony's claim of 66 million and Nintendo's of 6 to 12 million polygons. Of course, these are hardly apples-to-apples comparisons because Microsoft's competitors point out that the staggering figure does not indicate "real world" polygons with full shading and depth. However, the last company to underestimate what Nvidia technology can do, 3dfx, ended up walking off the playing field permanently. (Nvidia purchased 3dfx's remaining assets for $70 million in December 2000.)

Regardless of what the stats might say, however, this is a comparison that must be done with human eyeballs, and mine tell me that Xbox's 3D graphics rendering is clearly superior to GameCube and PlayStation. Of course, caveats exist: The graphics are highly dependent on the individual game designers and their ability to effectively harness the performance. In addition, the preference of one game system over the other is highly subjective. A person who prefers GameCube's visual quality over Xbox has every reason to feel that way, and need not be accused of indulging in hallucinogenic narcotics (a prevalent allegation used against both camps in online forums devoted to the respective platforms).

Memory

Once again, Microsoft has joined the hunt already loaded for bear. Xbox contains 64MB of total memory, compared to 40MB for GameCube and 32MB for PlayStation 2. In addition, Xbox's 4x32Mb DDR (double data rate) SDRAM memory is "unified," meaning that game developers can allocate it to the CPU or GPU functions as they see fit. Microsoft argues that this provides greater flexibility for game designers, and will result in improved game performance.

"The developer can decide how to allocate that (64MB), so if they have a game that's hugely graphically intensive, they can choose to take more of that memory and use it for video. If they have a game that's highly physics- or artificial intelligence-dependent, they can use it for that," Microsoft's O'Rourke says.

It gets a little tricky for game designs that are demanding in terms of both CPU and GPU functionality. "*Dead Or Alive 3* is a very graphics-intensive game; however, there is a fair amount [of] CPU horsepower at work also because of the fighting elements of the characters and how they react as 'people.' But it's not as intensive as, say, a racing game where you're doing calculations of velocity and momentum and trying to figure out when somebody goes around the corner, how much should the car slide, how much should it continue on when you apply the brake, etc. Those are very physics-intensive calculations compared to, for instance, an adventure game where a character is just sort of moving around. Fighting games do use up some of that (CPU) capability."

Predictably, Nintendo has begged to differ on the relative benefits of unified memory. Jim Merrick, a Nintendo technical manager who handles third-party relations, has gone on record saying that segmented memory is preferable because it guarantees the availability of memory and bandwidth for certain core functions, such as audio and animation. Nintendo has segmented its 40MB of RAM into a 24MB block for main memory and an additional 14MB set aside for audio/animation data.

The potential problem is that at some point, it's likely that both the GPU and CPU might want to use the same block of memory at the same time. Which request gets priority? Audio must win in the event of a tie, according to Merrick, even though it is a less bandwidth- and memory-intensive application than video. Drop a frame of video and the user might not even detect it, but if there is a hiccup in audio, the user will certainly notice the interruption.

The best experts to judge which scheme is better—unified or segmented—are actually the game developers, but like the hardware makers that support them, they appear to be largely split on the issue. Clearly, there is a trade-off either way, although many consumers readily accept Microsoft's position that more is simply better.

Microsoft Xbox technology officer Seamus Blackley underscored the memory issue during a public demonstration of Xbox capabilities at the Comdex computer trade show in Las Vegas a few days prior to the launch of Xbox. Blackley mesmerized the audience with the stop-action capabilities of *NFL Fever*. Zooming in on the ball, caught in midair during a Hail Mary pass, conference-goers could clearly discern the laces, the nubble of the pigskin, and even the NFL commissioner's signature.

"Our ball actually has more memory in it than PlayStation has video memory in it," Blackley boasted.

Of course, memory isn't just for rendering. You need to be able to save game data, too. GameCube and PlayStation both require the use of an optional memory card to save games, and anyone who aspires to achieve access to the advanced levels of a video game will soon learn that it's practically—if not actually—impossible to do so without such a card. However, Xbox's onboard hard disk can store as many saved games and levels as any player might ever wish. An optional memory card would be completely pointless, right? Well, not exactly. After all, hard drives can't make your saved games mobile. Memory cards are still the best means for taking your *Madden 2002* franchise over to a friend's house for play on his Xbox.

Microsoft sells an 8MB Xbox memory unit (see Figure 6.11) for $35, whereas third-party provider Mad Catz (www.madcatz.com) offers an "officially licensed" 8MB custom memory card for $30. (The Mad Catz card comes with "preloaded game saves" from EA Sports and other Xbox game developers to give the player a leg up on the competition.)

FIGURE 6.11
Despite the ability to save games to the hard drive, Microsoft hopes some users will still opt for an 8MB memory card.

FIGURE 6.11
Despite the ability to save games to the hard drive, Microsoft hopes some users will still opt for an 8MB memory card.

Input/Output

Another category in which Microsoft has distinguished itself is the area of external system I/O. Along with the expected audiovisual and game controller connections, Xbox is the only console that is broadband-ready right out of the box. At least, it is from a hardware standpoint. Currently, no authorized broadband service or online destination is available for the Xbox. In other words, with its Ethernet port and hard drive ensemble, Xbox is all dressed up with no place to go.

At least, that's the case so far as Microsoft is concerned. A group of independent software developers has taken the matter into their own hands, devising a somewhat cumbersome Linux-based application that can connect two online players via broadband Internet. Version 1.082 of Xbox Gateway can be downloaded at www.xboxgw.com. Gamespy.com has gone one better and introduced a "GameSpy Tunnel" software utility to allow Xbox owners to compete using a hosted online service.

Microsoft plans to offer its official connections to online multiplayer gaming sessions when it activates broadband capabilities in the summer of 2002. A DSL or cable modem will be required to participate, and the company has yet to divulge whether it will charge a subscription fee. Consider it highly likely.

In the meantime, the Xbox's Ethernet port has an immediate application: to connect to other Xboxes (see Figure 6.12). For Xbox games that are designed to accommodate multiple players, it is possible to daisy chain as many as four Xboxes together. This allows a total of 16 players to participate simultaneously in games such as the first-person shooter and sci-fi epic *Halo*.

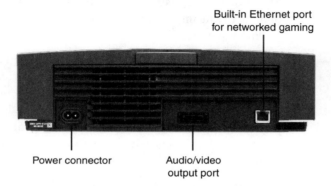

Built-in Ethernet port
for networked gaming

FIGURE 6.12
Xbox's rear panel houses an array of I/O choices.

Power connector

Audio/video
output port

In terms of Xbox's A/V output, Microsoft did not scrimp here, either. However, it might cost you a little extra to take advantage of some of Xbox's loftier output capabilities.

Dolby 5.1 surround sound is included free, along with Xbox's superior 256-voice capability and 3D audio, but Xbox's HDTV support requires the purchase of the High Definition AV Pack. Providing TV resolutions up to 1920x1080, the $20 High Definition AV Pack supports HDTV RGB video and a choice of RCA audio or digital audio via optical cable.

Microsoft also offers an Advanced AV Pack for $20 that provides optical digital audio output for Dolby Digital playback, as well as S-Video output. For older TVs that don't support RCA audio and composite or S-Video input, Microsoft sells a $20 RF adapter.

Storage

Like its HDTV features, using your Xbox as a DVD movie player requires an optional add-on kit. To turn the video game console into a home movie theater involves purchasing a $30 DVD Movie Playback Kit. The kit includes an infrared receiver and a remote control.

Although the onboard DVD movie playback is convenient and might take some of the edge off of coughing up $300 or more for the system, the real centerpiece of the Xbox's storage features is the internal 8GB hard disk.

161

For reasons unknown, Microsoft originally announced that the Xbox would contain an 8MB hard drive, quietly increased it to a 10GB hard drive, and then slimmed back down to an 8GB model for the final spec. Microsoft's terse statement on the final configuration decision said only that reducing the capacity from 10GB to 8GB was determined to be "more practical."

In any case, the integrated drive has numerous benefits, according to the company, a chief one being the ability to virtually eliminate "game loading" screens. By being able to cache, or temporarily store, large amounts of data on the hard drive, the system does not have to pause play every time it runs out of data stored in volatile memory and substitute a loading screen while it accesses new game data from the optical disk.

Microsoft also claims that certain special effects, such as the real-time audio play-by-play by veteran *CNN/Sports Illustrated* sports announcer Dick Stockton that accompanies Xbox exclusive title *NFL Fever*, can only be performed on systems that are equipped with a hard drive.

Controller

Although Microsoft is new to the field of game console manufacturing, it is, in fact, an old hand at making game controllers. After rolling out its first PC joystick controller in 1995, the company has produced a steady stream of the peripherals ever since. It added force feedback technology to its gaming repertoire through the acquisition of Exos Inc. in April 1996.

Considering the Xbox controller's lineage, it's hardly a coincidence that it bears such a striking resemblance to the PC-based Microsoft SideWinder Game Pad USB (see Figure 6.13).

Like any game controller, the success of the design is highly subjective. You either love it or hate it, and a major determinant will be what you are used to. If the Xbox is your first game console, or if you cut your videogame teeth on a PC using one of Microsoft's somewhat bulky, bat-shaped game pads, you're likely to find the Xbox controller comfortable and functional. If you're used to the smaller and lighter Nintendo and Sony controllers, you might feel the same as one disaffected Xbox owner expressed in an online discussion forum: "It's like holding a pumpkin."

FIGURE 6.13
For all practical purposes, the Xbox controller (left) could be this SideWinder Game Pad USB controller's long-lost twin.

Software

It's undeniable that Microsoft has tried to buy its way into the hearts of game developers, reportedly showering them with money in an effort to build a war chest of compelling game titles for Xbox. By and large, the strategy appears to be working.

At launch, Microsoft listed some 17 game titles. Another 18 or so were slated to ship in time for the holidays, and an additional 9 or 10 titles were listed for delivery by mid-2002.

Among the Xbox exclusive games on tap at the time of the system's debut were these:

- *Oddworld: Munch's Oddysee*
- *NFL Fever 2002*
- *Halo*
- *Dead or Alive 3*
- *Fuzion Frenzy*
- *Project Gotham Racing*
- *Mad Dash Racing*

Another exclusive software feature for Xbox is the addition of parental controls. Seamus Blackley, the former Dreamworks Interactive game developer who now heads up Xbox's hardware and software design efforts, says the parental control capability is critical—not just for parents, but for developers.

"The game developers, the guys I talk to, don't want to have to censor their thoughts," Blackley explained during a presentation at Comdex Fall 2001 in Las Vegas. "They don't want to have to put a violence slider in their games, so this takes care of that for them. That's why I think it's one of the most important features in the Dashboard."

The most significant piece of software Microsoft designed for Xbox is, in fact, the Dashboard itself. The "transparent, dynamic, 3D UI with a graceful feel," as the software maker describes it, appears upon system startup whenever the game slot is empty or when a standard CD or DVD is loaded (see Figure 6.14).

FIGURE 6.14
Xbox's Dashboard menu is Microsoft's first attempt at a 3D user interface.

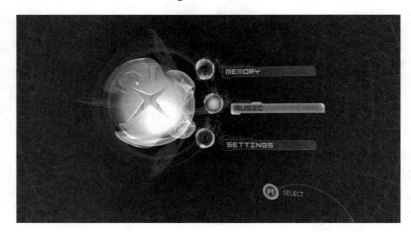

The interface—Microsoft's first to incorporate 3D graphics—was given its distinctive look and feel by Los Angeles design firm Rezn8. "The differentiating feature about the Xbox Dashboard is that it is a living and breathing component that can detect and interact with the software to offer higher levels of game interaction," says Rezn8's founder and president Paul Sidlo.

Xbox's Dashboard allows users to monitor and change parameters in three categories: Memory, Music and Settings.

The Memory menu (Figure 6.15) allows players to manage the use of both hard drive and memory card storage. The contents of each device can be viewed, moved, or deleted. In addition, the hard disk menu allows players to view a listing of all the games they have played, regardless of whether the game supports disk saves or use of the data cache.

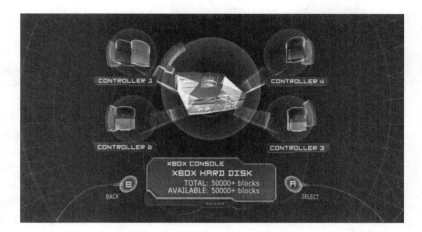

FIGURE 6.15
The Dashboard Memory menu offers choices for managing disk and memory card functions.

The Music menu, shown in Figure 6.16, provides controls for another set of features that are unique to Xbox: the ability to listen to audio CDs and record them to the game console's hard drive for use as custom game soundtracks. Audio tracks are recorded at 128Kb, 16-bit stereo quality, and are automatically normalized for consistent volume during playback. After tracks are recorded, they can be incorporated into Xbox games that support the Soundtrack feature.

FIGURE 6.16
The Music menu provides access to Xbox's CD ripping capability.

HOW TO RIP CDS ON XBOX

1. Insert an audio CD into the Xbox optical drive.
2. From the Dashboard display, select Music, Audio CD, Copy. Use the Xbox controller's joystick/trigger to move between Play, Pause, Select, Select All, and Copy functions.
3. Choose the Copy menu, and then select tracks from the CD to use for your soundtrack. Select Play or Pause buttons to audition tracks, and then use the Select or Select All buttons to mark tracks for copying. To save time, you can choose Select All and then use Select to toggle off any tracks you don't want to record.
4. After you have selected your tracks, choose Copy. The recording speed is roughly three times faster than playback speed. Audio tracks are now ready for use as a soundtrack in your favorite Xbox game.

The final Dashboard menu area, Settings is where the parental controls reside, alongside controls for the system's clock, language, audio, and video parameters. Choices include the ability to choose between mono, stereo, and Dolby SurroundSound audio characteristics, as well as letterbox and widescreen video settings.

Tips, Tricks, and Modifications

Like GameCube, too few Xbox games or players exist at this stage for a significant library of cheats and tricks to have been compiled. However, enterprising users have still managed to delve into some of the system's nook and crannies, and their labors have already produced some fruit.

Although Microsoft would like every Xbox developer to enable as many Xbox special features as possible, companies that are creating games for multiple platforms are unlikely to do so in every case. Anticipating this, Microsoft has created a backdoor capability to save games to the Xbox memory card, even if the game developer has neglected to enable the feature.

> **TIP**
>
> In the event that a game does not offer the option of saving game levels to the memory card, but it does support saving to the hard disk, users are advised to try the following:
>
> 1. From the Dashboard menu, choose Memory and copy the Save File from the Hard Disk to the Memory Card.
>
> 2. When you insert your memory card into another Xbox console, reverse the process and copy the Save File from the Memory Card Back to the Hard Disk.
>
> You should be able to resume play on the new Xbox system at the same point where you left off.

A number of cheats for specific Xbox games have also been uncovered. One of the most inspiring is for *Cel Damage*, a teen-rated racing and demolition title created by developer Pseudo Interactive and published by Electronic Arts. According to several online game cheat compendiums, entering your name as *ENCHILADA!* unlocks access to all cars, tracks, and modes.

To gain similar access to all cars and courses in *Project Gotham Racing*, the sports car auto racing game developed for Xbox by Bizzare Creations, try entering *Nosliw* (*Wilson* spelled backward) as your driver's name. Note: This is case sensitive.

An interesting cheat for *NFL Fever 2002*, an Xbox exclusive title developed internally by Microsoft Games, involves the ability to unlock all teams and stadiums. Simply enter the name *BROADWAY* at the Profile screen. And in the "something for nothing" category, try this cheat: Go to the Game Setup screen in *NFL Fever* and wait 30 minutes without pressing a single button. You might be rewarded with access to 125 extra created players.

As far as out-and-out hardware hacks, Xbox has so far proved an elusive target. In addition to the unofficial software releases that provide early access to online gaming (see the "Input/Output" section earlier, page 144), hackers have succeeded in documenting the substitution of a faster ATA-100 cable to speed up the connection between Xbox's hard disk and DVD drives.

Table 6.3 lists some of the promising Xbox hacking projects that are currently underway. However, the fresh nature of Xbox hacks makes it questionable whether each of the modifications will be independently confirmed and ultimately proven successful. Proceed at your own risk.

Table 6.3 – Sources of Information on Hacking the Xbox

Project Name	Description	Web Site
Xbox Hacker	Web site that is dedicated to documenting Xbox hacking and reverse engineering advances.	`www.xboxhacker.net`
X-64	Software emulator that allows Nintendo 64 games to be played on Xbox.	`www.x64.freeservers.com`
Andy + Luke's Xbox Information Area	Site that contains detailed documents and software utilities to describe and modify Xbox hardware. Downloads include: • Xbox File Dumper • Xbox IDE Sniffer	`www.tardis.ed.ac.uk/~lucien/computing/projects/xbox`
Icrontic	Site devoted to overclockers and gamers that has an excellent pictorial of the insides of the Xbox. It chronicles successful attempts to install an ATA-100 cable and more. The author also claims to be working on software to allow the Xbox hard drive to be mounted in a PC for transferring Xbox files to the PC.	`www.icrontic.com`
MrHack's Website	Site explains how to set up a virtual private network to connect Xboxes via the Internet.	`mrhack.realgamers.net`
Team Xbox Forums	Bulletin board for postings related to Xbox games and hacking.	`forums.teamxbox.com`

Sony PlayStation2

Officially introduced to the U.S. market in October 2000, Sony's PlayStation 2 shipments had topped nearly 20 million units by September 2001 (see Table 6.4). The numbers are exceptional, but this only marks the beginnings of Sony's plans for the game platform.

Table 6.4 – Sony Vital Statistics	
Status	Independent public company (SNE)
Business model	World's No. 2 maker of consumer electronics, Sony also has vast media holdings in the areas of television, motion pictures, and music
Founded	1946
Chairman and CEO	Nobuyuki Idei
Headquarters	Tokyo
Employees	181,800

Sony's President and Chief Operating Officer Kunitake Ando delivered a keynote speech during the Comdex Fall 2001 trade show in Las Vegas that clearly demonstrated the PlayStation 2, shown in Figure 6.17, evolving into something more than a mere gaming console.

In Sony's vision of the future, PlayStation occupies a revered place in the connected living room, serving as a hub for broadband communications and interaction between myriad consumer devices, ranging from network-enabled video cameras to high-definition plasma display televisions and computers for the desktop, laptop, and palmtop. (Yes, Sony's robotic dog, Aibo, figures in somewhere as well, but let's not even go there.)

To help realize that expansive PlayStation-centric vision, Sony enlisted America Online Time Warner, announcing at the event that the two giants will team on creating a next-generation home broadband entertainment hub. In a bow to Sony, AOL Time Warner CEO Steve Case beamed in via satellite to congratulate Ando on the deal, and to describe a major focus of their union: ease of use.

FIGURE 6.17
The Sony PlayStation 2 design leaves no question as to where Xbox derived its black louvered look.

"Nobody should have to be a systems integrator to make a convergence network work in their home," Case said. "It is still too difficult for most people to connect the dots."

Sony's primary answer to the issue appears to be a new wireless interface being developed under the name "feel". In a demonstration at the event, a Sony handheld computer was able to connect to a Sony notebook after each device sensed the other's proximity using a Bluetooth wireless network.

Ando also boasted of PlayStation's pervasive sales throughout Japan, and how Sony will continue to leverage that installed base to push other technologies into consumers' collective consciousness. Just as PlayStation's integrated DVD drive drove the adoption of DVD movies in Japanese homes, Ando said that PlayStation will act as the catalyst to finally convince consumers of the need for HDTV.

These pronouncements, combined with plans to introduce tailored online services and additional peripherals required for PlayStation to enjoy broadband connectivity, will make the console a formidable opponent in the battle for home gaming and beyond. The pronouncements also serve to underscore that, although Nintendo still seems content to sell toys, Microsoft and Sony have plans for their game devices that reach far beyond the traditional console business.

Hardware

As the successor to the original PlayStation that shipped in 1995, PlayStation 2 has been around long enough to leave little of its hardware territory unexplored (see Figure 6.18).

FIGURE 6.18
The interior of the Sony PlayStation 2 reveals a dual heat sink assembly shielding the motherboard, flanked on the right by the machine's onboard DVD drive.

PlayStation 2's physical attributes are summarized in Table 6.5.

Table 6.5 – PlayStation 2 Hardware	
Enclosure	12 in. (W) × 7 in. (D) × 3 in. (H)
	Black louvered front and side
	Can stand vertically or sit horizontally
Processing Power	CPU: 128-bit, 295MHz "Emotion Engine"
	GPU: 147MHz Graphics Synthesizer
Memory	32MB Direct Rambus (RDRAM) system memory
	8MB memory card

Table 6.5 – Continued	
Input/Output	Controller ports (2)
	USB (2)
	Memory card ports (2)
	FireWire
	Optical audio port
	Ethernet and 56K dial-up adapters (optional; not yet available in U.S.)
Storage	DVD/CD-ROM optical disk drive
	3.5-inch hard drive (optional; not yet available in U.S.)
Controller	Analog buttons allow incremental control of game features
	Built-in force feedback

Software

Sony's phenomenal success since showing up as a newcomer to the gaming IED business in the mid-1990s can be largely attributed to its ability to recruit major "killer-app" games to the platform.

The event that rocked the gaming world and truly started PlayStation's meteoric rise to the top of the console sales charts occurred in early 1996. Developer SquareSoft agreed to adopt PlayStation as the primary platform for the next version of *Final Fantasy*, its wildly popular role-playing game that had historically been available for various Nintendo consoles (see Figure 6.19). The defection was a severe blow to Nintendo, and public statements by Nintendo chairman Hiroshi Yamauchi indicate that the GameCube maker continues to view SquareSoft's move as an unconscionable act of treachery.

To this day, *Final Fantasy* is a mainstay of Sony's game lineup, as a look at the company's top-ten titles from November 2001 reveals (see Table 6.6). (Note that PlayStation 2 is the only gaming IED that provides backward compatibility to previous platforms; that is, it supports PlayStation 1 games.)

FIGURE 6.19
Final Fantasy X was the first installment of the best-selling series to appear on the PlayStation 2.

Table 6.6 – Top 10 Software Titles for Sony PlayStation 2

Rank	Title	Publisher
1	*Final Fantasy VII*	Sony Computer Entertainment
2	*Dragon Ball GT Final Bout*	Bandai
3	*Syphon Filter*	989 Studios
4	*Metal Gear Solid*	Konami
5	*Final Fantasy IX*	Square Electronic Arts
6	*Final Fantasy VIII*	Square Electronic Arts
7	*Syphon Filter 2*	Sony Computer Entertainment
8	*Gran Turismo 3: A Spec*	Sony Computer Entertainment
9	*Driver 2*	Infogrames Entertainment
10	*Gran Turismo 2*	Sony Computer Entertainment

Source: Sony Computer Entertainment of America

Despite Sony's inroads, Nintendo has managed to keep the predator at bay in some respects. The most recent figures from the Toy Manufacturers of America's indicate that for calendar year 2000, Nintendo dominated the list of the top 20 best-selling interactive entertainment software titles (see Table 6.7). However, when 2001 totals are eventually published in the first quarter of 2002, they might tell a different story. Nintendo will be shown to have relied even more heavily on its lead in portable handheld gaming, potentially benefiting from the introduction of the Game Boy Advance platform, although the transition from N64 to GameCube could potentially erode its console market share.

Table 6.7 – 2000 Top-Selling Interactive Entertainment Software Titles (Ranked by Units Sold)

Rank	Item Description	Platform
1	*Pokémon Silver*	Game Boy Color
2	*Pokémon Gold*	Game Boy Color
3	*Pokémon Yellow*	Game Boy
4	*Pokémon Stadium*	Nintendo 64
5	*Tony Hawks Pro Skatr2*	Playstation
6	*Legend of Zelda: Majora's*	Nintendo 64
7	*Tony Hawks Pro Skater*	Playstation
8	*Gran Turismo 2*	Playstation
9	*Pokémon Blue*	Game Boy
10	*Pokémon Red*	Game Boy
11	*WWF Smackdown!*	Playstation
12	*Tony Hawks Pro Skater*	Nintendo 64
13	*Pokémon Trading Card*	Game Boy Color
14	*Super Mario Bros. Deluxe*	Game Boy Color
15	*Madden NFL 2001*	Playstation
16	*Mario Party 2*	Nintendo 64
17	*Perfect Dark*	Nintendo 64
18	*WWF Smackdown 2*	Playstation
19	*Final Fantasy IX*	Playstation
20	*WWF No Mercy*	Nintendo 64

Source: Toy Manufacturers of America

Publisher	Release Date	Retail Price
Nintendo of America	October 2000	$27
Nintendo of America	October 2000	$27
Nintendo of America	October 1999	$26
Nintendo of America	March 2000	$59
Activision	September 2000	$40
Nintendo of America	October 2000	$60
Activision	September 1999	$30
Sony Computer Ent.	December 1999	$32
Nintendo of America	September 1998	$25
Nintendo of America	September 1998	$25
THQ	March 2000	$40
Activision	March 2000	$49
Nintendo of America	April 2000	$25
Nintendo of America	May 1999	$28
Electronic Arts	August 2000	$41
Nintendo of America	January 2000	$50
Nintendo of America	May 2000	$58
THQ	November 2000	$41
Square EA	November 2000	$40
THQ	November 2000	$60

Tips, Tricks, and Modifications

The most prevalent and radical modification available for the PlayStation 2 involves the installation of commercial "mod chips" that allow the user to circumvent certain limitations involving game and DVD movie media.

Generally known as *region controls*, these limitations prevent a PlayStation 2 purchased in the United States from playing games or movie disks formatted for sale in European and Japanese markets, and vice versa.

In addition, mod chips bypass the machine's baked-in copyright protection, allowing the use of copied game disks and opening the door to all manner of software piracy. Sony has reportedly undertaken some modifications of its own, working on the hardware side and with game developers to find ways of defeating mod chips. A cat and mouse game of firmware changes has ensued, with the result that a mod chip installation might or might not work on certain disks in certain countries.

As with any alteration of a consumer device that is not designed to be altered, installing a mod chip will automatically void the PlayStation warranty, leaving the user without recourse if their hardware ceases to function properly.

As for software cheat codes for PlayStation games, they are simply too numerous to attempt to list here. Interested players should check out any of the dozens of sites that are devoted to video game cheat codes (for a partial list, see Chapter 11, Table 11.4, page 268).

What's Coming Next

PlayStation 2 is entering middle age, according to Sony officials who expect it to have the same longevity as the 7-year-old PlayStation 1 (which is currently undergoing a marketing makeover as the newly portable, LCD-equipped PSOne). Meanwhile, the era of the GameCube and Xbox have just begun.

Sony intends to build out its PlayStation franchise as an entertainment hub for our 21st century homes, and Microsoft is hot on its heels with a multipronged effort to finally establish a Windows-based platform for consumer electronics.

Each of the three titans in this fight for conquest of the console market has introduced a platform that is capable of delivering on the promise of a true IED, and so far, none has acted on that promise.

Will game platforms eventually harness their own onboard intelligence to serve gamers better, observing their choices and responding to personalized needs and preferences? For instance, couldn't a video game console with the heart of a personal computer watch gamers' game-related struggles, diagnose their weaknesses, and gently, patiently prod them toward improvement?

On a broader note, why is it that, unlike their personal computer counterparts, so few video game developers strive to create games that are both educational as well as entertaining?

This author looks forward to the days when game machines will wake up to their own native intelligence and begin to look for ways to bolster gamers' intelligence. These days should soon be at hand.

Chapter 7

Intelligent Audio—Teaching Your Stereo New Tricks

Overview of Audio IEDs

Computerized home audio players have arrived, although they have not yet received quite the hero's welcome that video and gaming IEDs have enjoyed.

That could change rapidly as new service and distribution models come into play, including new satellite, broadband cable, and telephony-based subscription audio services.

Before taking off on an exploration of where audio IEDs are headed, it's time to take a snapshot of where they are today and how they got there.

The Basics

You probably learned in high school that sound, like light, travels in waves. However, science class might have omitted what happens to sound waves when they become "digitized" and placed on a compact disc. The undulating analog waveform of the sound is analyzed, and a digital file (code reduced to its binary elements of "ones" and "zeros") is created in its place.

Can a digital file provide an exact replica of an analog recording? Yes and no. Some audio purists might argue that, at some extremely minute level, the process of converting a continuous wave to a one or zero might sacrifice some tiny nuance of sound. However, it is generally accepted that these differences are far too subtle for the human ear to pick up. So, for all intents and purposes, the digital copy is an exact reproduction. It has the added benefit that it will never degrade. The physical medium on which it is stored could become corrupted over time (such as the CD developing scratches and skips), but the source file remains precise. This means that a digitized music file could be "burned" onto a *recordable CD* (a slang term for the process of encoding a file to a CD using a laser) an infinite number of times without variation.

These properties give digital recordings huge advantages over vinyl and magnetic tape recordings, which are not only subject to wear and tear, but which also suffer degradation when recorded, such that every successive recording generation sounds a little bit worse. Of course, the fact that digital music can be copied ad infinitum and always sound just as good is precisely what has sent the professional recording industry into paroxysms of alternating fear and rage (see the sidebar, "(Don't) Steal This Record," later in this chapter).

The Recording Industry Association of America (RIAA) and its international counterpart, the International Federation of the Phonographic Industry, historically took the quiet but effective approach of silently hobbling new digital recording technologies. This prevented new formats such as digital audiotape (DAT) from ever reaching critical mass in the consumer market. Usually, these organizations accomplished this through the judicious use of legal threats and backroom deals.

In 2001, the sudden and mostly unforeseen combination of file compression and easy peer-to-peer sharing of music files awakened the sleepy giant. The file compression technique that finally spurred the music industry to sit up and take notice was MP3 (see the next sidebar, "MP What?"), whereas the peer-to-peer distribution network that initially goaded the RIAA into action was Napster.

MP WHAT?

The compression technology that is known as MP3 got its start in 1987 at a German research facility. Patented two years later, it became part of the Motion Picture Experts Group's (MPEG) specification for audio and video compression systems in 1992.

What eventually drove acceptance of MP3 as an overwhelming de facto standard was its price: The Fraunhofer Institute, which had developed the standard, allowed free use and development of MP3.

An average MP3 file recorded at 128 kilobits per second (kbps) is roughly one-tenth the size of an uncompressed audio file. Thus, a 5MB MP3 file provides an acceptable representation of a 50MB source file.

The first MP3 player application came along in 1997. Called AMP, it became the model for Windows and Macintosh versions of the player, dubbed WinAmp and MacAmp. As these and other tools became popular, so did their use as a means of *ripping* CDs, a term for the process of automatically copying an entire compact disc into a series of compressed digital files. Additional tools were added to take those ripped music tracks and mix and match them for copying onto new audio CDs, sharing with friends and strangers via the Internet, and transferring to portable players.

This combination of free source code; widely available tools for encoding, playback, and sharing; and the capability to achieve a substantially reduced file size without compromising audio quality presented a winning blend of features, catapulting MP3 technology to the top of the charts.

MP3 and Your Stereo

Thanks to a young college dropout named Shawn Fanning and his ingenious software creation called Napster, the notion of digital music recording and ripping CDs became a household occurrence in 2000 and 2001—nearly as commonplace as copying a cassette tape. In fact, sales of recordable CD media have been setting records (see Figure 7.1).

FIGURE 7.1
Recordable CDs have become an international bestseller, with more than 4 billion units expected to be sold in 2002.

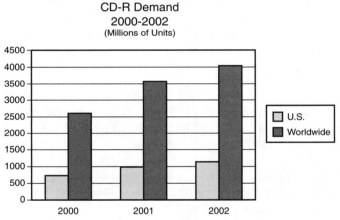

CD-R Demand
2000-2002
(Millions of Units)

Source: International Recording Media Association

Supported by the rising Internet "bubble" of inflated stock prices, Fanning turned his Napster file-swapping service into a multimillion-dollar private company, attracting huge investments from heavy-hitting dot-com financiers such as venture capital firm Hummer Winblad. Consumers came by the millions for free access to an unlimited library of commercial music. The unfettered file swapping—something the RIAA insisted on calling *piracy*—grew to staggering proportions as a hungry public gorged itself on the unauthorized largesse.

The Napster service, it's owners said, didn't copy or store the copyrighted material in question, it merely provided a conduit for individuals to share material. For example, if you have song files ripped from a CD on your computer, through the use of Napster software, you could make them simultaneously available to other Napster users around the globe. You could also browse freely from the files ripped by your peers (see Figure 7.2).

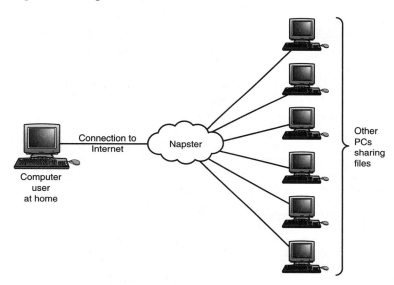

Connection to Internet

Napster

Computer user at home

Other PCs sharing files

FIGURE 7.2
How Napster worked before it became a subscription-based service.

Even though Napster later got its comeuppance in court, eventually closing its doors for free file swapping, a slew of new "open source" alternatives sprang up to take its place. Shutting down these communities of song traders, a conglomeration of private individuals using public domain software, has proved a much thornier problem for the RIAA.

However, despite the massive proliferation of MP3 music, demand for MP3-based home audio components has remained nascent.

People who created digital copies of music on their PC, primarily using the MP3 compression format, have been mostly content with burning the songs back onto audio CDs for use in their conventional home and car stereos. Alternatively, they suffice with listening to their MP3 libraries via their computer speakers or earphones plugged into portable MP3 players.

Although the electronics industry rubbed its collective hands in anticipation of growing consumer demand for devices that supported MP3 as a native format for audio playback, the trend has been realized only in the portable player category. Despite bullish projections, only a smattering of MP3-based car audio products have yet emerged, along with a few first-generation systems for piping MP3 music files into a home stereo system.

Although the latter category—home audio components that support digitally formatted and compressed music files—might be late to take off, analysts are betting that it will ramp steeply. In fact, Phoenix-based research firm Forward Concepts predicts that although shipments of console-type compressed digital audio players will be far lower than portable players through 2005, the category is poised for exponential growth (see Figure 7.3).

FIGURE 7.3

Forward Concepts expects the growth rate for home-based audio players to explode by 160% annually through 2005.

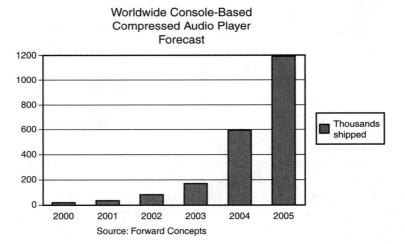

Source: Forward Concepts

Currently, the only category of home-based audio players with native MP3 playback capability that has achieved any market penetration is actually intended primarily as a video device: DVD players. DVD units that can also play audio CDs and recordable CDs containing MP3 files have become fairly common, although evidence is not available to suggest that many consumers buy DVD players primarily for their MP3 features. In fact, it's unlikely that the majority of buyers ever get around to using the built-in MP3 support. This is because the value of having a device play back MP3 files from a recordable CD is somewhat marginal. Even though a CD can store hundreds more MP3 audio tracks than normal digital audio tracks, the time required to actually record the CD is still the same. If the CD contains MP3s, you're still limiting yourself to players that are capable of reading the format.

The real promise of MP3 and other compressed digital music formats comes alive when the playback device interfaces directly with an Internet-connected computer hard drive. Outputting songs onto CDs—a tedious process at best, and generally beset by a high error rate—becomes superfluous. Music collections housed on a hard drive can be huge, yet poring over thousands of songs to find just the right one is the work of seconds, and new musical delights are just a click away on the Web.

Bring On the IEDs

What's holding back the market for audio IEDs? It has been a combination of the wrong companies offering the wrong products at the wrong prices.

Where Are the Big Brands?

Walk into your neighborhood electronics store and ask to see an MP3 playback deck from Marantz, Technics, Pioneer, or any of the companies that built the rest of your home stereo. The silence will be deafening.

The reasons that the major component audio manufacturers are absent from the MP3 space vary depending on who in the industry you talk to, but it's safe to assume that technology and licensing issues have played equal roles. For the majority of Japanese and European consumer brands, to roll out MP3 products would put them at odds with the rabidly anti-MP3 recording industry (see sidebar, "(Don't) Steal This Record"). In addition, building a high-capacity MP3 player involves the use of hard drives and other PC electronics and software that lie outside the core competence of these traditional appliance manufacturers. Finally, the adoption of compressed digital audio players in the home has the potential of cannibalizing their sales of more conventional and lucrative devices, such as tape and CD players.

(DON'T) STEAL THIS RECORD

It was a classic David versus Goliath battle, with startup file-swapping service Napster playing the small-but-wiry David, and the RIAA cast as the traditional heavy. The major difference from the biblical version, however, was that David went down.

After a protracted legal battle, the Napster service went on what seems, as of this writing, a permanent hiatus, leaving millions of record fans worldwide bereft. When the Napster site went dark, it was, as many described, "The day the music died."

Turned away from the Napster site in droves, many consumers went in search of alternatives, finding public domain file-trading communities such as AudioGalaxy and Morpheus to satisfy their musical cravings. Others were moved by the successful criminalization of Napster to stop or at least reduce their unauthorized file swapping.

Although the court's decision to refuse Napster the ability to continue trafficking in copyrighted materials had a chilling effect on many consumers, it had a downright glacial impact on existing and potential IED product manufacturers. Startups assessed their chances of winning a legal battle against the RIAA and quickly folded up their tents, and established hardware manufacturers instantly stifled any rebellious impulses to bite the hand that so richly fed them.

All eyes now are on the major music labels that make up the RIAA, and on how they will decide to fulfill the colossal and pent-up demand for online music roiling in Napster's wake. When the industry can decide on and deploy a sufficiently secure method of online distribution that protects the music royalty apparatus, hardware manufacturers will be ready in the wings with a second generation of audio IEDs designed to facilitate the online sale and consumption of commercial music.

In the vacuum created by most of the established home audio brands, a number of companies have taken a shot at trying to establish a new audio IED category. The product designs make it plain that the companies behind them have a background in computers and high technology, not in the real-world, low technology realm of consumer electronics.

The resulting products range from standalone stereo components that hold thousands of MP3s—and in some cases, require connection to a TV screen for viewing and managing that huge music library—down to devices that function primarily as PC peripherals, using a variety of networking technologies to deliver your PC's audio output to your stereo. None of the products offers a particularly easy, affordable, or intuitive solution for consumers. However, they do provide a sturdy foundation for future audio appliances and offer an intriguing set of capabilities for intrepid "early adopters" of the technology.

➔ For full descriptions of existing audio IED products, see Chapter 8, "Choosing the Right Audio IED for You," p. 189.

Another obstacle to a vertical takeoff for audio IEDs is the absence of prices that don't induce sticker shock. The AudioRequest and iPaq Music Center stand alone units, from Request Audio and Compaq Computer respectively, retail for around $800. Kenwood's announced Entre IED is expected to sport a hefty $1,800 price tag. Devices such as the SonicBlue Rio Receiver (also sold as the Dell Digital Audio Receiver) and Turtle Beach AudioTron (a.k.a., Gateway Connected Music Player) each sell for about $300—but they are useless unless connected to a $1,000-and-up personal computer. These are awfully pricey propositions for consumers who (let's face it) largely embraced the Napster/MP3 technology in the first place because it was free.

What's Coming Next

They might not be leading the charge, but the big brands don't plan to be far behind when it becomes clear that money can be made. Kenwood's arrival at the party, with a high-end audio IED similar to Compaq's iPaq Music Center, indicates that established audio manufacturers are finally starting to pay attention. One vice-president of business development for a U.S. audio IED designer said in the late summer of 2001 that he was receiving 10 calls a day from electronics firms interested in licensing and selling his products. Additionally, he had made six trips to Japan in as many weeks to follow up the leads.

Many companies that jumped early into the audio IED business learned some hard lessons about the retail electronics trade. Several were sent scurrying for cover, forced to hastily rewrite business plans when the venture capital largesse of the dot-com boom went bust. From these ashes, some interesting new business models are beginning to emerge.

In the early fall of 2001, companies such as DigMedia Inc. and AudioRamp Inc. transitioned from audio IED hardware manufacturers to new roles as service, software, and design providers. Essentially borrowing a page from the TiVo and ReplayTV playbooks, these audio companies hit upon new business models based on creating rich music- and Internet radio-related services, leaving the manufacturing to overseas partners with more experience in the consumer goods business.

The word that lights up the eyes of recording industry executives, computer companies, and audio IED designers is *commerce*. The RIAA's systematic drawing and quartering of Napster has left a vacuum for online music distribution, and the labels are planning to fill that void with the sweet sound of clinking coinage.

If the music industry has its way—and history indicates that it often does—audio IEDs will increasingly become Web-connected music vending machines. They will be able to quietly ascertain your tastes so they can provide you with opportunities to buy more of what you like, all at the press of a button on your remote control. For your purchase, you'll be rewarded with instant gratification as the song you want is delivered immediately to your stereo system. A word of caution to old-fashioned brick-and-mortar music retailers: Be afraid. Be very afraid.

But whether you buy into the RIAA's vision of a pay-as-you-go model for music consumption, or you're one of the unreformed pirates still thwarting the industry's apparent effort to wring every possible cent out of the listening public, the first generation audio IEDs warrant your close inspection. Perhaps you've even saved enough money skimming your music collection off the Web for free that you're ready to reward yourself with some shiny, new, great-sounding hardware.

Chapter 8

Choosing the Right Audio IED for You

Overview

It's a clear case of apples and oranges. Drawing comparisons between the various entries in the audio IED category is difficult because the products differ so greatly in what they can do and how they can accomplish their diverse design goals.

To be practical (and to get this book published in a timely fashion), it was necessary to look at only a subset of the growing pool of audio IEDs. The book focuses on those IEDs that hold the greatest promise, and on those few that have achieved some slight mind share or market share advantage in this fledgling business.

Here's the list of what all these products share in common:

- All of them play music stored in a compressed format, such as MP3 (see the sidebar, "MP WHAT?"), or Microsoft's proprietary Windows Media Audio. (WMA files are often designated with an .ASF extension.)
- All provide connectivity with a PC.
- All provide the capability of connecting to a home stereo system.
- Although a few of the systems are designed to facilitate online transactions, allowing consumers to buy music via the Internet directly from the IED, none requires subscription to a service. In this respect, the audio IEDs differ substantially from the video IEDs described in earlier chapters.

There ends the similarities between these computerized audio devices.

MP WHAT?

The compression technology known as MP3 got its start in 1987 at a German research facility. Patented two years later, it became part of the Motion Picture Experts Group's (MPEG) specification for audio and video compression systems in 1992.

What eventually drove acceptance of MP3 as an overwhelming de facto standard was its price: The Fraunhofer Institut, which had developed the standard, allowed free use and development of MP3.

The first MP3 player application came along in 1997. Called "AMP," it became the model for Windows and Macintosh versions of the player, dubbed WinAmp and MacAmp.

An average MP3 file recorded at 128 kilobits per second (kbps) is roughly one tenth the size of an uncompressed audio file. Thus, a 5MB MP3 file provides an acceptable representation of a 50MB source file.

This combination of free source code, widely available playback and encoding tools, and the ability to achieve a substantially reduced file size without compromising audio quality presented a winning combination of features, catapulting MP3 technology to the top of the charts.

The diversity that exists between various audio IED offerings is reflective of a market comprised of many startups, interspersed with a few established PC companies that are relative greenhorns in the home stereo business. As a result, consumers face a hodge-podge of products, all trying to define a new category in home electronics.

To decide which audio IED suits you best, you need to first make some decisions about how—and where—you envision using the device, and for what (in addition to actually hearing music) you want to use it.

For example, you need to consider the following:

- If you have an extensive CD library that you want to convert to MP3 or WMA files, you might want an IED with a built-in CD player, such as a Compaq iPaq Music Center. However, if your goal is to eventually transfer those encoded files back to a PC—and then perhaps out onto the Web or a PC-connected portable player—then consider something other than iPaq because its closed architecture doesn't support two-way transfers to your desktop. You might be better served with an audio IED such as an AudioRequest, or even an MP3 "jukebox" along the lines of Perception Digital's PD Hercules device.

- If you already have an extensive library of compressed music files on your PC's hard drive, either "ripped" from your own CDs or downloaded off the Web, you might be in the market for an IED that simply helps manage those files on your computer and makes them accessible to your home stereo. A device such as the Rio Receiver or Turtle Beach AudioTron does this job admirably, and by using HPNA (see the sidebar, "HPNA Phones Home") or Ethernet connections, your PC and stereo can communicate even when they are located at opposite ends of the house.

- Do you want a simpler way to hear the music stored on your PC in higher fidelity? Consider the Bose Wave/PC Interactive Audio System, essentially a high-end tabletop radio that connects via wires to your PC's serial port and allows you to play back MP3s on its impressive and compact internal speakers.

- Would you prefer not to have to boot up your PC every time you want to crank up some tunes? Some devices, such as the iPaq and Kenwood IEDs, along with the AudioReQuest Pro Digital Music System, can encode and store MP3s without a PC. The iPaq and Kenwood systems, both based on the OpenGlobe service (see sidebar, "World (Wide Web) Music, page 209), can even download songs and related information from the Web. But have a TV handy—they all rely on a TV screen to view and manage your audio library.

The good news is that with such a wide range of products offering so many different approaches and price points for listening to digital audio, there's sure to be one that suits your individual tastes and needs.

SonicBlue Rio Digital Audio Receiver

Alternatively sold as the Dell Digital Audio Receiver from Dell Computer, the Rio Receiver is manufactured by the Rio division of SonicBlue, the same company that acquired ReplayTV (see "ReplayTV Vital Statistics," page 44, Chapter 3).

In a market in which unknowns are battling other startups in a desperate attempt to build mind share, the Rio name actually means something. The MP3 music industry owes a debt of gratitude to Rio, which started life as a spin-off of Diamond Multimedia. As a graphics board maker that had taken a dangerous flyer on sales of CD-ROM upgrade kits, a market that boomed for a short time in the mid-90s, Diamond took an even greater risk in 1999 when it challenged the almighty music industry in open court and won.

The lopsided legal battle was a stunning victory for Rio, which walked away with court protection for selling its namesake portable MP3 player—a device designed essentially as a vessel for transporting and listening to copyrighted music files.

Protected by Rio's legal armor, other manufacturers copied and improved upon the design, flooding the market with portable players in every shape, size, and color. In 2000, Rio's parent company, failing graphics chipmaker S3, changed its name to SonicBlue and began to reconfigure itself as a digital consumer electronics company. The Diamond brand has since faded into obscurity, but SonicBlue continues to market its audio-specific product under the Rio moniker.

Hoping to expand its leadership status into the untried home MP3 console market and perhaps to recapture some of its early cachet, Rio unveiled its Digital Audio Receiver in May of 2000 (see Figure 8.1). The unit is compact and functional, and relatively easy to set up and configure. For an effective way of harnessing your PC-based MP3 library and enjoying it via your existing stereo system, the Rio Receiver is an excellent choice.

Hardware

The Rio Receiver has achieved an impressive degree of simplicity. You might expect that installing its bundled phone-line networking adapter would be daunting, but it's child's play. Simply open your PC, insert it into an empty PCI slot, and close the case. After the hardware install is complete, reboot your PC. Windows should detect the new device and request a driver disc (located on a CD-ROM included with the card). Then plug a phone cord between the wall jack and the Rio card. Back in the living room, switch on the Rio device, and watch as it "shakes hands" (establishes communications) with your PC, and then mines it for available MP3s. The process is painless.

You also might fear that the Rio's HPNA adapter will conflict with your existing DSL broadband connection to the Web, but it won't. The DSL and HPNA data will share your telephone lines in a gentlemanly fashion, and neither will impinge on your ability to place voice calls over the lines—another pleasant surprise.

You can even tempt fate by installing a wireless network adapter in the same host PC that contains the Rio adapter. Despite all the curves you might throw at it, the Rio equipment functions flawlessly. You can even transfer new MP3s to the Rio by dropping them on your PC's hard drive and browse the Web for more music via DSL, all while the Rio Receiver plays sweetly in the background.

FIGURE 8.1
Front and rear views
of the Rio Digital
Audio Receiver from
SonicBlue.

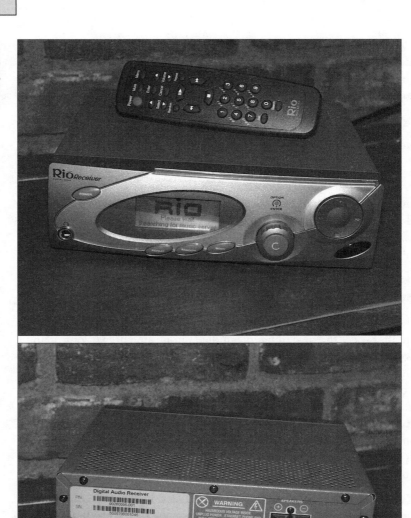

HPNA PHONES HOME

Several of the major audio IED offerings have been designed to take advantage of Home Phoneline Networking Alliance (HPNA) adapters.

These network adapters—available either as cards that plug into a PCI slot in your desktop computer or as a dongle that connects via your PC's USB port— make use of your home's existing copper phone wiring, literally turning your telephone lines into a data network that can be tapped from any phone jack.

Note that all HPNA adapters are not created equal: HPNA 1.0 adapters transfer data at a slow 1Mbps, whereas HPNA 2.0 devices run at 10Mbps.

Key features of the Rio Receiver IED include the following:

- Compatibilty with Ethernet and HPNA adapters
- Support for MP3 and WMA audio formats
- Upgradeable software to support future audio formats
- Internal 10 Watt-per-channel amplifier for attaching speakers directly, without the need for a separate amplifier or stereo receiver
- RCA output for connecting to an amplifier
- Capability to manage up to approximately 10,000 songs
- A full-function remote control
- Capability to search by artist, genre, title, or album

The Rio Receiver cannot run as a stand-alone player because it requires connection to a live host PC for storage, management, and playback of compressed music files. (Table 8.1 lists the configuration requirements of that host.) However, unlike the competing Turtle Beach AudioTron, the Rio does not require a stereo receiver or external amplifier. Just hook up a pair of speakers, and it's ready to go (see Figure 8.2).

FIGURE 8.2
The Rio Receiver contains an internal amplifier, so it does not require use of an external amplifier to drive a pair of speakers.

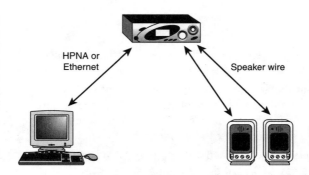

HPNA or Ethernet

Speaker wire

Table 8.1 – Rio Receiver: Minimum Requirements for Host System	
Operating System	Windows 98/98, SE/Me, or 2000/XP
Processor	Intel Pentium 200MHz MMX or higher
Memory	32MB of RAM
Storage	• 16MB of available hard drive space • CD-ROM drive
Network Adapter	HPNA or Ethernet

The SonicBlue Rio Receiver is based on a Cirrus Logic EP7212-CV-D ARM 32-bit embedded CPU chip, comparable to a 100MHz Intel Pentium in terms of horsepower, coupled with 32MB of EDO DRAM and 1MB FlashRAM. The primary DRAM is made up of two Integrated Silicon Solutions Inc. (ISSI) IS41LV16100-50T 16Mbit EDO DRAM chips, running at 50ns and drawing 3.3 volts. A broadcom BCM4210KTF chip provides the networking for the unit, in the case of HPNA connectivity, and a Crystal LAN CS8900A-CQ3 chip on the Ethernet side.

Internally, the Rio Receiver is extremely similar to the Turtle Beach AudioTron, down to the same brand of CPU and networking chips. Independent reviewers have rated the Rio as having a slight performance advantage over the AudioTron in terms of buffering, however. Hardware Web site ExtremeTech.com labeled the Rio as having a 20-second buffer time on 128Kpbs music files, compared to a 40-second approximate buffer time for the AudioTron.

The Rio also appears to have a better showing in the area of screen display. It provides a bitmapped display resolution of 64 by 128, compared to the AudioTron's 40-character, 2-line graphics display.

However, despite the higher resolution, the Rio is actually much more difficult to read from across the room than the AudioTron's alphanumeric liquid crystal diode (LCD) display.

Software

The Rio Receiver runs an embedded Linux-based operating system. This has the side effect of rendering the device easily hackable, as demonstrated by programmer Jeff Mock (see Chapter 11, "Audio IEDs," page 268).

Rio's setup and installation software for the PC handles the job quickly and efficiently. Just be sure to read the poster-size Quick Start Guide from top to bottom rather than left to right.

The only downside is that variations in the naming conventions for your MP3 files can stymie the machine and render its music sorting and selection menu meaningless. Essentially, the Rio Receiver uses the ID3 tags that are embedded in your MP3 files to sort music by artist name, album name, genre, and song title. Unfortunately, not all MP3s contain ID3 tags.

TIP

The Microsoft Developer Network defines ID3 as "a fix-sized 128-byte tag that is located at the end of an audio file. It can include title, artist, album, year, genre, a comment field, and other metadata. It is mainly targeted at files encoded with MPEG-1/2 layer I, MPEG-1/2 layer II, MPEG-1/2 layer III, and MPEG-2.5, but it might also work with other types of encoded audio. ID3 refers to the family of frame-based tagging methods that use the 10-byte header beginning with "ID3" followed by version information."

Whether your MP3 files contain ID3 tag data is a function of the music ripping software used to create the files. If the data is missing, the Rio Receiver will not display the songs in any of its search results, rendering them essentially invisible to the player.

If some of your MP3s don't show up in the Rio's search screens, try editing or adding ID3 tags using a shareware utility. An easy way to locate an ID3 editor is to run a search for "ID3" at a site such as www.download.com. You will find dozens of choices.

197

In general, if you want to navigate around a large library of music, be sure to use consistent spellings, titles, and format information when naming your files, and be prepared to rename and recategorize any compressed music you pull in from the Internet.

Turtle Beach AudioTron

Also sold as the Gateway Connected Music Player for piping digital audio from your PC to a audio receiver, the Turtle Beach AudioTron is similar in features and functionality to the Rio Digital Audio Receiver.

Like the Rio Receiver, the following characteristics are true of the AudioTron:

- Requires a running host PC for storage of the compressed audio files
- Supports HPNA and Ethernet connections to the host PC
- Supports MP3 and WMA audio formats
- Manages thousands of songs
- Has a full-function remote control
- Searches by artist, genre, title, or album

Figure 8.3 shows both front and rear views of the AudioTron.

The company behind the AudioTron is a respected name in PC audio, having been one of the premier brands of high-function sound cards for PCs since the late 1980s. In fact, Turtle Beach was a pioneer in the field of PC-based hard-disk audio recording, delivering systems that professional musicians once prized.

In 1996, Turtle Beach was acquired by Voyetra Technologies, a maker of software for recording, sequencing, composing, and scoring music. The merged company adopted the name Voyetra Turtle Beach Inc.

Hardware

The AudioTron design is conventional, but attractive. Its alphanumeric LCD readout is visible from across the room, in contrast to the Rio Receiver's bit-mapped LCD display, which requires much closer inspection to discern which song title or artist they are choosing. (In fact, Rio's remote control seems somewhat pointless, since you have to be close enough to push the buttons anyway to read the choices on the small screen.)

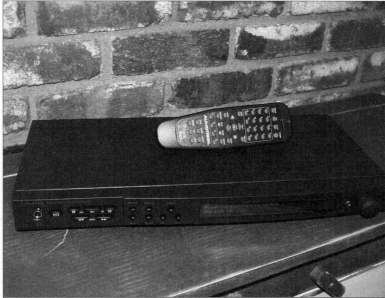

FIGURE 8.3
The Turtle Beach AudioTron contains most of the same connections as Rio's player, with the exception of speaker jacks—the AudioTron requires the use of an external amplifier.

NOTE

An Internet Protocol (IP) address is a numerical designation in the form of xxx.xxx.xxx.xxx that is used to identify a device across a network (not unlike your street address that identifies the location of your home). In some cases, this device is configured for you automatically; as is the case with the AudioTron, however, some addresses must be manually configured.

Unlike the Rio Receiver, which also lists for $299 (although street price extends down to the $150 range), the AudioTron does not include an HPNA adapter.

It took hours of trial and error to get the AudioTron to work with my HPNA hardware, while the Rio Receiver installation was remarkably trouble free.

The problems I experienced turned out to be completely surmountable. As with most problems of this nature, it was all a matter of locating the correct documentation—and hitting on the correct interpretation of that documentation. In my case, the default configuration of the AudioTron was wholly unsuited to my existing HPNA setup. Feeling very much like a reluctant dairy farmer delivering a stubborn calf, I was forced to roll my sleeves up to my shoulders and reach deep into my PC's network parameters to get things sorted out.

If a phoneline network adapter is configured for "Auto IP," the AudioTron finds this state of affairs deeply offensive. Unfortunately, the test utility included with the device gave only scant clues as to how the problem could best be corrected. Eventually, I found that you must change the adapter's TCP/IP configuration to hunt for a particular static IP (an IP address that does not change) rather than automatically generating a new one each time it attempts to connect. I was further instructed to set the static IP address as 192.168.0.1 and the subnet mask to 255.255.255.0. After rebooting so these changes could take effect, I then had to reconfigure the AudioTron to match the new settings.

Reconfiguring the AudioTron requires that you disable Dynamic Host Configuration Protocol (DHCP), the term used to describe devices whose IP addresses are automatically configured. DHCP is turned on at the factory in the vain hope that the system might be able to essentially configure itself, allowing you to get right to the activities for which you acquired the unit. Following the instructions that are included with the device, you must access the AudioTron Options menu to disable DHCP, using the existing IP address and configuring the subnet mask to match the parameters that are set on the PC, as explained earlier.

Your next challenge will be to make sure that the AudioTron can actually find your PC-based MP3 collection. The AudioTron is extremely particular in where it will and will not look for music files. The first order of business is to ensure that the folders that contain your MP3s have been "shared," so they are accessible to other devices across the network. The next step is to make sure that the files are stored in a directory where AudioTron will look for them.

The audio IED looks for music in various directories, including those named the following:

- Audio
- Music
- My Music
- My Documents\My Music
- Program Files\MusicMatch\Music
- Program Files\MusicMatch\MusicMatch Jukebox\Playlist
- MusicMatch Jukebox\Playlist

After you make sure that your music collection is stored in one of these folders, your AudioTron should immediately begin filling its musical coffers.

When the device is properly configured and working, you're left to enjoy all of its key features, some of which include these:

- Multiple AudioTrons can simultaneously play different music. This could be useful for larger installations in which people want to play different music in different "zones" within their home or business.
- AudioTron includes Voyetra's AudioStation media player software. Although it appears that using the AudioStation software is at least intended to be optional, it is highly recommended for smooth operations of the AudioTron.

NOTE

Sharing a folder on your PC means configuring it so that attached network devices can also read the folder across the network. The process for doing so varies based on your version of Windows, but in the most recent version, Windows XP, you must simply right-click the folder in My Computer and choose Sharing and Security. From there, use the Sharing tab to make the folder available on your network.

- AudioTron recognizes standard M3U playlists (see the Tip that follows).

- The system is sized specifically to be compatible with conventional, 17-inch-wide home audio components. In fact, a peek inside the chassis reveals that it's mostly wasted space—the circuit board takes up only about half of the AudioTron's footprint. Engineers made a design decision to create an enclosure that is the right size for your stereo cabinet or equipment rack.

Like the Rio Receiver, the Turtle Beach AudioTron requires connection to a live host PC for operation. Table 8.2 lists the configuration requirements of that host.

Table 8.2 – Turtle Beach AudioTron: Minimum Requirements for Host System	
Operating System	Windows 98/98, SE/ME, NT 4.0/2000/XP
Processor	Intel Pentium 233 MHz MMX or higher
Memory	32MB of RAM
Storage	Sufficient hard drive space for storing your digital music files
Network Adapter	HPNA or Ethernet

The AudioTron relies on Cirrus Logic EP7312 ARM processor as its CPU, along with the venerable Crystal Semiconductor CS8900A for its 10mbit Ethernet support and the BroadCom BCM4210 for HPNA capabilities.

For system memory, the AudioTron relies on two 8MB SDRAM chips: a pair of 64Mb Micron MT48LC4M16A2 3.3-volt chips. Interestingly, the circuit board features two sets of empty pads—most likely to allow an engineering change to higher density chips, such as two 16MB, 32-bit SDRAM chips. The SRAM chips are accompanied by 2MB of Flash RAM.

One major functional difference between the Turtle Beach AudioTron and the Rio Receiver is that the former does not include an internal amplifier. It is designed to be used in conjunction with a home stereo receiver or self-powered speakers (see Figure 8.4).

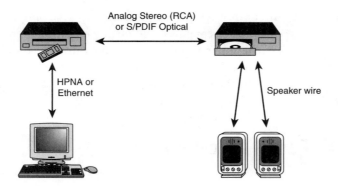

FIGURE 8.4
Typical setup for the AudioTron involves routing its audio output through an external amplifier, such as the receiver of your stereo or home theater.

Software

AudioTron's embedded operating system is Windows CE 2.12. The AudioTron ships with the company's own MP3 jukebox software, AudioStation.

This built-in software compatibility can come in handy: Although the Rio might fail to recognize the playlists you create using jukebox packages, the AudioTron is designed to be compatible with the playlist structure that the AudioStation application supports. Unless you really like your own third-party jukebox package, you can save yourself a lot of headaches by using the adequate AudioStation if you want to get the best results from your AudioTron.

TIP

A **playlist** is a roster of songs that you want to listen to, customized in the order in which you want to hear them. The playlist is actually a text file that your jukebox application creates; it then stores the songs you want to hear and where they're located on your PC. Some of the most common types of playlists include the following:

- .pls (WinAmp MPEG playlist File)
- .m3u (MusicMatch MPEG URL playlist file)
- .asx (Active Streaming File—Windows Media)
- .wvx/.wax (Windows Media metafiles)
- .m2a (MPEG Archive Enhanced .M3U Playlist File)

After you have the AudioTron properly configured, it works well and provides acceptable sound quality over your stereo speakers. However, no consumer should have to go through complicated configuration maneuvers. The absence of better software configuration utilities and documentation is keeping this product from attracting mainstream consumer acceptance and unnecessarily limiting its market to tech-oriented audiophiles.

iPaq Music Center

Compaq has enjoyed world renown as a premier brand in the PC space ever since its founder, Rod Canion, introduced the original lunchbox-sized Compaq portable PC in 1982.

The Houston company crested $42 billion in sales in 2000, but got caught in the PC industry ebb tide in 2001. Harking back to the old adage "misery loves company," Compaq celebrated the Labor Day 2001 weekend by announcing a merger with ailing competitor Hewlett-Packard. The two plan to combine into the world's largest PC company, eclipsing leader Dell Computer.

If and when the historic merger is consummated—the deal was in dire peril at the time this book went to press—the Compaq brand name will likely be retired. The future of Compaq's groundbreaking iPaq Music Center could also be called into question. In June 2001, Hewlett-Packard announced plans to deliver its own home console for digital music, called the HP Digital Entertainment Center. Many of the iPaq Music Center's features are duplicated by its HP counterpart, as both platforms enable consumers to do the following:

- Easily store, manage and automatically catalog hundreds of CDs and thousands of individual audio tracks
- Transfer music to select MP3 players
- Use built-in connectivity to download music and artist information and access streaming audio from the Internet
- View music selections and other product features through a consumer-friendly onscreen TV display and simple remote control
- Connect to stereo and TV components

The HP unit's ace in the hole is its built-in CD-writer, allowing users to record custom music audio CDs.

As this book goes to press, the merger plans are too amorphous to answer whether HP will continue to market the iPaq Music Center in the event that shareholders approve the deal (by no means a foregone conclusion, at his point). However, it seems unlikely that two such competitive products are likely to survive in an integrated product line.

FIGURE 8.5
Regardless of whether the Compaq iPaq Music Center is eventually eclipsed by the HP Digital Entertainment Center, the iPaq will have earned its place in audio IED history by being the first product in this category to offer an integrated online service.

Hardware

Whereas the Turtle Beach and Rio IEDs (marketed by Compaq competitors Gateway and Dell, respectively) require a host PC to provide even the most basic playback features, the iPaq Music Center stands alone as a full-function digital music recording and playback device. It doesn't need a PC because it already is one.

Manufactured for Compaq by First International Computer Inc. of Taiwan, a well-known contract manufacturer and supplier of PC motherboards, the iPaq Music Center features an onboard 20GB hard drive, CD player, and software. Its music processing engine is based on a programmable Internet Audio digital signal processing (DSP) chip from Texas Instruments, a member of TI's low-power TMS320C5000 processor family. The chip's firmware supports a variety of widely used digital audio formats, including MP3, WMA, Advanced Audio Coding (AAC), ATRAC3, and others.

All you need to fully take advantage of the unit is $800 and the following:

- A dial-up Internet service provider account (a pending software upgrade is expected to add support for broadband modems via the iPaq's USB port)
- A TV set with composite or S-video input
- An amplifier or stereo receiver
- Speakers
- A credit card number (if you want to make online music purchases)

This PC-dressed-up-like-a-stereo features an impressive roster of input and output options. Output choices include coaxial digital-audio, optical digital-audio, RCA-type analog audio, and two forms of video for the unit's television display: composite and S-video. The iPaq IED also accepts audio input via RCA-type analog jacks, coaxial digital-audio, and optical digital-audio. Additional data I/O can be routed through the system's two USB ports: its built-in modem port or the HPNA phone jack.

The iPaq Music Center ships with 2 AA batteries (for the remote), a 3-prong AC power cord, a composite-video cable, a stereo analog RCA interconnect cable, an RJ-11 phone cable, a phone-jack splitter, a remote control, a quick-setup poster, and a user's manual.

One of the most unique attributes of the iPaq is its capability to establish a direct Internet connection via its onboard V.90 modem.

I had planned to leave this feature alone and instead opt for using the system's built-in HPNA support. As with the AudioTron, I had a great deal of difficulty getting the iPaq to communicate through HPNA, despite innumerable hours of trying and countless phone calls to both Compaq and my HPNA device vendor.

In general, the first level of support that Compaq customers receive when they call in with questions about their iPaq Music Center is adequate only for rudimentary issues, such as how to turn the device on. If your problem goes beyond the basics covered in the still-evolving manual, the sooner you can get your problem escalated to second-tier support, the better.

To its credit, Compaq has tried to build a core group of Music Center support providers at its Ottawa, Canada call center. To that end, the company has devised a system for routing all Music Center-related support calls to that facility—no small feat for a company as dispersed as Compaq.

Despite having concentrated its training resources on the personnel in a single facility, the level of familiarity with the device among Compaq technicians fluctuates widely. In the worst case, a technician asked me whether, by invoking the iPaq Music Center, I might be referring to "that black box?" On hearing the affirmative, he promptly disconnected my call. I finally bonded with a senior support specialist, who e-mailed me long articles describing my symptoms, and over the course of a week, asked me to change various settings and to check and recheck configuration parameters.

The final resolution was reached by means of a series of conference calls involving me, the Compaq technician, and his counterparts at OpenGlobe (see the sidebar, "World (Wide Web) Music") and at 2Wire. 2Wire is the company that manufactures the combination Ethernet/HPNA/802.11 wireless LAN gateway through which I was attempting to connect the Music Center to my home network and out to the Internet.

Over the course of a day, IP settings were tweaked and retweaked until the magic formula of network parameters was eventually reached. Although all parties were finally able to agree on a solution, there was no such agreement on the nature of the problem. Compaq concluded that my ISP was exhibiting a DNS error that was causing the Music Center timeout before it could complete registration with the OpenGlobe server. 2Wire assured me that the phone company had botched my DSL installation. I generally complicated matters by intermittently failing to plug things in correctly or mistyping IP settings into the computer and the Music Center.

Although my experience was hardly typical because of the 2Wire HPNA gateway, Compaq technicians admitted that I was not the first to attempt to use this device with a Music Center, and I was not alone in finding myself challenged by the process of configuring the IED for use on a network. Music Center users who similarly want to utilize their broadband connections might face similar difficulties. The basic problem is lack of software support for autoconfiguration with a broad selection of home networking adapters, and in lieu of that, the absence of detailed documentation for tweaking the Music Center's network parameters to match these devices.

TIP

Want to take a peek at your iPaq Music Center's secret settings screen? Just follow this procedure:

1. From the main screen displaying the Music Guide listings, press Setup on the remote control.

2. At the first setup screen, press 5555 on the remote.

3. Choose the Configuration Information item in the menu, and then press Select. The Configuration Info screen (see Figure 8.6) displays a variety of information about your device, including its current software version and network settings for your dial-up, Ethernet, or HPNA connection.

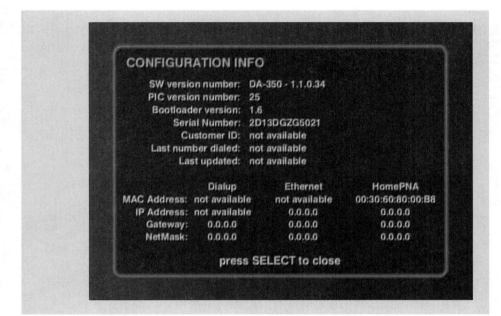

FIGURE 8.6
The iPaq Music Center's Configuration Info screen displays detailed information on your system's software and network settings.

Software

Although the iPaq features a front-panel LED readout, it is designed to make use of an adjacent TV set to display its colorful and graphics-laden interface. As you navigate through the setup process, you are "treated" to numerous promotional messages congratulating you for buying such an advanced device, and generally lauding you for living "*la vida tecnología.*"

The iPaq's most intriguing software feature is its support for OpenGlobe Entertainment Services, an online hub for sampling and buying digital music (see the following sidebar).

WORLD (WIDE WEB) MUSIC

Indianapolis-based OpenGlobe has been quietly orchestrating what it intends to be a sea change in how consumers acquire music.

Partnering with electronics manufacturers, OpenGlobe's Web-hosted services are designed to simplify access to online entertainment media products, allowing consumers to purchase music and movies "without having to leave their chairs."

Compaq's shipment of an OpenGlobe product has been followed closely by stereo maker Kenwood, which announced plans to ship the Kenwood Sovereign Entre during the summer of 2001. Combining many of the features found in the iPaq/OpenGlobe product—and with the added ability to burn its own audio CDs—the Entre will also come with a much heftier price tag: $1,800. At that price, it is truly an item for the man or woman who has everything.

Along with the support for e-commerce activities (see Figure 8.7), the OpenGlobe architecture offers the following:

- Access to Internet radio stations
- Access to Internet media databases, such as CDDB Music Recognition Service and OpenGlobe's MovieDB
- Downloading of graphics and related content pertaining to CDs, DVDs, and artists

FIGURE 8.7
OpenGlobe allows consumers to discover and purchase music directly from their audio IED.

The iPaq Music Center is one of the most truly innovative audio IEDs available. Even though it has been commercially available since mid-2001, it's still early days for the device. For instance, documentation for the device is still in its formative stage. Consider the mysterious process of programming the IED's remote control to operate your TV or stereo/home theater A/V receiver.

The manual advises you to simply "Press the Code Set button on the remote control and follow the on-screen directions." The problem is that no onscreen directions are available. A procedure for programming the remote does exist, but it bears no resemblance to the instruction manual. Subsequent online versions—and presumably new printed versions—of the Music Center's "Getting Started" guide now document the following steps to set up your remote control:

1. Press and hold the Code Set button on the remote control for three seconds. The LED will blink twice.

2. Press the TV PWR button, enter the first four-digit code for your brand (found in the Appendix to the startup guide). The LED will again blink twice, confirming that a valid code has been received.

3. Press the TV PWR button. Your television should turn off. If your TV does not respond, repeat steps 2–3, trying each code listed for your brand until you find the correct one.

4. To program an A/V receiver, repeat steps 1–3, substituting the A/V PWR button for the TV PWR button in steps 2 and 3.

As you can see, this is an instance where doing it "by the book" does not get you far.

TIP

Point your remote control away from the iPaq Music Center while you enter control codes. The remote was apparently intended to use onscreen interaction during remote control setup procedures, as the early manuals suggest, because it continues to send IR transmissions to the Music Center while being programmed. Unfortunately, the feature apparently was never supported by the device's operating system software, so you need to be sure that the remote can't transmit to the IED during the programming process.

AudioReQuest Pro Digital Music System

Founded in Troy, New York in 1998, Request Multimedia made headlines as the first to introduce a standalone home audio component designed from the ground up to capitalize on MP3 music compression.

Hyperbole concerning the company's flagship product, the AudioReQuest ARQ1, knew no bounds:

"AudioReQuest will revolutionize the way people listen to music by making songs easily available in a convenient centralized location. Listening to music will no longer require the effort of changing CDs and deciding what to play next."

The electronics trade press bought into the concept, heaping the ARQ1 with praise and awards. Since then, the company has had time to reflect on the difficulties of blazing a new trail into consumers' living rooms.

The company has retrenched and refocused its business plan from one targeted at consumers to one aimed at commercial installers. The ARQ1, with its 20GB hard drive and $800 MSRP, has been replaced with the ARQ Pro line, featuring 40GB and 60GB configurations and prices of $2,500 and $3,500, respectively (see Figure 8.8).

Hardware

Even in its original consumer-oriented version, the ARQ looks industrial—an essentially featureless black box, devoid of any contours or frills. It comes as no surprise that the device ships with rails for rack mounting. It's unimaginative appearance looks more at home in a wiring closet than a living room.

But looks aren't everything, as the ARQ Pro amply proves. Inside its barren black façade lurks a true audio IED, precisely the kind that breeds a fiercely loyal community of devotees—and provides an inviting platform for benign hacking (see the section "Audio IEDs," in Chapter 11, "Hacking Your IED," page 255).

In the nature of a true IED, the ARQ Pro requires no PC connection, although connectivity is provided via Ethernet or an included LapLink parallel port cable. Installing the PC software and hooking ARQ up to your personal computer allows you to transfer music files back and forth, and to make use of the awe-inspiring CDDB online music database (see the following sidebar, "Name That Tune") to automatically identify individual tracks from your commercial compact discs.

FIGURE 8.8
The AudioRequest ARQ Pro is a pricey audio IED that is being aimed at professional audio system installers.

NAME THAT TUNE

Created in 1995 by a pair of musically minded software developers, the Compact Disk Data Base (CDDB) was fueled by submissions from the online community. Now privately maintained and licensed by Gracenote in Berkeley, California, the database boasts nearly 28,000,000 unique users each month, all logging on to access an estimated 885,000 records.

The ability to have your audio IED automatically recognize the CD you insert, and then to have it effortlessly sort all your encoded digital music files by track, artist, and album, is both simple and powerfully seductive.

The popularity of the CDDB service accounts for the backlash that occurred in the spring of 2001, when Gracenote decided to take the database private, locking out certain software and hardware vendors and their customers. A lawsuit and countersuit erupted between Gracenote and CD-burner software provider Roxio.

The case's outcome could also determine the fate of two open-source alternatives to CDDB: Freedb.org and MusicBrainz.org.

The ARQ Pro earns its "professional" distinction in great part by virtue of its storage capacity. Its onboard 40GB or 60GB hard drive, providing up to 275 or 450 hours of high-quality MP3 audio, respectively, explains why the device makes sense for a high-end audio installation, such as a store, bar, or restaurant. The hard disk is complemented by a 40X CD drive for ripping audio disks to the main storage device.

Output ports include an Ethernet and a parallel port for data connectivity, and for audio, a pair of RCA-type analog output jacks. S-video and composite-video out ports feed the TV display, and a VGA port is provided for running a PC monitor. Input is handled via a pair of RCA-type analog input jacks, a microphone jack for voice recording, an AT-style keyboard connector, and a USB port, also for a PC keyboard. The device also ships with a full-featured remote control.

Software

Although the printed documentation for the ARQ seemed somewhat disjointed and poorly organized, the device's excellent onscreen interface makes the manual mostly superfluous.

The main screen provides a portal for navigating through your music collection and adding to it (see Figure 8.9).

FIGURE 8.9
The ARQ's "navigator" screen is the IED's primary interface for manipulating music files.

After music files are selected and the remote control's Play button is activated, the music begins playing and the unit switches to a player screen (see Figure 8.10) that can be customized according to five different interface "themes."

FIGURE 8.10
The ARQ's Player screen is shown with the "Classic" interface theme selected.

Users can move between the Player or Navigator screens, and access other features of the ARQ by activating the Main Menu (see Figure 8.11) from the remote control.

FIGURE 8.11
The ARQ's Main Menu screen provides access to a variety of additional screens and functions.

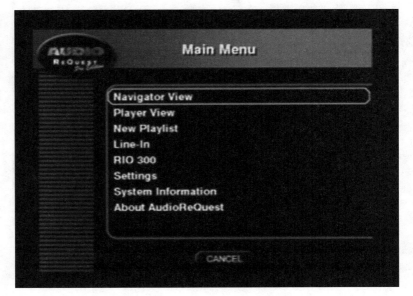

The Main Menu screen also provides access to the ARQ's system settings interface, which allows users to set parameters such as recording quality (a lower bit rate provides less audio quality but allows room for more recordings), date and time settings, network and TV display configuration, and more.

> **TIP**
>
> Want to know what your ARQ Pro is up to? The System Info screen (see Figure 8.12) can clue you in to what version of the software your system is running, how much and what type of media is stored on your system, and how much free storage capacity remains.

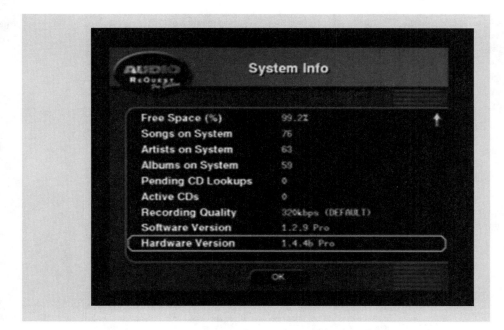

FIGURE 8.12
The ARQ's System Info screen gives you a snapshot of your IED's status.

Additional Audio IEDs and Related Components

If the Compaq iPaq music center and the AudioRequest ARQ Pro are too rich for your blood, but you still crave a standalone audio IED that does not require a running PC host system to play music, you might want to consider a lower-end solution, such as the PD Hercules or the DigMedia MusicStore.

Perception Digital's PD Hercules

Although it has yet to make a showing in U.S. retail locations, the PD Hercules from Perception Digital of Hong Kong is a digital audio jukebox that deserves a look and a listen.

Unlike the ARQ, the PD Hercules is designed to grace the living room with a curvaceous metallic bezel and a matching clam-shell-style two-way remote control that will delight the gadget lover in your family (see Figure 8.13).

FIGURE 8.13
The Perception Digital PD Hercules is designed to complement your other home audio/video components.

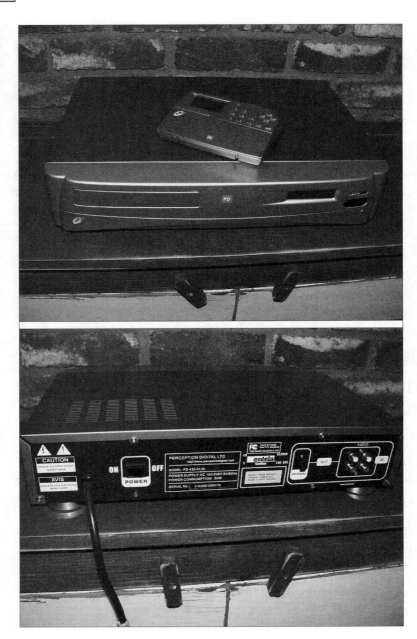

The interface is simple and well thought-out, and the unit is designed for two-way file transfers with a PC, unlike the iPaq, which does not permit encoded music files to be transferred to a personal computer. The PC connects via a supplied USB converter. In addition, PD Hercules has a SmartMedia slot for outputting compressed music files onto wafer-thin flash memory cards that can be inserted directly into a portable player.

The Hercules interacts well with a Web-connected PC that runs the company's PD Jockey software. The arrangement is useful for tasks such as looking up CDs using Gracenote's CDDB system (see the sidebar, "Name That Tune," page 214) and for transferring music files to and from the device and the PC.

The 20GB unit can be purchased online via the company's Web site at www.pdhercules.com for $699 plus international shipping.

DigMedia's MusicStore

You might have some difficulty laying your hands on one, but the "temporarily discontinued" (manufacturing rights have been transferred to a UK-based vendor) MusicStore tabletop console from DigMedia could be the perfect match for cost-conscious consumers who want to add compressed music files to their repertoire without breaking the bank.

The 5GB MP3/CD player can record, play, store and manage up to 90 hours of music encoded at its highest fidelity (128Kbps), or 180 hours of music ripped at 64 Kbps, although audio quality will suffer at those levels. The unit is designed to connect to a conventional stereo amplifier, self-powered speakers, or headphones. In addition, the unit contains a docking port for DigMedia's portable SoulMate player (see Figure 8.14).

MusicStore's unique 12-key pad layout is similar to that of a telephone, and uses the same T9 predictive software provided in many cell phones. An option is available to turn off T9, but its ability to guess at what search term you might be inputting is quite effective after you get used to it.

FIGURE 8.14
The DigMedia
MusicStore and
SoulMate portable
companion.

Although it initially retailed for as much as $500, the MusicStore IED has been seen advertised on ComputerShopper.com and other sites for as little as $130.

Bose Wave/PC Interactive Audio System

Not a true IED, but still deserving of a mention is Bose Corp.'s Wave/PC Interactive Audio System. The Wave/PC is essentially identical to the famed Bose Wave Radio, a compact tabletop radio imbued with Dr. Amar Bose's award-winning Acoustic Waveguide Speaker technology (see Figure 8.15).

The player device connects to a host PC via a 15-foot serial and analog audio cable. A software application allows the user to control the sound output via a mouse or the Wave/PCs credit-card-sized remote control unit, switching between Web radio stations, digital music files, CD audio, and the device's onboard AM/FM receiver.

The $449 unit lacks the onboard computer of a proper IED and requires the services of a tethered PC. On the other hand, it is a fully functional, self-contained audio output unit. Unlike any other audio IED profiled in this book, it does not require a separate set of speakers.

FIGURE 8.15
The Bose Wave/PC Interactive Audio System.

Coming Attractions

Along with the debut of the Kenwood Sovereign Entre, Hewlett-Packard's Digital Entertainment Center, and The Rio Advanced Digital Audio Receiver, the late fall of 2001 and winter of 2002 should be a fruitful period for audio component makers as they cautiously begin to cash in on the MP3 craze.

The next step in added features for the iPaq Music Center calls for new software to support a multi-disc changer, such as Sony's CDP-M555ES and CDP-M333ES 400-disc Megastorage CD changers, allowing the mass storage of CDs in addition to the digital files stored on the system's hard drive. Compaq sources say that the company planned to release a software upgrade—which the IED would install during its nightly check-in calls—in the fourth quarter of 2001 and another, more sweeping revision of the iPaq's operating system in early 2002. Among the new features are the ability to apply "fuzzy" logic to CDDB searches, improving consumers' chances of locating the correct album cover art and track information for digital music files.

Japan's music mogul, Yamaha, has launched a device that combines CD burning with audio and MP3 playback in a high-end component styled for your stereo cabinet. The CDR-HD1000 is priced at $999 and features a 20GB hard drive and an accelerated encoding engine that stores CD audio in a digital format at 10 times normal playback speed.

Those who want to add a new form of digital radio to their digital home audio system can also consider tapping into the satellite-delivered radio service being rolled out by XM Satellite. (A competing service, Sirius Satellite Radio, is designed initially only for listening in your vehicle.)

The Sony DRN-XM01H is designed to let you receive XM Satellite Radio's 100 digital audio stations via your home stereo, using its AUX or TAPE inputs. The $299 unit displays and memorizes program information, such as song title and artist, and can be removed from its cradle for use in your car. An XM Satellite antenna is included. Be sure to budget for your subscription to the nationwide service. It costs $10 per month.

Finally, expect the other shoe to drop in digital audio programming from existing cable, satellite TV, and broadband Internet providers. Many are quietly teaming up with former and future makers of audio IEDs, designing "stereo-top boxes" that will deliver customized and on-demand audio and associated video and graphics. Of course, you can expect to pay an extra monthly fee for the content, and don't be surprised if your new programming service embeds lots of enticements to buy additional downloadable music, concert tickets, and related paraphernalia featuring your favorite artists.

Chapter 9

Other "Convergence" Devices

What Else Is There?

In segmenting the IED marketplace into video, gaming, and audio categories, I stumbled across a certain number of intelligent devices that simply didn't fit neatly into the bins I had created. Either they spanned multiple categories, such as a combination of music and video, or they struck a different path entirely.

Regardless of whether these devices have taken an orthodox design approach—in a market that is far from orthodox—these IEDs might deserve consideration in your search for the perfect intelligent entertainment companion.

ZapStation

One of the most intriguing new entries is ZapStation, the initial hardware product of Atlanta-based ZapMedia. ZapMedia is a privately held media platform developer that aims to provide "instant access to customized news and entertainment through a common point of access."

One of the most ambitious IEDs of them all, ZapStation is designed to do all of the following:

- Surf the Internet via a broadband connection
- Play CDs, DVDs, and MP3s
- Enable secure online purchases of audio and video content
- Tune in Internet radio stations
- Surf the World Wide Web
- Manage and store audio and video media

To do all this, ZapStation operates as a full-featured digital jukebox, serving up content in the form of streaming audio and video off the Web, CD audio, and DVD video. If you tire of audio and video entertainment, you can use the device to tune in a daily news feed courtesy of ZapMedia investor Gannett, the parent company of USA Today.

All this, obviously, requires a fair amount of storage. Fortunately, ZapStation comes equipped with a 30GB hard drive able to store up to 10,000 MP3 songs—all of it accessible via your television set and a remote control.

Hardware

ZapStation made its debut as a commercially available product in November 2001, shipping only from the company's Web site at www.zapmedia.com (see Figure 9.1). Its initial price point could come as a shock to those who recall the company's first rumblings back in spring of 2000. At that time the company was touting plans to release a unit for approximately $300. The systems are available now for about $1,500—a considerable leap!

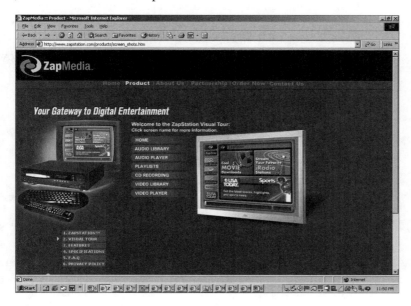

FIGURE 9.1
ZapMedia's ZapStation is available only from the company via its Web site at www.zapstation.com.

Although the high price point will certainly turn off many potential customers, ZapStation's specs indicate a potential for high performance. The IED's Linux-based operating system runs on an 800MHz Intel Celeron with 128MB of PC100 SDRAM, a respectable processor platform for such a device. Its 30GB Quantum Fireball Quiet Drive hard disk is complemented by an optical drive, something that to date is normally not found in a video IED. The inclusion of a playback-only combination CD/DVD drive is unique in this category.

In terms of audiovisual I/O, inputs exist for stereo audio, USB devices, a 10/100 BaseT Ethernet port, and a modem. Outputs accommodate RCA-type and digital audio (SPDIF), along with composite, S-Video, and SVGA video connectors. Finally, a connector is available for plugging in headphones.

ZapStation ships with all the accessories needed to connect and operate it, including a handheld remote control, a wireless keyboard, a power cable, stereo RCA cables, composite video cable, S-Video cable, and batteries.

Software

ZapStation does not currently require a subscription to a dedicated ZapMedia service, although this was originally part of the company's business model. Instead, users are encouraged to frequent the ZapMedia Portal, called the ZapZone, where they can access music, movies, streaming video, video downloads, and Internet radio. Access to the ZapZone must be accomplished through the user's own ISP account, and although dial-up accounts are supported through a home network connection, the company recommends customers use an always-on broadband connection such as DSL or cable.

ZapStation is innovative in its ability to support Windows Media streaming content and DVD playback on a Linux platform, as well as in its integration of a direct news feed from *USA Today*. However, don't confuse this device with TiVo, UltimateTV, or ReplayTV because ZapStation is missing a major ingredient: the ability to record video programming to the hard disk.

Conclusions

ZapStation is billed as an IED that "can do it all"; however, it still can't function as a digital video recorder.

Although it was announced that respected audio component maker Harman Kardon would introduce a ZapStation-based DMC (Digital Media Center) 100 in the third quarter of 2001, it is rumored that the electronics maker backed out of the deal. ZapMedia had to cut about a quarter of its 80 employees. In addition, reports surfaced in July 2001 that ReplayTV's parent company, SonicBlue, was considering a buyout offer for ZapMedia. Whatever the company's true status and durability prove to be, the degree of retrenchment that ZapMedia has been forced to do over the course of 2001 is enough to give any potential customer pause.

On the other hand, the system does have many promising features. If you're someone who is more interested in audio/video jukebox features and the ability to surf the Web through your TV than you are in the ability to record every available episode of *Hawaii Five-O*, it might be the perfect IED to complement your home entertainment system.

Internet-Enabled Set-Top Boxes

Although customers acquire a few set-top boxes through retail channels (see the next section, "Open Season for Set-Tops"), they acquire most of them directly from their cable and satellite service providers. In this way, these devices seem to choose us, rather than the other way around. However, the following information on some new developments in the set-top space might help you make a more informed choice when choosing a programming source for your home.

Open Season for Set-Tops

While video IEDs TiVo, ReplayTV, and UltimateTV have made inroads into the retail channel for consumer electronics, makers of set-top boxes have remained shut out and relegated to making industrial-sized deals with cable and satellite service operators.

As a result, Motorola's General Instruments division, Scientific American, and other mainstays of the set-top business have virtually no consumer awareness and no access to the higher-margin retail business.

That's why these companies are turning to an industry-supported non-profit test and design laboratory for help. Cable Labs, based in Denver, has championed an initiative called OpenCable, which has three stated goals:

- Provide a blueprint for "the next generation digital consumer device."
- Encourage competition among set-top box suppliers.
- Create a retail hardware sales channel for set-top devices.

Cable Labs determined at the project's outset that retail sales of set-top receivers would not be possible until a standard for interoperability was available. Simply put, people won't go out to an electronics store and buy set-top boxes (no matter how cool they are) until they are certain that they will run with whatever cable TV system they have at home.

Today, such systems are proprietary and seldom comply to open standards, with the result that a set-top box configured and manufactured for use on one particular cable system is highly unlikely to work on another.

To overcome this hurdle and open the door to the retail world, Cable Labs and the major cable systems operators that fund the labs are in the process of creating a standard application platform to support a laundry list of competitive features:

- Interactive, electronic program guides
- "Impulse" pay-per-view
- Video-on-demand
- Interactive sports, game shows
- Web access and communications features such as e-mail, chat, instant messaging
- Interactive games
- Services such as shopping and home banking
- Personal video recorder capabilities

Companies that are creating interoperable set-top boxes based on the OpenCable Application Platform (OCAP) include LG Electronics, Microsoft, SCM Microsystems, Motorola, Panasonic, Philips, Samsung, Scientific-Atlanta, Sony Electronics, Thomson Consumer Electronics, and Zenith.

Under the OpenCable architecture, after a consumer purchases an OCAP-compliant set-top, he is issued a credit-card-sized device to activate the box. Called the "Point-of-Deployment (POD) module," the device allows the set-top to decode and display encrypted content. Companies that are making POD modules include Mindport, Motorola, Nagra, NDS, Scientific-Atlanta, and SCM Microsystems.

On the software side, OCAP efforts to blend Web access with cable modem-based broadband services are primarily aimed at delivering interactive television services to cable customers. The specification is made up of two major software components: an "execution engine" that provides a programmable environment, and a browser-like "presentation engine" that supports standardized markup and scripting languages, such as Hypertext Markup Language (HTML) and ECMAScript.

To date, Sun Microsystems has directed development of the execution engine, whereas Liberate and Microsoft have taken the lead in defining specifications for the presentation engine.

The motivation behind the OpenCable initiative goes deeper than a simple desire to create a competitive retail market for set-top boxes. In fact, the cable industry would probably never have funded such an effort if it hadn't received a firm kick in the pants from Uncle Sam. Cable operators have been under pressure from the Telecommunications Act of 1996, which directed the Federal Communications Commission to enforce the creation of an open marketplace that would allow consumers to obtain set tops and other equipment from multiple sources, including retailers and manufacturers—not just cable operators. The FCC mandated that cable operators make removable security modules (PODs) available to the public.

Integrated Devices

Set-top boxes with integrated digital video recording capabilities, such as the Dish Network-based DishPlayer and DirecTV-based UltimateTV and "DirecTivo" (a nickname for the combo DirecTV and TiVo IED/satellite receiver), offer some serious advantages for the consumer.

These devices—and the many that will follow in their footsteps —provide a "baked-in" satellite receiver and full integration between the hardware and the service provider's electronic program guide. Just connect the device to the output of your roof dish, and you are ready to slice and dice your programming with no further ado.

Ease of setup is the first advantage to these combo receiver IEDs. A lot can be said for combining two separate boxes, each requiring its own complex set of inputs and outputs, into a single device. That act alone eliminates innumerable setup steps and a bag full of hardware accessories. Comparing a DirecTiVo setup to the configuration of a ReplayTV standalone ShowStopper, for example, the DirecTiVo does away with one set of audio cables, an S-Video cable, and an IR Blaster. It also takes up one less electrical outlet and eliminates a phone jack (not to mention, one less device ties up the phoneline to check in with the head office every night). In addition, the DirecTV integrated IEDs can automatically tell you what's on the Pay Per View channels, whereas ShowStopper cannot.

More importantly for the IED manufacturer, having the cable or satellite provider as a partner opens up a new and effective direct sales channel into consumers' homes. Offers to buy the combo devices often arrive in the same envelope as your satellite TV service bill, and might be accompanied with telemarketing, targeted infomercials, and other effective direct marketing techniques.

For the programming services, adding the capabilities of a hard drive-based video IED to their set-top offerings is also a win because it helps differentiate their service while giving consumers ways to milk more value from those services. For instance, Microsoft's UltimateTV design group estimates that DirectTV customers have access to approximately 1,000 movies each week. Without powerful sorting and browsing capabilities (Microsoft and TiVo have just improved these qualities in their video IEDs), consumers can only capture and view a tiny fraction of the films that are available to them on a daily and weekly basis.

Cable and satellite operators are slowly coming around to the conclusion that video IEDs—integrated or otherwise—help their customers see more of what they're paying for, so they're likely to be more satisfied with the service. Because they derive more from their TV experience, IED users are more likely to order additional upgrade services. For example, "We've found there's a very high correlation between UltimateTV owners and people who subscribe to NFL Season Ticket from DirecTV," said UltimateTV's director of strategy Mark Mullen.

SurfReady NTV-2500

Somewhat akin to the DishPlayer—that "missing link" between Microsoft's early WebTV offering and its UltimateTV successor (see "Sights Set On Set-Tops," Chapter 3, page 22)—the SurfReady NTV-2500 from Neon Technology is a set-top box with PC aspirations (see Figure 9.2).

Neon bills its $649 device as "the complete Internet and entertainment solution." In addition to surfing the Web, writing e-mail, and chatting on the Internet Picture Phone, the box boasts "advanced entertainment features" such as karaoke and playback of DVDs, CDs, and MP3s.

FIGURE 9.2
The SurfReady NTV-2500 combines Web browsing, audio CD and DVD playback, video telephony, karaoke, and more in a full-feature set-top box.

Based on a 266MHz Intel Mobile Pentium with MMX, the NTV-2500 includes a TV tuner that is capable of displaying six different channels at once, a DVD/CD drive, and a 56K modem, along with support for 10/100 Base-T Ethernet. The device also supports RealNetworks' RealPlayer streaming media content.

The NTV-2500 comes with a digital camera, wireless keyboard, and remote control. It is the only IED in this book that is specifically designed for karaoke support (although the manufacturer warns that this feature requires a separate karaoke disk).

The SurfReady NTV-2000's browser supports frames, tables, JavaScript, Secure Socket Layer (SSL) 3.0 for secure e-commerce transactions, and RealNetworks' RealAudio 5.0 for streaming audio, in addition to a streaming MP3 audio player. The browser also serves as a portal for online upgrades to the SurfReady's system software.

As versatile as the SurfReady is, manipulating live television is not on its résumé. If you want to pause, record, rewind, or fast-forward live television, the SurfReady 2500 is not equipped for the job.

A TASTE for Tuxia

Several partnerships that were announced in mid-2001 could bear interesting fruit in the months and years to come, extending the reach and scope of set-top entertainment devices.

One such partnership involves Canadian visual media software provider MGI (see listing in Table 4.2, "Video Capture/TV Tuner Software," Chapter 4, page 106) and Tuxia, an embedded Linux systems company.

In July 2001, the companies joined forces to complete a software platform for home entertainment devices designed to combine the following features in a single, all-in-one set-top box:

- Optimized Linux-based operating system
- Digital VCR
- Time-shifted TV viewing
- DVD playback
- Web browsing

Roxio, best known for its CD recording software, has since acquired MGI. The deal, announced in December 2001, could derail the Tuxia partnership because the set-top box development is somewhat peripheral to Roxio's core focus of providing packaged consumer software.

Shortly after the MGI deal, Tuxia announced details of another, related initiative, also based on Tuxia Appliance Synthesis Technology (TASTE). TASTE incorporates a Linux Kernel 2.4 operating system and the company's embedded Mozilla browser, called Nanozilla. In the latter announcement, Tuxia revealed it is working with video technology company Focus Enhancements on a reference design for "an Internet media gateway and interactive TV" set-top box. The resulting device will offer the following features:

- Picture-in-picture capability
- Web browsing, with support for Macromedia Flash, Java, and RealNetworks' Real Player streaming media playback
- MP3 audio playback
- DVD playback
- MPEG-2 video playback
- Simultaneous LAN services
- Support for antennae, cable, or satellite TV programming sources
- Gaming and other home entertainment/management applications

No manufacturers have yet been named to produce the systems, which would be based on an Intel Celeron processor.

Motorola Digital Convergence Platform 500 Series

Motorola upped the ante for its set-top box division, General Instruments, in June 2001 with the announcement of its Digital Convergence Platform (DCP) 500 Series product (see Figure 9.3). The DCP500 family will combine an interactive digital cable receiver with home theater system entertainment technologies, such as DVD and audio CD playback, and a built-in A/V receiver.

FIGURE 9.3
Motorola's DCP500 Series aims to ease consumers' experience integrating home theater acoustics with digital video and interactive cable services.

The DCP500 Series is set to include the following models:

- The DCP501, with a single-disk DVD/CD player
- The DCP503, equipped with a three-disk carousel player
- The DCP510, featuring "an integrated personal video recorder hard drive for storing files." The DCP510 is scheduled for introduction late in 2002.

Motorola says the designs are the result of extensive consumer research, pointing toward a major spike in demand for home theater products and interactive cable programming services. Consumers also indicated a pronounced desire "for a single-unit solution that enhances the A/V experience by merging and simplifying remote control and wiring operations." (Do I hear an "Amen"?)

The under-$1,000 set-tops will include the following:

- A DVD player
- A CD player
- Motorola's DCT-2000 Interactive Digital Cable Terminal
- An audio/video receiver and amplifier (5×100 watts/channel)
- A Dolby digital decoder
- Composite video outputs for all input sources

Motorola is also planning to add digital video recording support to its DCT5000 family of set-top boxes sold by cable operators (see Figure 9.4). The cable modem-equipped devices are all designed to allow consumers to simultaneously experience interactive video, audio, and high-speed data access. The systems are powered by a RISC-based microprocessor in the 300-plus MIPS (millions of instructions per second) speed range, complimented by a 32-bit 3D graphics processor and memory expandable up to 90MB. The company has not divulged specifics about the personal video recorder (PVR) features that it plans to install into the DCT 52X0.

FIGURE 9.4
Motorola's DCT5000 family is scheduled to add video IED capabilities in mid-2002.

The company also announced in November 2001 its DCT2600 model, which will combine a hard drive for video recording and timeshifting, along with a 175MIPS, 175MHz RISC CPU and 64MB of DRAM configured as unified memory (see "Xbox: Memory," page 158 in Chapter 6). The device is slated to ship in mid-2002.

Simple Devices SimpleFi Wireless Broadband Audio Player

Motorola has also decided to partner with Simple Devices to bring a wireless digital audio receiver/player to market. Motorola is an investor in the Burlingame, California, company, along with wireless networking firm Proxim, and consumer electronics manufacturer Casio.

The SimpleFi (pronounced "simplify") reflects the confluence of those investors' corporate DNA. It combines local area wireless networking—reminiscent of Proxim—with broadband connectivity that smacks of Motorola's Broadband Communications set-top box operations (formerly General Instruments), and it all comes wrapped up in the attractive styling of a table-top consumer device worthy of Casio (see Figure 9.5).

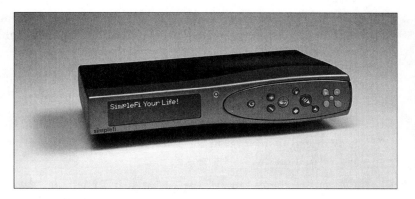

FIGURE 9.5
The Motorola SimpleFi wireless audio receiver is being marketed to cable operators as a way to offer subscribers new media-related services, such as "preference-based" content and information, and music downloads.

To be marketed through cable and broadband service providers, the Motorola SimpleFi receiver will be aimed at broadband subscribers who want to stream high-quality audio from the Web to their existing stereo equipment, distributing digital audio files wirelessly throughout their homes.

Upon introducing the device at the Western Cable Show in Anaheim, California in November 2001, Motorola Broadband's Director of Home Networking Vince Izzo said it represents "an emerging class of devices that leverage the computer and a broadband connection to move digital media away from the PC and into other areas of the home." In this way, people can experience MP3 and Web-based audio in the place and manner to which they are accustomed.

The SimpleFi wireless receiver features a unique "TagIt!" button that marks streaming content for later review, allowing subscribers to perform related searches for concert tickets, CDs, or artists' biographies.

Conclusions on Convergence

As the consolidation of electronics companies continues to accelerate, IED features that are now the province of dedicated entertainment appliances will increasingly merge with desktop PCs and digital set-top boxes. PCs will begin to look more like appliances, while appliances and set-top receivers will look more like PCs.

Call it convergence. I call it inevitable. Just as inevitably, some of these multifunction devices will end up integrating too many functions for their own good. Consumers will be wracked with indecision about such matters as whether they want to record their own DVDs in their kitchen while watching a movie, toasting bread, and engaging in an online chat session. Ultimately, many products that are too highly integrated will fail.

Those products that survive will do so because they have hit upon ways to significantly enhance the things we already like to do, rather than trying to revolutionize the way we do everything, by forcing us to adopt new behaviors that are unfamiliar and uncomfortable. Successful growth and innovation in the IED marketplace will be evolutionary, not revolutionary.

Of course, there's always the caveat that something truly brilliant might come along, astounding us all and forcing us to beat a path to the electronics store. It is the dream of creating precisely that kind of magic that continues to drive these "convergence" companies forward.

Chapter 10

Customizing Your Digital Entertainment Experience

Understanding the Pieces of the Puzzle

As electronics companies go through the exercise of creating new products, they diligently test them in hundreds—sometimes thousands—of different configurations, trying to pinpoint and correct potential problems the consumer might encounter. At least we like to think they do.

If I can claim any particular skill in the field of evaluating and reporting on high-tech products, it is my unerring ability to fall right through that safety net, to automatically gravitate to any hole in the fabric of product testing, no matter how tiny.

No prescience is involved. I claim no sixth sense about this. In fact, I am always desperately hoping the product will simply work as advertised, and I'm bitterly disappointed when it does otherwise. No, I believe that my strange and unfortunate gift of putting my finger directly on any product's secret weakness comes from my approach to testing these products, not as a laboratory researcher, but as a consumer.

Consumers don't read manuals. We don't plugs things in correctly, and when we do, we generally bend the pins. Above all, we don't start with a clean workbench. In other words, we bring baggage. Like the emotional baggage that we inevitably tote along into our human relationships, consumers bring another type of baggage into these electromechanical relationships, such as preinstalled hardware and software that might conflict or compete for resources with the new product. We also bring the baggage of our preconceptions and expectations for the product, and these can be wildly at odds with the product's true capabilities.

Unfortunately for both vendors and consumers, that's the real world. These new products aren't destined for installation in sanitized labs and temperature-controlled cleanrooms. They are coming home to our living rooms, where anything and everything can occur—and most of it isn't covered in the manual.

One thing that manufacturers always seem to overlook is that their cherished device is not being installed in a vacuum. For instance, none of the documentation that accompanied the video, audio, or gaming IEDs discussed in this book took into account the possibility that consumers might also choose to install one of the other video, audio, or gaming IEDs discussed in this book. Heaven forbid you should want to connect a TiVo, an Xbox, *and* a RequestAudio device to the same television set. However, this is precisely the scenario these manufacturers *should* anticipate; who is more likely to buy a computer-enhanced video recorder than someone who already owns a computer-enhanced game console or stereo?

How Does It All Fit Together?

If you happen to be lucky—and perhaps foolhardy—enough to consider owning multiple IEDs, how would you go about making them all work together?

As ever, the first step is deciding what you want to do with each device, and then devising a plan to accomplish it. Prepare to be flexible. Assume that the manufacturers did not anticipate your needs and objectives, and then find yourself pleasantly surprised when you discover that the connector you need is actually where it belongs.

Logic will take you a long way. If you want to transfer digitally recorded TV shows from your video IED to a VCR, for instance, you need to connect the output of your IED to the recording device. The manuals instruct you how to do this; however, they might neglect to mention how to direct the output of your VCR back into your TV, even though it's logical to assume that eventually, you'll actually want to watch some of that archived videotape.

Other common activities also seem to have mysteriously escaped documentation. The desire to connect an Xbox, GameCube, or PlayStation alongside your TiVo, Replay, or UltimateTV does not seem unreasonable or unusual. Naturally, I tried it, throwing a VCR into the bargain as well. Several hours and a trip to the local RadioShack later, the slapstick antics of Goofy's Fun House for PlayStation 2 were finally gracing the screen of our playroom TV. (When it comes to tough audiences, no crowd is uglier than a roomful of frustrated grade schoolers, their fingers twitching for the game controller.) Getting there was no easy feat, however.

Although Panasonic's ShowStopper technicians were unable to confirm or explain the nature of the problem, my ReplayTV unit stubbornly refused to pass through a PlayStation signal to the television.

Although the problem had Panasonic reps scratching their heads, I learned that I was not alone in encountering a mismatch between the game console and the ReplayTV. Postings to the alt.video.ptv.replaytv newsgroup and the ReplayTV bulletin board at AVSforum.com indicate that other ReplayTV owners have had similar experiences. The universal experience was that of "a blue screen, no-video-signal detected message," as one newsgroup poster accurately described it.

Although you won't find the explanation in the manual, the AVSforum did eventually yield the answer: "PlayStation video is not NTSC-standard," wrote Mike Kobb, a ReplayTV employee who helps police the forum. The PlayStation's output is a single field, not a "proper 2-field interlaced frame," Kobb explained. "So, we can't encode it, although your TV can display it."

Even if you could route the game IED's video through your video IED (and some users have had success using a combo TV/IED unit, or routing the game video through a switchbox), Kobb says you wouldn't want to. ReplayTV leaves about a 1-second lag behind live TV due to the buffering process. This, of course, has a negative impact on gameplay, where timing is usually everything. In other words, the ReplayTV's modus operandi of recording all signals passed through it onto the hard drive causes a small delay that prevents it from displaying the output of the game machine in real time.

The best solution is to simply bypass the video IED, which, in my case, was connected to the television set via composite video and RCA audio cables. I coupled the PlayStation to the VCR via the same cabling scheme, and attached the VCR to the TV's RF "cable/antenna in" connector (see Figure 10.1). Of course, this isn't the only possible solution. The important thing is to make sure that your video IED doesn't come between the signal from your game console and your television. If, for example, you have an audio/video receiver with available video input connections, you can connect your game console through it to bypass your video IED.

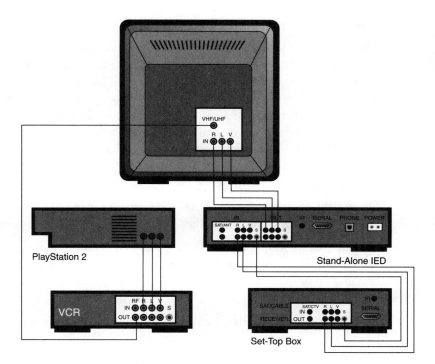

FIGURE 10.1
To display the PlayStation's output on the TV, you might need to bypass the ReplayTV unit.

This is functionally fine, except that it requires the constant use of two remote controls—one to control every function *except* switching the TV to its A/V input mode, and the television's original remote control to do exactly that. This setup constantly confused the kids, who frequently forgot to switch the TV's A/V inputs, thus finding themselves unable to access their beloved ReplayTV Scooby-Doo Theme Channel, or thwarted them in their attempts at improving their cart-racing skills on the PlayStation. Quite by accident, I discovered that the ReplayTV remote was capable of switching the television's input source—not by pressing the INPUT button as one might expect, but by pressing the TV/VCR button. Go figure.

In a world of myriad home audio/video components, snaking cables, and three dozen remotes to control them all, more often than not you'll encounter scenarios like this. In these cases, your only recourse is often to simply remain calm and patient and be as creative as possible in how you decide to connect these devices.

Overprotective Copy Protection?

This brings up the other reason that it's often necessary to bypass your video IED: to watch commercially recorded videotapes. My first attempt at testing the Replay unit with my VCR brought me to jarring hard-stop. When I popped in the first videotape lying around (a new-ish, store-bought copy of Mary Poppins), I saw a few seconds of the video before it was unceremoniously replaced by a dire-looking warning screen indicating that I had no right to be attempting to watch copy-protected material.

ReplayTV's onboard support for Macrovision's anticopying technology was the culprit. It prevents the IED from displaying any encrypted video. Replay has documented this "feature" in its manual, as follows:

"When Macrovision or CGMS-A (Copy Generation Management System-Analog) copy protected signals are available for TV broadcasting, the show is NOT viewable in LIVE TV mode, nor can it be recorded."

Of course, the hitch is that I was not watching a live, copy-protected broadcast, but a commercial videotape that I had purchased for the express purpose of (silly me) watching.

Elsewhere in the Panasonic ShowStopper manual, the issue is stated in plainer language:

"The Hard Disk Recorder does not record copy protected programs. A warning screen will appear if you try to playback a copy-protected program."

There you have it. The problem lies in the fact that the ReplayTV records everything it displays. Even if your intent is to watch the program—without the least intention of recording it to sell thousands of copies on the black market—the machine can't help recording it as it passes through the video playback system. Macrovision senses this and kicks in, leaving you staring at a warning screen instead of your videotape. The same problem occurs when trying to play back a Macrovision-protected DVD.

Panasonic acknowledges the glitch, but makes no apology for it. The only apparent workaround for viewing copy-protected material appears to be by adding an inexpensive splitter to the RF signal. Of course, most new televisions have multiple inputs for video signals, which can make using a splitter unnecessary. Simply connect your video IED to one input and your Macrovision-protected DVD player or VCR to the other. For example, if your TV has an S-video input and inputs through RCA plugs, connect the DVD signal to your TV via an S-video cable, and your video IED through the RCA inputs (or vice-versa), as shown in Figure 10.2.

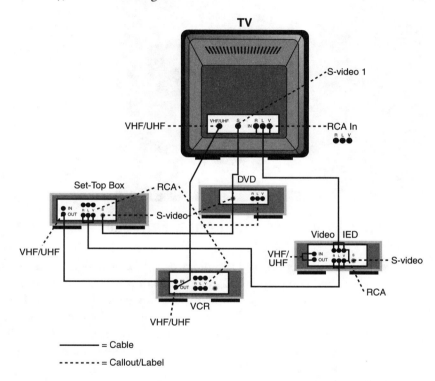

FIGURE 10.2
Macrovision-protected VCRs and DVD players need to stay on a separate wiring path from your video IED.

It's true that applying the ShowStopper's disk-caching schema to your videotape playback signal would be pointless (your VCR already offers you all the timeshifting features you might desire). However, it seems that Panasonic should have given more consideration to the fact that most people have VCRs and a library of tapes, and would obviously want to use them in conjunction with their new IED. Separate RF or A/V jacks specifically for this purpose should have been part of the back panel design. The additional cost would have been minimal, and the source of user frustration could have been easily eliminated.

In the meantime, this workaround will allow you to connect the output of your VCR or DVD player to a direct input on your television, bypassing your video IED altogether. Otherwise, you could find yourself with nothing to look at but a puzzling advisory that you don't have permission to watch your own video (see Figure 10.3) .

This show is copy protected and cannot be viewed or recorded.

To watch another show, press CHANNEL GUIDE.

To watch recorded shows, press REPLAY GUIDE.

For more details on copy protection, please refer to the user guide.

All About Macromedia and Fair Use

The obstacle that was briefly discussed in the Mary Poppins example earlier in this section is a technology called Macrovision, from a company of the same name. The copy-protection software is what makes your aging dub of Snow White go suddenly dark, then bright. It also triggers a filter in ReplayTV and other Macrovision-enabled devices to stop viewers in their tracks. Additional versions of Macrovision technology are used to "protect" DVDs and audio CDs, as well as live pay-per-view programming.

According to Macrovision, "Major Hollywood studios, independent home video companies, and special interest, corporate, and educational program providers use the company's videocassette copy protection technology to protect against unauthorized home copying of rental and sell-through videos." The site does not specifically address the technology's unfortunate side effect of occasionally preventing IED-equipped consumers of these products from viewing the stuff they legitimately paid for.

You can defeat Macrovision, but the methods of doing so are mostly expensive and illegal. Sites such as www.lik-sang.com offer relatively inexpensive devices that are designed to filter out Macrovision signals that trigger the IED's blocking function. Lik Sang International's DVD Video Decoder (Macrovision remover) is one of the less expensive devices on the market—around $40 plus shipping from Hong Kong. Although more expensive, Sima Products in Oakmont, PA also manufactures devices that will do the job, such as the $170 Pro-Series ColorCorrector.

If you're handy with a soldering gun and a schematic, you can even construct your own Macrovision-stifling device from plans available at sites such as http://home.quicknet.com.au/andrewm/macro or http://www.gratis-tv.com/esquemas/macrovision/eivnaess/ines.html.

Finally, several brands of DVD players, and even some older VHS decks, can be modified through software or hardware to ignore the Macrovision "flags" that are embedded into the media. Models manufactured by Apex are notorious for their ability to turn off the Macrovision filter.

Don't expect manufacturers of these products to brag about or even document their products' anti-Macrovision features. Sima (online at www.simacorp.com) makes no claims regarding the use of its products to defeat Macrovision. It does, however, acknowledge the potential illegal use of its SCC Model with the disclaimer, "Use of this product for unauthorized duplication of copyrighted material from DVD, VHS or other media is prohibited under federal copyright laws unless the copy qualifies as a fair use under the Copyright Laws."

What constitutes fair use? The jury is, in a fairly literal sense, still out on that one. Fair use used to mean that a consumer could make a copy of a copyrighted work that he owned, for his own use. Although legal challenges to that limited meaning seem to be ongoing with no clear resolution in sight, there's no reason to believe that you will suffer legal consequences if you stay within that narrow definition. If you plan to make mass copies of a commercial video or DVD and sell them without the express permission of the copyright holder, you are definitely infringing and you are inviting prosecution. Anything in between—including copying such material and distributing it for free on the Web—is a legal gray area, unfortunately.

Don't expect the problem to go away any time soon. Macrovision-type copy protection is growing at a rate that would make cancer blush: According to Macrovision, more than 20 million households worldwide already have copy-protection features on their set-top decoders, including virtually all of the digital set-tops in North America.

As more of these set-top boxes adopt hard disk recording features, it will be up to Macrovision or its competitors to create a more intelligent copy protection scheme—one that can distinguish between the real-time recording used in IED playback and attempts to make illegal copies.

In fact, Macrovision is moving in that direction. As this book goes to press, the company is expected to announce a new version of its copy-protection technology for audio CDs that places duplicate copies of digital music tracks on a single disk. One copy is formatted for a conventional CD player, whereas the other is a compressed and encrypted computer file. When consumers attempt to rip the file to a PC's hard disk, the computer will only see the encrypted file. Rights-management technology that is embedded in the file will dictate what kind of copies the user is authorized to make.

According to a Macrovision spokeswoman, consumers will be able to play the CD in a PC's CD-ROM drive, and if they are "authenticated" as the disk's rightful owner, they will be allowed to transfer it to a portable player.

If Macrovision is able to successfully deploy the technology for CDs, the company is likely to try to extend that to video media as well.

The A/V Receiver

The way that most manufacturers seem to handle the issue of wiring up additional devices is by blithely suggesting that the consumer should throw an A/V (audio/video) receiver into the mix. Just plug everything into the all-purpose switchbox, the manual suggests, and you will be miraculously delivered from design flaws, such as providing insufficient input/output capabilities.

Although those who already own a "home theater" speaker set for their television are likely to have purchased an A/V receiver of some description, buying one with sufficient inputs and outputs can add anywhere from about $80 to as much as $3,000 to your IED installation costs. That investment can, however, save you a lot of headaches by significantly easing the setup process. Instead of worrying about how you're going to connect your DVD player, TiVo, and VCR to a two-input television, a good A/V receiver allows you to plug all the devices into it. This allows you to use the receiver's remote control to decide which signal to pass on to your television.

A word of caution: Even in this scenario, you are limited to the input/outputs on your receiver, and many receivers still leave you with rather limited I/O options. In addition, you'll be adding yet another remote control to clutter up your coffee table (see the following section, "Seeing Infrared"). Finally, it's one more electronic device that must be left on full-time, sucking up juice and ratcheting up your growing electric bill.

Your best bet is to draw up a diagram of your components and how you plan to connect them, and then bring that with you to the electronics store. This could potentially save you additional return trips to the store for connectors—or a new receiver altogether.

Seeing Infrared

As you attempt to marry multiple IEDs and related A/V equipment, you might need to give some thought to the proliferating number of remote and wired controllers that are cluttering up your coffee table.

Your game console should provide the only controllers that remain tethered to the device, and at least these are difficult to lose. Your video IED's remote control should be able to replace your separate remote controls for the cable/satellite receiver box, the VCR, and the TV (unless, like me, you happen to own what might be the only TV in the world that the Sony-built UltimateTV steadfastly refuses to support). But the remote control for your TiVo/Replay/UltimateTV, or any "IR Blaster" attachment that came with it, is highly unlikely to have any interest in controlling your audio IED.

➜ **For more on infra-red devices, check out "What's Coming Next," in Chapter 2, p. 19.**

Is it possible to get around this unfettered propagation of remote controls? Is there no "universal remote" that is truly universal?

You can give some consideration to a programmable remote, such as the Yamaha RAV 2000 or the Remote Commander Control Unit from Sony, but plan to spend some quality time with the unit (and some quality dollars to purchase it). My brief encounter with the Yamaha entry to the category confirmed the conclusion that the device would have no trouble controlling my standard appliances, that is, my TV, VCR, and stereo receiver. Operating my UltimateTV—a task that sometimes seemed to challenge even the device's original remote control—seemed to be a distant and time-consuming dream.

For the determined tweaker, however, the goal of a single remote control that operates every function on every device—video, audio, and gaming IEDs, plus your VCR, DVD players, A/V receiver, and stereo components—is apparently within the realm of possibility. Sites such as www.remotecentral.com list .CCF files (Cabernet Configuration Files. Believe it or not, Cabernet was the codename that developers used for the Philips Pronto TS-1000 Remote Control) to control devices ranging from PlayStations to ReplayTVs and most electronics in between. Several high-end programmable remotes with PC software connections accept .CCF code files.

FIGURE 10.4
Yamaha's $400 RAV 2000 connects to a PC's serial port, allowing it to be customized for serious remote controlling.

I don't hold out much hope for most multi-IED households to slim down to a single remote control any time soon. The very nature of the true IED's ability to download new operating systems overnight would seem to work against this goal. In the case of these unique appliances, the leopard really can change its spots, providing a moving target for IR codes, and consequently, all attempts to program a truly universal remote control.

Instead, let us all take solace in the fact that Lillian Vernon and other fine catalog retailers continue to offer an attractive selection of baskets and organizers to hold our burgeoning collection of remote controls.

Making Web Connections

In each of the key IED categories described in this book—video, gaming, and audio—the most advanced hardware devices offer Web connectivity to enhance the experience. In each case, the Web offers certain capabilities that uniquely extend the device's feature set (see Table 10.1).

Table 10.1 – How Web Connectivity Enhances the IED Experience	
Type of Device	**Supported Web Activities**
Video IED	Remote programming and device management
	Interactive services related to programming (Web lookup of program details, real-time polling, and game show participation)
	Interactive ads, e-commerce, and shopping for program-related items
	Communications such as e-mail, chat, and instant messaging
	Web browsing from the TV
Gaming IED	Online gaming
	Purchasing and downloading of game software and related e-commerce activities
	Communications such as e-mail, chat, and instant messaging
	Web browsing from the TV

Table 10.1 – Continued	
Type of Device	**Supported Web Activities**
Audio IED	Internet-enabled identification of CD audio and MP3 music tracks
	Purchasing and downloading of music tracks, and online shopping for related items (concert tickets, T-shirts, and more)
	Communications such as e-mail, chat, and instant messaging
	Web browsing from the TV

Not all IEDs in a given category support all of these features. In fact, some devices support all or nearly all of the online enhancements, whereas others offer few or none.

It is important to point out that demand for most of these capabilities is completely unproven. Will consumers like you and me find them useful and habit forming? Or will these capabilities become simply another set of features that sound great on the side of the box but offer no real utility? It is likely that in the end, some features will prove vastly popular, forcing all manufacturers to support them, whereas other features will meet with indifference from consumers and quickly fade from the scene.

The Value Proposition

Of the three major IED categories, video devices seem to offer the weakest value proposition for their online capabilities.

Online gaming has already spread like wildfire among PC and even cell phone gamers. Millions meet every day in online arenas to test their skills against remote competitors or to join online teams in pursuit of a common goal. For users of audio IEDs, access to the CDDB database and its ability to automatically identify and categorize song tracks is an instant "killer app," another tried-and-true capability already made popular by music lovers on their PCs.

For people who are watching their TVs, however, what is the killer app for online connectivity? Microsoft is at the forefront of trying to answer that question, looking for a niche to occupy with its WebTV capabilities.

➜ See the discussion entitled "Internet Access and Interactivity" in Chapter 2, p. 36 for more about Microsoft and WebTV.

Although standard Internet communications—mail, chat, and instant messaging—are likely to be enabled on gaming and audio IED platforms that roll out in early 2002, UltimateTV already supports those features. Unfortunately, these are add-ons that are unlikely to get much usage. Research has failed to show that many consumers are interested in using their televisions for two-way communication.

How to Connect

Although the reasons for connecting your IED to the Web might seem somewhat tenuous, it might be worth a try to see if set-top computing fits your lifestyle. Likewise, if you want to send and receive e-mail and surf the Web but you don't own a personal computer, a Web-connected IED can save you the trouble of buying a PC.

Some IEDs provide integrated modems for establishing dial-up connections to the Internet, whereas others—principally audio IEDs—might rely on a connected PC to do the connectivity dirty work. A few promise future upgrades to support "broadband" connectivity, allowing consumers to connect directly via their home's DSL or cable modem.

Regardless of how you connect, the question to be answered is what you will connect to. Most IEDs that support Web access allow users to enlist their existing Internet service provider (ISP) for access. A few, such as Microsoft's UltimateTV, offer an option of contracting with a "captive service," such as MSN. UltimateTV users pay a different price for their monthly service fee, depending on whether Internet service is rolled into the subscription or the user is contracting with an independent ISP.

Here's the basic trade-off: Using a dial-up connection to an integrated ISP will be the easiest to configure. Such a connection comes preconfigured to work in most areas. Users simply connect the IED to a phone jack, enter a few tidbits of information—such as their area code and credit card number—and the device is ready to dial out and log on. The potential downside is that you might already be paying for ISP service on your PC. This is definitely the case if you have broadband service.

Paying for multiple ISP accounts is clearly folly, and anyone with a broadband connection in the home is unlikely to be happy settling for using their IED's browsing features via a slower, dial-up connection that inconveniently ties up the phone line. However, configuring your IED to take advantage of your existing dial-up ISP account can be challenging—and getting it to recognize your existing broadband service can be nigh to impossible. This was certainly my experience in trying to force the iPaq Music Center to recognize my home's broadband DSL gateway via its onboard HPNA connection.

➡ **For details, see a discussion of the iPaq's hardware features in Chapter 8, p. 206.**

If you don't already have an ISP account, then take the path of least resistance and sign up with the service that comes bundled with your IED, if such is offered. If you already have an ISP account, let your pocketbook and your appointment calendar be your guide. If you can't afford a second ISP fee simply for your IED, consider canceling your existing service and making your IED's access service your primary means of accessing the Web. Or if time is no object, go ahead and try to configure your IED to connect via your existing service. Doing so might require a phone call or two to both your IED manufacturer and your ISP to make this work, in addition to some serious fiddling around with setup screens on your IED. However, you'll probably end up with a less expensive and more satisfactory online connection scheme for your household.

Future Trends

Getting electronic devices from multiple manufacturers to talk to each other is a challenge under the best circumstances. That's what industry standards are for, but incompatibility problems will arise even when all parties scrupulously adhere to these standards.

In general, a single-vendor solution will inevitably provide tighter integration than an entertainment system that is pieced together from a patchwork of electronics from multiple vendors. For example, without a doubt, the remote control for your Sony-built UltimateTV video IED will contain codes to control a Sony television and VCR. However, the device was unable to control my off-brand Korean-made TV.

In the future, expect to see new alliances that enhance the integration of in-home entertainment and connectivity offerings. Just as cable and satellite programming providers have branched out to offer us broadband Internet connections as well as integrated set-top boxes with video IED capabilities, we will see them trying to incorporate additional intelligent gaming and music subscription services. Phone companies are also moving into the entertainment space, although some of their vertical integration efforts have been hampered by economic factors in 2001.

Consumer-grade wireless technologies are advancing on both the bandwidth and standards adoption fronts, providing another potential solution for connecting audio, video, gaming, and data devices into flexible networks that blanket the home.

The future is bright for entertainment systems that present a broad spectrum of engaging programming services in a tightly integrated, easy-to-navigate offering. In the meantime, consumers who welcome IED technologies into the home are essentially pioneers who crave the cutting edge. Lack of integration is one of the prices for having the coolest equipment long before our neighbors.

Chapter 11

Hacking Your IED

Are You a "Tweaker?"

No sooner did the ReplayTV and TiVo video IEDs ship from their respective factories than did technically gifted hobbyists throw warranty concerns to the wind and crack open the cases, eager to learn how the machines worked and ravenous to know how they could expand and enhance their capabilities.

The same fate awaited the first audio and game IEDs. Although few successful exploits have been widely documented, hackers are out there now, tinkering away on the new UltimateTV, GameCube, and Xbox platforms.

Why do some people feel driven to try to improve upon existing products, cure their flaws, boost their storage and power, and gain access to content and features they didn't pay for? That's a question better left to the hackers. To some, it's a hobby. Others find it an obsession. A few actually derive their livelihood from it, but for the most part, these are the criminal element. Their activities take place in the twilight world of the black market, and they are not documented in this book.

Most of the so-called hackers described in this book are essentially normal, law-abiding citizens, whose only peculiarity might be that they like to tinker with their home electronics. They do not necessarily run in the same circles as script kiddies, crackers, cypherpunks, cryptorebels, or phone phreaks. In fact, perhaps they deserve their own phylum or subspecies classification: tweakers.

However, like those other categories of netherworld geekdom, tweakers tend to keep their activities quiet. They don't hold rallies, and for the most part, they don't publish detailed histories.

That said, tweakers do manage to collaborate through a variety of newsgroups, chat rooms, and user forums, and in the best tradition of the Open Source software movement, they can often build successfully upon the works of their peers toward the advancement of common goals. Those goals typically include finding ways to expand and enhance the capabilities of their IEDs and in more extreme cases, defeating copyright protections and other barriers to their enjoyment of the machines in question.

Before you remove that first screw and begin the process of modifying your hardware, you should take the "Are You a Tweaker?" quiz:

- Do you feel you have a divine right to do anything you damn well please with a product that you paid for?

- Do you believe that the movie studios and record labels are in league to defraud you or force you to pay as much and as many times for their content as they possibly can?

- Are you handy with replacing disk drives and modifying system-level software?

- Are you prepared to kiss your purchase price and warranty good-bye?

If you answered yes to all or at least some of the questions, then read on.

> **CAUTION**
>
> I do not condone or encourage readers to do anything that might result in injury, voiding their manufacturer's warranty, or disobeying copyright or anti-tampering law or agreement to which they might have deliberately or unwittingly given their consent. In other words, you're on your own.

Weighing the Risks

The biggest potential danger of hacking into your sealed-box IED unit is not merely voiding the warranty and potentially turning your device into an expensive doorstop. The most serious hazard is that of electric shock.

Unlike PCs, which are designed from the outset to allow consumers to open the box and tamper with the contents, sealed appliances are prone to have unprotected and ungrounded power supplies, which can deliver a potent shock even when turned off and unplugged. If you decide to blithely disregard every other word of caution in this chapter, please heed this warning: Touching the power supply inside your IED can result in severe injury or even death. (Although it should be of less concern, it can also severely damage your IED.)

Now that that bit of unpleasantness is out of the way, the would-be tweaker would do well to carefully review the potential benefits of performing a "field upgrade" of their device, and consider whether those possible gains adequately off-set the lesser dangers of unauthorized IED manipulation. In a nutshell, you could damage your IED beyond repair, and if you do, no one will lift a finger to help you undo it.

Some of the hacks discussed next might be technically unlawful, or at least legally questionable. However, exactly what is or isn't legal is something best left to lawyers. Judging from existing case law, it would appear that people who are not actively engaged in acts that result in copyright infringement or out-and-out mayhem on a large scale have no reason to be overly concerned about being the target of a civil or criminal complaint. Common sense comes into play here: If you are doing anything that could result in freely distributing copyrighted materials, and you do not have the permission of the rights holder, you could find yourself in hot water. Likewise, if you deliberately create malicious code that results in damage to other people's property, you deserve to be prosecuted. If you are simply modifying a device that you purchased for your own enjoyment, it's unlikely that you're breaking any laws, or that anyone really cares one way or the other. (Just don't call your manufacturer's tech support line expecting help if your tweaks do more harm to your equipment than good.)

Weighing the Benefits

Most seasoned tweakers recommend having some hands-on experience messing around inside a PC before undertaking the hacking of your entertainment appliance. If you've swapped the disk drive out of your desktop before, and even better, if you have some familiarity with Linux or another Unix-derived operating system, you'll have a much better chance of success in accomplishing the hacks discussed in the following sections.

Tweaking Your Video IED

What are the potential rewards of hacking your video IED? The primary reason for opening the case and voiding your warranty is the promise of significantly extending your recording time, perhaps up to hundreds of hours.

In addition, you might be able to record a program using your video IED, and transfer that digital copy onto a PC. Why would you want to? The copy protection crowd would have you believe this is mostly the activity of Digital Age pirates, plundering the work of Hollywood studios for their own gain. Personally, I haven't stumbled across any thriving black market for PC files containing reruns of Get Smart. However, IED manufacturers are already well aware of the utility of recording a show on your ReplayTV ShowStopper, for instance, and being able to transfer it to your laptop to watch on your next cross-country flight. This kind of file transfer has no technical barriers, only legal and artificial software obstacles—precisely the kind of hurdles that hackers relish jumping.

Table 11.1 lists a few major milestones for tweakers of video IEDs.

Table 11.1 – Great Moments in Video IED Hacking

Date	Event
March 2000	Individuals first claim to have successfully upgraded a TiVo hard drive.
July 2000	"Mr. Belboz" releases a Linux program that does the entire job of "blessing" a hard drive for placement in a TiVo, greatly simplifying the storage upgrade process.
November 2000	Australian hacker Andrew Tridgell allegedly breaks the TiVo files system, but agrees not to release the code.
December 2000	A group of Open Source developers unveil rtvpatch, a software package for upgrading ReplayTV systems.
January 2001	Hacker d18c7db posts PlayStream, the first software tool to reverse engineer TiVo's video storage techniques.
February 2001	TiVoNet boards—Ethernet cards that allow TiVo data to be shared across a network—become widely available.
	Users of the EchoStar Dishplayer (forerunner of Microsoft UltimateTV) discover the joys of unauthorized hard drive upgrades.
June 2001	Hackers release ExtractStream, a software program that allows TiVo users to transfer compressed copies of TV shows into their computers and beyond.

In addition to recording and transferring files, some hacking projects are aimed at leveling the playing field between the various IED platforms, allowing users of one type of video IED to enjoy a coveted feature that is supported on a competing platform. For example, the TiVo Web Project (http://tivo.lightn.org/) is working to allow TiVo owners to program and manage their IEDs remotely via the Web, a feature already available to users of the ReplayTV.

Because of the sheer volume of material it would require and the fact that most tweakers are only interested in hacking into one particular brand and type of IED, it would be impractical to detail every conceivable hacking "exploit" available for every IED discussed in this book.

Does It Work?

In addition to the sheer volume of hacks that can be performed on a video IED, the reality also exists that the method and viability of each individual exploit might be valid one day and completely outdated the next. Regarding this latter concern, two factors are at work: the nature of the device and the nature of the hacker community involved. The IEDs—particularly in the video category—are designed to check in nightly to download new features or an entirely new operating system, potentially rendering the most ingenious exploit completely useless overnight. The tweakers that dream up and execute these hacks are equally mercurial. They do not operate on rigid and predictable development schedules. They are often students and hobbyists. As is so often true in the hacking world, a brilliant new piece of code can suddenly materialize at any time, instantly obsoleting everything that came before it.

Still, it can be useful to study a specific exploit in greater detail, giving all would-be tweakers an inside look at how hacks are accomplished; what skills, tools, and materials are required; and the amount of work that is involved. In this spirit, this chapter will now take a closer look at what is by far one of the most popular and best documented IED exploits to date: expanding the video storage capacity of a TiVo device.

Adding Storage Space to a TiVo

With both 20- and 30-hour units available, most TiVo devices offer more than enough storage space for casual users. But really, who wouldn't want to see their device store double or triple that amount? If you're interested in a little home improvement of your TiVo, you'll need the following ingredients:

- 1 Phillips screwdriver
- 1 Torx screwdriver set (or interchangeable bits); Torx size 10 and 15

- 1–2 high-capacity hard drives (minimum 5200 RPM rotational speed recommended)
- 1 hard drive mounting kit (for adding a second drive to a single-drive TiVo)
- 1 blank CD-R disk or 2 blank floppy disks

CAUTION

The following steps are condensed and do not address many of the specific idiosyncrasies of each type of TiVo, or how to deal with the many things that can go wrong with the upgrade process. This process is in no way supported or endorsed by any manufacturer. It has been pieced together from hundreds of trial-and-error experiences documented in places such as the TiVo Underground section of www.avsforum.com/.

You should refer to such a resource before undertaking an exploit like this, to find out the most current methods and mishaps that TiVo tweakers are encountering. Additionally, this cat can be skinned many different ways. The method outlined here is not necessarily the fastest or easiest way to upgrade. It is a conservative approach that uses numerous safeguards to help ensure a positive outcome.

As a final note of caution before you begin, do understand that the processes described next are fairly complex and require a firm understanding of how PC components are connected and configured. If you could use a good technical reference on how PC components work—hard drive technologies in particular—check out Scott Mueller's *Upgrading and Repairing PCs, 13th Edition* (ISBN: 0-7897-2542-8).

Step 1: Typing Your TiVo

TiVos come in a variety of shapes and sizes and are made by multiple manufacturers. To successfully upgrade your TiVo, you must first determine its type by answering the following questions:

Is it a standalone or combo unit? The latter units have an integrated satellite receiver, such as the DirecTV/TiVo unit colloquially known as a DirecTivo by users. The information you need to collect about your TiVo device includes:

- Who is the manufacturer?
- What is the recording capacity?

- What is the current software version?

➔ **To determine this method, see it described in "TiVo: Software," p. 75.**

- Does your TiVo have one or two hard drives?

If your TiVo has two hard drives the next important distinction can be a little more difficult to ascertain: Are the two drives cross-partitioned at the factory, effectively creating a single logical device? A TiVo configured in this fashion is also referred to as true *factory dual-drive standalone TiVo* in documents such as the meticulously detailed "Hinsdale How-To TiVo Upgrade" guide offered by 9th Tee Enterprises Inc. (www.9thtee.com).

The author of "Hinsdale How-To TiVo Upgrade" asserts that a factory dual-drive DirecTiVo does not exist. Like many standalone dual-drive TiVos, all dual-drive DirecTiVos are *factory married* units, indicating that a primary, or "A" drive, contains the system software, and a secondary "blessed" (TiVo formatted) hard drive stores additional video. Although you might be able to make an educated guess as to whether you have a true factory dual-drive or a factory married TiVo, based on the reports of other tweakers' experiences with like models from like manufacturers, your hypothesis won't be confirmed until you actually make a backup.

Step 2: Making a Backup

Backing up your original TiVo hard drive (or drives) is essentially an insurance policy. No matter what goes wrong—whether you fail to correctly "bless" or format your new drive with the proper information to make TiVo recognize and accept it, or if the company should introduce new download code in the future that nullifies your modifications—your backup provides a way to restore your TiVo to its original state.

Backing up your TiVo's hard drives used to be a cumbersome, time-consuming process. The necessity of devoting many hours and many gigabytes of hard disk space to the backup task changed with the advent of tools that can compress the backup process to a few minutes and a few floppy disks, or a single recordable CD.

This is a major advance for TiVo tweakers, who used to advise each other that the ideal time to make a backup copy of their TiVo's disk was before ever having used the device. The primary benefit of copying the TiVo disk in its pristine, or "virgin" state was that the backup could be accomplished using a single recordable CD (less than 650MB). After the TiVo had been turned loose to record TV programs, that backup could balloon up to potentially dozens of CDs.

Today, using new utilities such as Mfs Tools and tweaker-acclaimed TivoMad software, it is irrelevant whether a TiVo has been used for a year, or is fresh out of the box. The backup process compresses the file size to a fraction of the total contents of the original TiVo disks, preserving important data such as channel line-ups, season passes, guide data, and thumbs-up/thumbs-down preferences, but jettisoning bulky video files. (You might find your old recordings still listed in the "Now Playing" screen after you've restored your backup file to a new disk drive, but they will no longer play.)

The basic steps for backing up your TiVo are as follows:

1. Download the latest upgrade utilities. (Currently, these might include Mfs Tools, TiVoMad, or Kazymyr's boot CD image version 2.6i, but please check postings on the sites listed in Table 11.2 for the most up-to-date information). If you plan to use a Quantum or Maxtor hard drive, you might also need to obtain the "qunlock" utility to open up access to the drive's total storage capacity when it is reformatted as a TiVo device.

2. Use the utility program to create a boot disk (either on floppy disk or recordable CD, depending on the software you select and whether your PC has a recordable CD drive). You can also buy a pre-made boot CD from companies such as 9th Tee.

3. After recording the software version displayed by your TiVo (see Figure 3.20 on page 85), remove the hard drive(s) from your IED. This is accomplished by powering down and unplugging the IED, removing the size 10 Torx screws, and prying off the top lid. (The lid might be tightly fitted and require some careful work with a flathead screwdriver to loosen it.) Remember: *Do not touch the power supply*—it can deliver a nasty shock even when the machine is unplugged. Disconnect the IDE and power cables

from the TiVo drives and remove the drive brackets with a size 10 or size 15 Torx screwdriver. If you are removing two drives, label the "A" drive before removing it. It is usually connected to the end of the IDE cable (the "B" drive is connected in the middle of the cable) and might have jumpers set to "Master" or "Cable Select."

4. Install the TiVo drive(s) into your home PC. You can configure the drives in your PC in several ways. When upgrading a single-drive TiVo, Hinsdale recommends keeping your PC's primary C:\ drive configured as the primary master IDE drive and your original TiVo hard drive as your secondary master. Then attach your new, larger replacement hard drive as the primary slave, and your CD drive as your secondary slave. If you are upgrading a dual-drive TiVo, you will initially connect your TiVo's A drive as the secondary master and the B drive as your primary slave. Any way that you configure the drives, be sure to use the proper IDE cable connections (refer to your IDE controller documentation or AVS Forum for details), and make sure these settings match the jumper switches on the drives.

5. Insert the boot CD or floppy you created in step 2, and power up your PC. After following the onscreen prompts and entering the correct parameters, a small compressed backup file—generally called tivo.bak—will be created in the root directory of your PC's C:\ drive. Hinsdale recommends running the Mfs Tool backup utility with a command-line prompt that includes the instruction "-6so." In the case of a factory-married two-drive TiVo system, this will result in your drives being effectively "divorced," with their merged contents stored in a backup file containing a single drive image. This image can be restored on any disk that is at least as large as the original A drive. In the case of a true factory dual-drive TiVo, the utility will have no effect, and Mfs tools will not report an "upgraded to" file size. You will need to rerun the backup command, omitting the *s* (that is, placing *-6o* in the command-line string). This image will need to be restored on a disk that is at least as large as the combination of the original A and B drives put together. (It's useless to restore the merged drive image of a factory dual-drive system to a larger disk because you

cannot currently use the remaining space on the A drive. However, a larger B drive can now be "blessed" to provide room for expansion.)

Step 3: Test Your Backup

Hinsdale and other conservative tweakers recommend testing your backup before blessing a new, larger drive for your TiVo. This is accomplished by running the restore utility to expand the compressed backup file onto your new, larger upgrade drive, and then unmounting and disconnecting the drive from your PC and installing it into your TiVo. Be sure to check your IDE and jumper connections to ensure that the drive is designated as the master before powering up the TiVo. If your Tivo behaves normally, you have a usable backup file.

Step 4: Bless a New Drive

Now that you have made and tested a backup file, you're finally ready to perform the upgrade. Power down your TiVo, remove the upgrade drive you were testing, and reinstall it into your PC. Your upgrade options will depend on the type of TiVo you are upgrading. If it is a single-drive unit, you can replace the original TiVo drive "as is" and simply bless and install a new B drive. For maximum storage, you can create a new A drive and (optionally) a new B drive as well. Simultaneously "expanding" a new A drive and blessing a new B drive also applies when upgrading an existing dual-drive unit. After the new drive or drives are reinstalled into the PC as described in step 2, reboot the PC and run the expand utility. If you are using TiVoMad software, you will be prompted for a variety of information, including the location of the new A and B drives. When this process is complete, you are ready to unmount the drives, power down the PC, and transplant the drives to their final destination inside your TiVo. Power up and celebrate by recording a few hundred hours of your favorite shows!

Where to Go from Here

Now that you are familiar with the general process, you need to double-check that you have the latest software and instructions for carrying out the tasks. Table 11.2 lists some of the resources for obtaining the most up-to-date information on hacking your video IED.

Table 11.2 – Ample Resources for Hacking Your Video IED Are Readily Available on the Web

Site/Organization	Platform	URL
Tivo Hack FAQ	TiVo	`http://tivo.samba.org/`
9th Tee	TiVo	`www.9thtee.com/tivonet.htm`
Personal TV Underground	TiVo	`http://pvrhack.sonnik.com/tivo/`
Ptvupgrade	TiVo	`www.ptvupgrade.com/`
TiVo Web Project	TiVo	`http://tivo.lightn.org/`
Avs Forum	TiVo, ReplayTV	`www.avsforum.com/`
Prman's Replaytv Advanced FAQ	ReplayTV	`http://replayfaq.reidpix.com/`
Replaytv Hard Drive Upgrade FAQ	ReplayTV	`http://rtvpatch.sourceforge.net`
Dish Hack	DishPlayer	`www.vap0r.com/html/dish-hack.html`
How to Upgrade Your Dishplayer's Hard Drive	DishPlayer	`http://ben.reser.org/dishplayer/upgrade-howto.html`

Game IEDs

Many of the hacks involving game platforms are aimed at stealing—or perhaps "liberating"—game content, so it can be played on other machines or swapped across the Internet. The cracking of the Sega Dreamcast in the summer of 2000 by a group identifying itself as "Utopia" was just such a feat. It allowed gamers to substitute a home-made boot disk that would fool the Dreamcast unit into recognizing and accepting recordable CD-ROMs containing pirated games, rather than insisting on its own proprietary "GD-ROM" format. The resulting loss of game revenue for Sega might have been a major determinant in the ultimate withdrawal of Sega and its Dreamcast platform from the gaming IED marketplace.

Table 11.3 lists a few major milestones for gaming IED hackers, tweakers, emulators, and cheaters.

Table 11.3 – Great Moments in Gaming IED Hacks

Date	Event
June 1997	Sega Genesis software emulator Genecyst Version 0.12 for DOS is released, allowing PC users to play Genesis games.
January 1999	Connectix releases Sony PlayStation software emulator for the Macintosh. Connectix is initially sued by Sony, which later acquires the software.
	The initial release of Nemu 64 and UltraHLE, software emulators for the Nintendo 64 console.
July 2000	Chat room discussions break out reporting the successful hack of the Sega Dreamcast, allowing users to freely copy and trade game software.

Dreamcast has been a popular target of emulators, as have the Nintendo 64 and Sony PlayStation platforms. Emulation uses software to mimic hardware, for instance, allowing a game that is created for one platform (such as Dreamcast) to be played on another (such as the PC).

Other types of game-related hacks involve changing hardware parameters of the game devices, such as modifying the Sony PlayStation 2 to provide multiregion DVD playback, or disabling the embedded Macrovision copyright protection scheme that prevents people from pirating DVD content.

Finally, many sites cater to the popular traffic in "cheat codes." Sometimes available as software-only manipulations and in other cases requiring hardware adapters (such as Game Shark and Pro Action Replay cartridges), cheat codes allow players to override the game console's internal memory and, well, cheat. Common cheat codes let players change important game information, such as the number of lives remaining, status of shields, ammunition, current game levels, and so on. As Cheat Code Central editors explain it, the codes enable you to "override the values in those memory locations, allowing the game to be played with unlimited lives, always full shields, unlimited ammunition…" You get the idea. It might not be very gentlemanly, but it's amazing what people will resort to after they've been shot down, blown up, carved into pieces, beaten to a pulp, or turned into a spiralling fireball a few hundred times, without ever having progressed past the first game level. Then again, if cheating can transform a seemingly impossible game into something that's actually fun to play, it could be a worthwhile approach.

Table 11.4 lists a few sites that contain information on game console hacks and cheats. Note that many gaming IED hacks are offered as for-pay services and products. Other hacking activities, such as trading actual pirated game discs and files, are highly illegal and tend to be conducted in relative secrecy. To avoid prosecution, such transactions are generally conducted on a person-to-person basis via game-related discussion forums, newsgroups, and IRC messaging groups.

Table 11.4 – Web Sites That Are Exclusively Devoted to Video Game Cheats and Hacks

Site/Organization	Platform	URL
Cheat Code Central	All major game platforms	`www.cheatcc.com`
GameShark Home Page	PlayStation, Nintendo 64, Dreamcast, and others	`www.GameShark.com`
The Official GameShark Discussion Board	PlayStation, Nintendo 64, Dreamcast, and others	`http://ubb.gameshark.com/UBB`
Rage Games	PlayStation, Nintendo 64, Dreamcast, GameBoy, and others	`www.classicgaming.com/ragegames`

Audio IEDs

Audio IED hacking is a relatively new sport, but this year's crop of intelligent audio machines presents the same "call of the wild" for tweakers that led them to delve into their video and game IEDs.

Table 11.5 lists a few major milestones for audio IED tweakers.

Table 11.5 – Great Moments in Audio IED Hacking

Date	Event
December 2000	Christopher Richmond (a.k.a. "Crichmond") begins documenting extensive information on hacking the AudioRequest IED.
	Several sites document the extremely accessible back doors that allow hacking of Apex DVD/CD/MP3 players, making them a favorite among tweakers.

Table 11.5 – Continued	
Date	**Event**
February 2001	Jeff Mock releases a set of Perl CGI scripts for hacking the Rio Receiver (also sold as the Dell Digital Audio Receiver).
March 2001	A protocol guide is released for hacking the Creative Nomad Jukebox.
October 2001	Reed Esau releases a Java servlet-based open source-hosting program for the Rio Receiver.

One of the best documented hacks of an audio IED is Jeff Mock's creation of new control code for his Rio Receiver (a.k.a, the Dell Digital Audio Receiver) based on the Perl development language.

Building on Mock's preliminary work, chronicled at www.mock.com/receiver, Reed Esau released an open source project called JReceiver, a Java-based host program that allows non-Windows machines—currently a Linux PC, although a Mac version is planned—to act as the Rio's host. Esau has published his software at http://jreceiver.sourceforge.net, along with his reasons for creating the hack. Along with his primary goal of supporting additional operating systems—SonicBlue has shipped software with the product that only supports Windows—Esau stated that he wanted to protect his investment in the audio player by ensuring "that the device never goes obsolete."

The AudioRequest IED has also succumbed to determined hackers, yielding up its secrets, most of which are recorded by Christopher Richmond at http://sharky.ne.mediaone.net/arq/arq_hacking.html.

TIP

The nature of hardware hacking—an "unsupported" activity that some manufacturers choose to ignore and others actively try to stamp out—makes the information difficult to find, and often deliberately so.

You might receive some kind of DNS error when you try to load a page listed here in your browser, indicating that the page is no longer at that location or can't be viewed. If this happens, try going to a search engine such as Google.com, and entering the title or the actual URL of the page you are seeking. Then instead of clicking on the primary link to the page in the entries that are returned by the search engine, click on the link for a "cached" version of the page. This allows you to view the content of the page as it was stored in memory by the search engine, even if the actual page has been removed or its server is offline.

Chapter 11

Although much information is available on how the AudioRequest operates and how it was constructed, the real piece de résistance for tweakers is the discussion of how to install a larger hard drive and how to overclock the system's CPU.

Although the benefits of a larger hard drive are self evident, the payback for overclocking (increasing the clock speed) of the ARQ's processor is less obvious. Richmond stated that speeding up the CPU might help prevent the unit from the occasional skipping and stuttering that some users experience while running the ARQ's visualization screens or ripping a CD, although he admits that the problem is more likely caused by low available memory. "Of course, the other reason to do it," Richmond says, "is because it *can* be done… and it's cool."

One of Richmond's motivations for attempting to overclock the ARQ in the first place was in response to a cryptic posting by AudioRequest's Webmaster and chief information officer Brutus Youn. The posting on an ARQ discussion board stated that "neat things happen when you have a faster processor in the ARQ. Of course, we'll leave that to you to explore."

Finally, even though they might not fall under the strict definition of "intelligent entertainment devices," ample resources are available on the Web for customizing MP3 playback devices, such as the Creative Labs Nomad portable MP3 jukebox, and particularly hacker-friendly DVD/MP3 combo playback decks, such as the Apex AD-600A.

A few Web sites offering greater details on these exploits are listed in Table 11.6.

NOTE

Youn later said that his comments regarding neat things happening when overclocking the AudioRequest were "overblown." The "neat things" he was referring to were "basically just faster visuals and slightly faster encoding," Youn said. "If you can squeeze some more usefulness out of something without having to pay much extra, it's always 'neat' to me," he explained.

Table 11.6 – Web Sites That Offer Detailed Descriptions and How-to Instructions for Hacking Audio IED

Site/Organization	Platform	URL
Hacking the Rio Receiver	Rio Receiver (Dell Digital Audio Receiver)	www.mock.com/receiver
Hacking the Rio Receiver	Rio Receiver	http://jreceiver.sourceforge.net
ARQ1-20 Hacking Page	AudioRequest	http://sharky.ne.mediaone.net/arq/arq_hacking.html

Table 11.6 – Continued		
Site/Organization	**Platform**	**URL**
Nomad Jukebox USB Protocol	Creative Labs Nomad	www.aracnet.com/ ~seagull/NJB/index.html
Apex AD-600A Home	Apex DVD/MP3 Combo Player	www.nerd-out.com/ apex/index.html

Final Options

Do you yearn for the expanded capabilities of a hacked IED but hate the thought of doing your own dirty work? Several commercial enterprises have sprung up that offer ready-to-go reconfigured video and gaming IEDs.

Naturally, you'll pay a premium for the surgically enhanced TiVo, Replay, or PlayStation. In some cases, these businesses operate on a "service and repair" model, where you ship them your device, and they alter and return ship it to you.

Like hacking your own IED, this option has inherent risk. Because these people do this kind of thing for a living—or at least a serious hobby—their success rate in performing the hack should be pretty close to 100%. However, apart from the basic risk of doing online or mail-order transactions with a small, unfamiliar company, another issue looms: If it's not downright illegal, altering these products for profit is a practice that operates in the gray area of copyright infringement. Although no widespread efforts are currently being made to crack down on these companies, it's always a possibility these companies could disappear in a heartbeat if IED manufacturers decided to exert legal pressure.

If this option still sounds attractive to you, Table 11.7 lists a few examples of companies offering these "hack for hire" services. Let the buyer beware!

Table 11.7 – "Hack for Hire" Operations Might Offer an Easy Way to Obtain a "Modified" IED

Company	Products/Services	URL
STARFIRE.tv	Upgraded TiVos (to 250 hours) and self-install kits	http://www.starfire.tv
DigitalRecorder.tv	Upgraded TiVos and self-install kits	http://www.digitalrecorder.tv
Weaknees.com	Upgraded TiVos, self-install kits, and upgrade services	http://www.weaknees.com
PTVupgrade.com	Tivo upgrade kits and installation services	http://www.ptvupgrade.com
Techtronics (UK)	PlayStation 2 with multiregion DVD playback upgrade	http://www.techtronics.com
Vguys' Electronics	Modified PlayStation 2 devices and self-install "modchip" supplies	www.vguys.com

Chapter 12

How Did You Ever Live
Without It?

Overview

It's funny how quickly we become accustomed to new technologies when they fit neatly into our lives. Like a pair of new shoes that are so comfortable we simply decide to wear them home from the store, a major innovation can suddenly become so ingrained in our lifestyle that it's as if we always had it.

This is certainly the case with video, gaming, and audio IEDs. Ask anybody who owns them. Most will tell you they can scarcely remember how they ever survived without them.

In the beginning of this book, we set out to define how video, audio, and gaming IEDs are fostering a revolution in our living rooms. In this final chapter, we assess the nature of this revolution and find that in the continuum of uprisings—say, measured on a scale from minor insurrection to violent revolt—history will probably record the IED revolution as a bloodless coup. The change might be profound, but it's occurring quietly, and we're going along willingly.

Video IEDs

Leading the intelligent entertainment revolution are the video IEDs, whose advent has been universally hailed by all who are lucky enough to have gotten their hands on one. These devices for our television sets—TiVo, ReplayTV, and UltimateTV—have been able to seamlessly mesh with our lives because they managed to present new capabilities that offer great utility, while only subtlely changing the way we were used to consuming broadcast programming.

The designers and marketers of these pioneering devices deserve credit for accomplishing this feat. They offered us the ability to pause, rewind, and fast-forward a live, real-time television broadcast. To consumers, this was presented as simplicity itself, a natural extension of the features from their trusty VCRs, overlaid onto live television. The fact that it required the investment of hundreds of millions of dollars and the development of a revolutionary new computer-based platform is irrelevant to most consumers. And this is as it should be.

The introduction of television was probably similar, in a fashion. Although the addition of moving pictures to the family radio was an eye-popping, exciting, and even a life-changing event, it was rapidly adopted into our routine. It simply fit.

Video IED Outlook

Fast-forward to today's retail landscape. TiVo, ReplayTV, and Microsoft have developed the core technologies that were needed, and have proven that the video IED concept is viable. Sony, Panasonic, Thomson/RCA, Philips, and other major multinational consumer electronics makers have come to understand that hard-disk recording is a natural extension of their TV-related appliance businesses. As the march of time and the increase of unit volume drive prices down, these features are likely to become increasingly pervasive in set-top boxes, satellite receivers, and televisions.

Based on these developments, researchers are predicting bullish growth for IED adoption. Market analyst Forrester Research predicts that the estimated 900,000 units that were in the field in 2001 will increase more than 46-fold in the next three years (see Figure 12.1)!

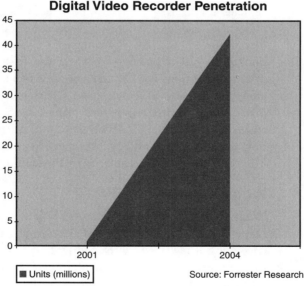

Digital Video Recorder Penetration

■ Units (millions)   Source: Forrester Research

FIGURE 12.1
According to Forrester Research, a steep incline is predicted for digital video recording technology, potentially rocketing up to 42 million units in 2004.

Some of the events that will fuel the steep ascent of video IED technology have already occurred. For example, TiVo was able to clinch a deal in November 2001 with AT&T Broadband, the nation's largest cable provider, that will potentially put TiVo's technology into the hands of millions of cable subscribers through a custom AT&T-branded set-top box. The pact mirrors TiVo's previous arrangement with satellite programming service DirecTV. TiVo also sought new licensing relationships with major manufacturers; it landed a contract in September 2001 that will allow Sony Corp. to embed TiVo's digital video recording technology into consumer electronics devices such as camcorders and DVD players.

ReplayTV has taken the position of staking out the high end of the video IED space, announcing a 4000 Series that is as ambitious as it is contentious (see "ReplayTV Rerun," Chapter 3, page 49). ReplayTV's ability to allow users to erase TV commercials from recorded material and to share that material freely across the Internet has acted as a lightning rod, bringing a storm of legal action against the company from the established entertainment community.

For its part, Microsoft has also been making inroads with cable providers since the late introduction of its UltimateTV device in March 2001. The company sees UltimateTV as one of many delivery vehicles for its larger television-related software strategy, organized under the heading of Microsoft TV. At the 2001 Western Cable Show in late November 2001, the company gave its first public demonstration of several advances—including the first showing of Microsoft .NET applications for TV, and a preview of a new Microsoft TV-powered interactive TV service from Charter Communications. Earlier that month, Charter announced plans for "the largest deployment of advanced interactive TV services in the U.S. to date," citing its intention to deliver technology based on Microsoft TV Advanced and Microsoft TV Server to more than 1 million U.S. cable subscribers.

What About "Surf TVs"?

What Charter intends to launch as a field trial in early 2002 for its hometown St. Louis market closely resembles the old WebTV experience, with a few new twists. Subscribers will be able to personalize their TV experience, using e-mail, Internet browsing, and custom content such as on-demand local and national news, weather, sports, entertainment, shopping, and games. The trial will also include streaming-media services featuring (naturally) Microsoft Windows Media platform.

Although the underlying computer architecture has made available a broad selection of secondary features—primarily Web surfing, e-mail, and other electronic communications—these capabilities are likely to remain secondary for some time to come.

Although we have seen PC adoption in homes surpassing our wildest dreams from a decade ago, we have yet to see e-mail or Web surfing take off on non-PC platforms, despite efforts to embed the technology in everything from telephones, TVs, and kitchen appliances to wireless, home-roaming clipboards. Only cell phones and other extremely portable devices—such as wireless personal digital assistants/organizers and two-way pagers—have shown any promise of luring us away from our PCs for any significant amount of time. And even in those devices, Web browsing is often seen to be a highly touted but little used feature.

Why do Bill Gates and company continue this incessant barking up the interactive TV tree? People demand it—but not consumers. The demand is from programmers and content providers, television networks, Hollywood movie studios, and cable and satellite access providers who see the old advertising model for TV ebbing away.

Research shows that only about two out of every five TV watchers actually pay attention to commercials these days, despite the massive budgets that are increasingly allotted to creating these TV ads. These ads frequently feature the kind of top-notch talent and special effects that used to be reserved for major motion pictures, yet they still cannot succeed in capturing consumer interest (see Figure 12.2) .

Will interactive TV truly replace conventional advertising as a way to extract money from the viewing public? Microsoft certainly hopes so, as does its growing list of clients for interactive TV trials. Perhaps consumers should hope so, too. The alternative to conventional advertising means "paying more at the pump." This translates to increased subscription fees, including fees for content we are used to getting for free.

FIGURE 12.2
Our growing inattention to TV commercials has companies that rely on advertising revenue worried.

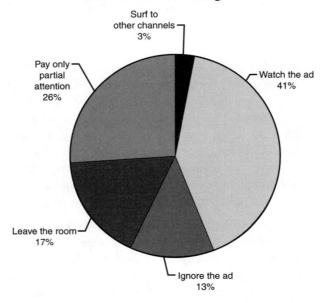

TV Commercials No Longer Effective

Surf to other channels
3%

Watch the ad
41%

Pay only partial attention
26%

Leave the room
17%

Ignore the ad
13%

Source: Forrester Research

Where's the Service?

In the beginning of this book, I charted the total cost of ownership for a video IED (see Chapter 1, Table 1.1, page 6), and attempted to draw attention to the *real* cost: subscription fees. Long after your IED is installed, Microsoft, Replay, and TiVo will still be nickle-and-diming you with their relentless monthly charge (unless you opt for a "life-time" subscription that doubles the up-front costs).

What do you have to show for the $120 a year in fees? The senior director of Microsoft's UltimateTV strategy Mark Mullen was surprisingly candid about it. "Right now we are just barely holding on to this proposition of 10 dollars a month," he said. "It's very hard to escape the accusation that we are just renting you access to the hard drive you've already paid for."

Of course, an admission such as this only comes when you're ready to talk about how all that is about to change. That's precisely the point that Microsoft had reached when they contacted me—ironically on the day I was putting to bed the final chapter of this book—to offer me a briefing on their secret upgrade plans.

Winter CES in Las Vegas, the annual Consumer Electronics Show in January, would become ground zero for the unveiling of significant new additions to the UltimateTV platform, Mullen confided, although the actual features will not be available to consumers until sometime "in the first half of the year." Mullen said he was prevented from being more specific about the availability date, citing the difficulties of creating software that runs on different hardware platforms provided by multiple manufacturers. "You want to make very sure that any kind of an upgrade doesn't break someone's box."

When it does finally ship out, what are the features that will be rolling out on new Sony and RCA DirecTV video IEDs in 2002? Here are the highlights:

- UltimateTV Movies—Although search capabilities are already available within UltimateTV, a new movie tool will make it easier to sift through the more than 1,000 movies displayed each week on the DirecTV service. The upgrade will allow more granular searches, such as specifying not just a keyword, like an actor or title, but also categories such as genre, year, and even production values, such as whether the movie has Dolby Digital sound. New "AutoRecord" searches, similar to ReplayTV's "ReplayZones" (see Chapter 3, page 49), will allow UltimateTV viewers to set up persistent searches that constantly scour the program guide looking for specific shows. Finally, the service will add daily movie recommendations by category and integrated reviews from independent film site E! Online.

- Satellite Remote Record—This is like ReplayTV's MyReplayTV.com service (see Chapter 3, "Programming ReplayTV from the Road," page 59), but with a significant advantage. Using the PassPort identification service that is central to Microsoft's overarching .Net initiative for Web-based software applications, viewers will be able to log on to a secure site where they can operate their home video recorder via satellite!

  Mullen talked about his favorite example. After accepting a last-minute dinner invitation on his cell phone, he uses a Microsoft Web-enabled PocketPC device to tell his UltimateTV to record an important show he would otherwise miss. Most of this is possible today using ReplayTV's Web remote service, with one important exception: The ReplayTV wouldn't receive the record command until it makes its nightly call to the server in the wee hours. Mullen's example wouldn't work under ReplayTV's model because the home unit would not receive the information in time to record the show that evening. However, using DirecTV's satellite system, the commands are relayed "nearly instantaneously," Mullen says.

- Increased speed and performance of UltimateTV—This will be welcome news to UltimateTV subscribers, whose most frequent complaint is that the machine simply takes too darn long to respond to commands (see Chapter 3, "UltimateTV Software," page 86).

UltimateTV is also working to improve its sports-related interface—possibly with a view to introducing features that will allow viewers to watch one game while monitoring every other game currently on TV. In one scenario the live picture might occupy two-thirds of the TV screen while the left column provides a stream of scores from other games that are being televised on other channels.

The kicker is that certain graphics elements and text alerts would keep the viewer in touch with the action from all the games, and clicking on the alert or the score listing would automatically switch you to the other game. Picture this: You're watching a football game, when elsewhere in the league, another team is about to complete a touchdown drive. A red football icon appears next to that team's score, letting you know that the team has just rushed to inside the 20-yard line and is in scoring position. With one click of the remote, you're watching the other game. (For baseball, a diamond diagram might show you when a runner is about to score). Text messages could appear to alert you to when a big play has occurred on another channel, or when Barry Bonds is about to step into the batter's box.

Taken together, these new features will go a long way toward comforting UltimateTV owners who feel they are not yet getting the ultimate value for their subscription dollars.

Beyond that, the additions to the UltimateTV platform underscore just how committed Microsoft remains to its growth and potential, tying it in closely to the company's most cherished plans for the future:

.NET. Features such as sports-related screen alerts are only the start, Mullen says. In the future, onscreen alerts could be completely unrelated to what you're watching—anything from stock quotes to incoming messages to weather advisories.

The Microsoft .NET Alert capabilities allow the delivery of messages and alerts from any service to which you subscribe, to any device you happen to be using, regardless of whether it's a computer, a cell phone, a handheld device, or a television, Mullen says. The true value of this platform will be determined by the quality of new software applications that are created to use it. "It's a chicken and egg scenario…hopefully developers will decide to jump onto this architecture down the line."

Gaming IEDs

You can't argue with the phenomenal success of home video game consoles. Ever since Nolan Bushnell first whetted our collective appetite with his primitive game of Pong, we have lusted for more powerful electronics with which to while away our leisure hours.

Game makers have continued to deliver that power in an uninterrupted stream, from early devices that required acetate overlays affixed to the TV screen to today's systems that are essentially high-end computers with game controllers instead of keyboards and televisions instead of computer monitors.

Game consoles are now a fixture in middle-class homes all around the world. In fact, it's not unusual for a family to own several different models and makes, with a shoebox full of game cartridges for each machine. The gaming IED makers are actually counting on multiconsole households for a significant portion of their sales. Nintendo of America Vice President George Harrison estimates that 25%–30% of video game buyers will end up owning more than one console. In another Seattle suburb a short distance from Harrison's headquarters, Microsoft is creating its own stratagems to place Xbox alongside GameCube and N64. "As a matter of fact," Xbox Director of Sales and Marketing John O'Rourke told me, "Many of the people that are going to buy Xbox we know will have cut their teeth playing their first video games on Nintendo."

Gaming IED Outlook

By any measure, 2001 was a watershed year for electronic gaming. Events of the past year have forever changed the complexion of this industry built on the pursuit of fun and programmers' flights of fancy. The exit of mainstay manufacturer Sega from the hardware side of the business and the arrival of take-no-prisoners Microsoft into the fray are ample proof that this game is now being played in deadly earnest. Toy company Nintendo has suddenly been thrust into a life or death battle against two of the most powerful brands in the world. Can the company that started out making playing cards from mulberry tree bark survive the transition into its third century?

What about the passionately creative developers who drive the game business? As developers are swallowed by large conglomerates, can they maintain the freedom of expression to continue creating games that fire the fertile imaginations of young adult and teenage males? Not only that, can they come up with new ideas for titles that will widen console gaming's narrow male demographic?

Figures 12.3, 12.4, and 12.5 demonstrate the peculiar resilience and prolificness of the video game software sector. From 1995 to 2000, game consoles saw only modest increases in unit sales, which plateaued in 1999 and fell slighty in 2000, according to NPD Group's annual study in conjunction with the Toy Manufacturers of America. Meanwhile, software sales skyrocketed in 2000, from 33 million games to 100 million, or more than 10 games for every console sold. However, part of that popularity came at the expense of high software unit prices. The average selling price (ASP) of a hardware console during that 6-year period fell only 16%, whereas the ASP for a video game cartridge plummeted by 36%.

Looking at these charts, it's plain to see how the stage was being set for 2001. The flat sales in 1999 turning downward in 2000 could only mean that the gaming public was losing interest in the increasingly geriatric hardware offerings from Sony, Sega, and Nintendo. It was clearly time for the hardware industry to steal a page from renowned TV chef Emeril Lagasse and "kick it up a notch!"

Video Game Units 1995-2000
Hardware Versus Software

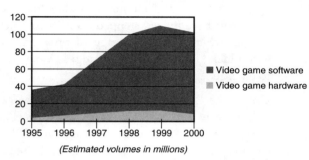

(Estimated volumes in millions)

Source: The NPD Group/Toy Manufacturers of America

FIGURE 12.3
The modest slump that hit the video game market in 1999–2000 did little to dent software unit sales.

Video Game Sales 1995-2000
Hardware Versus Software

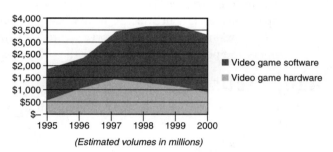

(Estimated volumes in millions)

Source: The NPD Group/Toy Manufacturers of America

FIGURE 12.4
Although software sales volume increased substantially, hardware continued to garner a disproportionate share of the total dollars spent on electronic games.

Video Game Average Selling Price 1995-2000
Hardware Versus Software

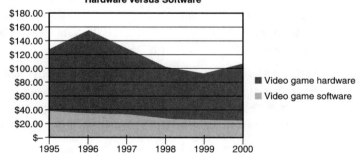

Source: The NPD Group/Toy Manufacturers of America

FIGURE 12.5
The popularity of video game cartridges ballooned during the latter half of the 1990s, yet game developers saw games prices erode substantially.

Sega chose discretion over valor and beat a hasty retreat from the hardware business, while Sony trumpeted a potentially successful band-aid approach to its still eminently viable PlayStation 2. Nintendo and Microsoft have indeed stepped up with completely new consoles, neither of which carries baggage of providing backward compatibility with older, "legacy" game cartridges. A new world order is beginning to emerge.

Unlike the PC industry, where change is a constant, the video game industry experiences change in fits and starts. The growth spurt in hardware capability that occurred during late 2001 is likely to settle down. Complacency will set in, R&D costs will be recouped, and then another cycle of upheaval will take place. That is, at least, if newcomer Microsoft plays by the rules. Having come from a different industry and bringing with it a different genetic code, it's possible that Microsoft will keep up the pressure with regular upgrades to its Xbox system. The impact such a shift in strategy would have on this old and extremely cyclical business would be unprecedented—perhaps good for consumers and potentially disastrous for the old guard.

Audio IEDs

Unlike video and gaming IEDs, intelligent audio devices are something that most consumers of home electronics are still quite comfortable living without.

Video game consoles have become a standard home appliance because of their irresistibility to males between the ages of 6 and 36. Digital video recorders might have some catching up to do before they reach the adoption rate of game boxes; however, most people with whom I spoke about TiVos, ReplayTVs, and UltimateTVs in the past year at least coveted one of their own.

Audio IEDs, however, have a tougher row to hoe. Whereas "wearable" players of digital music have achieved some measure of success, MP3 players have yet to make significant inroads into our cars (the place where most Americans listen to music), let alone our living rooms.

As far as computerized home audio appliances were concerned—true IEDs—most of my friends and acquaintances were blissfully unaware that these even existed, and I have yet to meet anyone outside the immediate industry who admits to actually owning one outright.

However, if user group bulletin board postings are any indication, customer satisfaction is extremely high among the lucky few who have actually purchased the devices.

For the right individuals—people who listen to music frequently, and when they do, listen to a lot of it—these devices could be a godsend. For a busy journalist and author with a house full of underage overachievers, however, spending hours preening my music collection just isn't in the cards. I can only hope these devices are still around when I finally reach an age where I have time to enjoy them.

Like most middle-aged Americans, I accumulated the bulk of my music collection when I was in my teens and 20s—I had a lot less money, but evidently more time on my hands. There lies the rub: The demographic group most likely to want these devices has been completely priced out of the market for them. After all, how many high schoolers can afford (or convince their parents they need) an $800–$1,000 device to store the music collection that they downloaded for free off the Internet?

The mismatch between target audience and their ability to acquire the device is less pronounced with video and gaming IEDs. Both tend to cost hundreds less, and although parents are a softer touch for the game consoles, it's the parents who are snapping up the TiVos, ReplayTVs, and UltimateTVs for their own enjoyment.

Although that might be oversimplifying a complex issue, at the end of the day, we are left with the injustice of a great product in search of a market.

Into this bleak and somewhat barren landscape, a new victim—or perhaps a prophet—has apparently blundered. Enter Hewlett-Packard with its own entry for the audio IED space: the HP Digital Entertainment Center, or de100c for short.

Once again, as fate would have it, I was interrupted in the middle of my final day of writing this penultimate chapter. No sooner than I had hung up from hearing the confessions of Microsoft's head UltimateTV strategist did HP representatives contact me. They wondered if I'd still like to see some details about the mysterious audio IED project announced at PC Expo the previous June (see the section in Chapter 8, "iPaq Music Center," page 204).

The new unit is designed to "slide comfortably into anyone's home entertainment center," according to the reviewer's guide, and indeed it looks as though it could sit alongside a VCR, DVD, and any number of other entertainment appliances without attracting undue notice (see Figure 12.6).

FIGURE 12.6
With its de100c, Hewlett-Packard competes with its acquisition target Compaq Computer in the manufacture of dedicated audio IEDs.

The de100c (the name, unfortunately, is not likely to greatly improve its distinguishability) is designed to do most of the things that the Compaq iPaq Music Center and the Kenwood Entre (see Chapter 8, "iPaq Music Center," page 204) have been designed to do, namely:

- Operate independently of a host PC, including a built-in modem to log onto the Web
- Rip CDs and store the music as digital media files on a local hard drive
- Allow online music purchases
- Play Internet radio
- Create personal playlists
- Transfer music to select portable MP3 players
- Allow remote control operation

Where Hewlett-Packard has gone its competitors one better is by including an item that has long been a staple of HP's far-reaching manufacturing and development efforts: a recordable CD.

The HP offering contains a 40GB hard drive, with enough capacity to store 9,000 music tracks—roughly equal to approximately 750 CDs compressed as 128Kbps MP3 files. Windows Media is expected to be supported at a later date. HP also reports that the unit has the ability to display streaming video clips when connected to a TV.

Some initial reviews of the pricey $999 device found fault with the fact that you must listen to each CD while ripping it, and all other functions of the device are disabled during that ripping process "to ensure that all tracks are recorded without errors."

Interested parties should also note that, like the iPaq Music Center, the HP Entertainment Center allows copying to the unit from a PC over a network, but does not allow files on the IED to be copied back to the PC. Of course, this is a minor inconvenience because the HP unit is equipped with a CD-RW burner—unlike the iPaq.

The de100c uses a Linux operating system, running on a 566Mhz Celeron processor with 64MB RAM.

Although it's gratifying to see that companies like HP are continuing to test the IED waters, one can't help wondering if it is a wise use of limited resources during this time of economic recession and general misery in the high tech sector.

Unlike gaming IEDs—and to a certain extent even video IEDs— intelligent audio devices are far from being a slam dunk these days. Why not instead offer a potentially more innovative, less expensive device that simply marries hard drive recording technology to a radio? As my learned colleague, former CNET Radio host Alex Bennett has often suggested, the ability to timeshift, rewind, and record a live radio show would likely constitute a "killer app" for audio IEDs. I have no doubt that this would also give the Recording Industry Association of America serious conniptions. In fact, it probably already has (which might explain why no such device has yet come to market) .

And The Hits Keep Coming

While they came on the scene too late to be fully analyzed in this book, there were two additional IEDs that demanded our notice: The Rio Advanced Digital Audio Center from SonicBlue and the Moxi Media Center from Moxi Digital.

The Rio product competes with Hewlett-Packard's HP Digital Entertainment Center at the top of the class in the audio IED category. Shipping in early 2002 with a 40GB hard disk and an integrated CD-RW drive, the $1,500 device Rio Advanced Digital Audio Center is designed as a standalone audio jukebox console. In other words, it does not require a PC, but functions as its own server. It can be connected to multiple Rio Receiver units to provide music from room to room using a built-in 10Mbps Home PNA network adapter. At its debut, the Rio Advanced Digital Audio Center allows connection to the Internet through an ISP solely for identifying CD audio tracks using the CDDB database. The company, however, expects to enable the devices to acquire music and perfrom other online functions in the future.

The Moxi Media Center promises to give current video IEDs a run for their money. The device, which was unveiled by WebTV founder Steve Perlman at the Winter 2002 Consumer Electronics Show in Las Vegas, combines the best features of a "DirecTiVo" or UltimateTV box with up to four satellite tuners and the ability to handle compressed audio files and DVD playback. Onboard support for a broadband modem and wireless networking allow the device to double as a Web access "hub" for the home, while broadcasting a wireless video signal to multiple TVs around the house. Designed to be distributed by cable and satellite operators, such as launch Partner EchoStar, the Moxi Media Center device will cost about $425 plus $75 for the wireless adapter (called an MCx) required for each additional TV. Enabling use of the device's 80GB hard drive to record and playback media on four separate televisions would cost only about $180 per room—considerably less than equipping each room with a TiVo, ReplayTV, or UltimateTV.

A Final Rant

Perhaps it can be attributed to the aging of the computer industry, but it appears that increasingly, the obstacles to introducing revolutionary new products are less technological and more often than not, political and economic. Like highly efficient automobile engines whose designs were quietly squelched by car makers that feared anything that might threaten their comfortable cartel, new technologies and services that are eminently feasible—and even extremely desirable from a consumer standpoint—can languish indefinitely waiting for sufficient backing to nudge them toward launch.

As the chief technical officer of AOL Time Warner said to me in November 2001 regarding the media giant's ability to offer vast archives of on-demand video and music content via cable lines into our homes, "The technology is available now. You could do it today. But it's going to take a very long time."

His frustration was palpable and quite understandable. We are on the threshold of realizing fantastic new capabilities that have the potential to fundamentally change the lives of millions of people. The only obstacles that are hindering these efforts, unfortunately, won't be solved in the lab, but in the boardroom.

Index

Symbols

3D objects
  gaming IEDs, 134
  polygons, 135
9th Tee Web site, 266

A

A/V
  output, Xbox, 161
  receivers, 246-247
access
  online, gaming IED, 8
  recording options, video IEDs, 33
accessing Internet
  IEDs, 251
  TVs, 37
ACTiSYS IR200L Remote Control, ShowShifter, 109
adapters, HPNA
  AudioTron, 200
  iPaq Music Center, 207
  Rio Receiver, 193
adding storage space, TiVo, 260, 263-265
advertising, IED, 11
All-In-Wonder, ATI, 103
AMP, MP3 player, 181
Apex AD-600A Home Web site, 271
ARQ Pro (AudioReQuest Pro Digital Music System), 192, 211
  CDDB (Compact Disk Data Base), 212
  connecting, 212
  hardware, 212-214
  I/O, 214
  interface, 214
  memory, 214
  screens, 216
  software, 214-216
ARQ1-20 Hacking Page Web site, 270
ASIC (application-specific integrated circuit), hardware, 70

ATI
  All-In-Wonder, 103
  ATI-TV Wonder, 103
  image quality, 103
  installation, 103
  motherboards, 103
  processors, 104
  timeshifting, 104
  TV tuner card, 99, 103-104
  TV Wonder, 103
  video compression, 104
audio
  IEDs, 8, 12, 183
    ARQ Pro, 211-216
    AudioTron, 198-204
    Bose Wave/PC Interactive Audio System, 220
    brands, 185-187
    considerations, 191-192
    costs, 187
    digital recordings, 180-182
    DigMedia MusicStore, 219
    features, 190
    future of, 187, 221-222, 284, 287
    HP Digital Entertainment Center, 204
    HPNA (Home Phoneline Networking Alliance), 195
    iPaq Music Center, 204-211
    marketing, 185-187, 285
    MP3, 182, 185
    Perception Digital PD Hercules, 217
    remote controllers, 247
    Rio Receiver, 192-198
    tweaking, 268-271
    Web connections, 250
  processing, GameCube, 143
  streaming, ZapStation, 224
AudioGalaxy, MP3 files (sharing), 186
AudioRequest IED, 269-270
AudioReQuest Pro Digital Music System. *See* **ARQ Pro**
AudioStation, 203
AudioTron, 8, 191
  AudioStation, 203
  Auto IP, 200

  configuring, 200
  CUP, 202
  DHCP (Dynamic Host Configuration Protocol), 200
  features, 198, 201
  hardware, 198, 201-202
  host systems, 202
  HPNA adapters, 200
  LCD readout, 198
  memory, 202
  MP3, 201
  software, 203-204
Auto IP, AudioTron, 200
Avs Forum Web site, 266

B

backdoor
  codes, TiVo, 75-80
  mode, TiVo, 76
backups
  making, TiVo (tweaking), 262, 265
  testing, TiVo (tweaking), 265
bit rates, CPUs (central processing units), 135
Blocked Channel, security features (TiVo), 89
Blue Skin, ShowShifter, 109
Bose Wave/PC Interactive Audio System, audio IED, 192, 220
boxes, set-top boxes, (video IEDs), 22-23
broadband, gaming IED, 11
buffers, video IEDs, 33
buttons, GameCube, 142

C

C-C-E-E 2, CCEE code, 77
C-C-E-E-8, CCEE code, 78
C-E-C Fast Forward, CEC code, 77
C-E-C Thumbs-Up, CEC code, 77
C-E-C-5, CEC code, 77
C-E-C-O, CEC code, 77

Cabernet Configuration Files (CCF), programmable remote controllers, 248

Cable Labs, 227

cables
coaxial (coax), 28
component video, 28
composite video, 28
S-video, 27-28
selecting, video IEDs, 28
video IEDs, installing, 27-29

cards
graphics, PC displays, 101
memory cards, GameCube, 142-144
TV tuner
ATI, 103-104
Hauppauge, 103
Matrox, 104
nVidia, 105
PC hardware, 101, 106
screen playback, 98
timeshifting, 99
tuner chips, 102
USB (Universal Serial Bus) connections, 102
video capture, 99

CCEE codes, backdoor codes (TiVo), 77

CCF (Cabernet Configuration Files), programmable remote controllers, 248

CDDB (Compact Disk Data Base), 212-214

CDs
audio, Macrovision, 246
playing, Xbox, 165-166
recordable, 286
ripping, 181, 286
ZapStation, 225

CEC codes, backdoor codes (TiVo), 77

central processing units. *See* **CPUs**

CFP field (Claw Foot Portal), 49

Channel Settings, security features (TiVo), 89

channels
custom, ReplayTV, 52, 58-59
deleting, ReplayTV, 55-56
priorities, ReplayTV, 56
show-based Replay (ReplayTV), 56-58
theme, ReplayTV, 52
virtual, 8

Cheat Code Central Web site, 268

cheat codes, game IEDs (tweaking), 267

chips, tuner (TV tuner cards), 102

Christopher Richmond Web site, 269

CinePlayer DVR Plus (WinVCR), 110-111

Claw Foot Portal (CFP field), 49

clocks
ReplayTV, 48
TiVo, 78

coaxial (coax) cables, 28

codes
backdoor, TiVo, 75-80
CCEE, TiVo, 77
CEC, TiVo, 77
cheat, game IEDs (tweaking), 267
Claw Foot Portal (CFP field), 49
Thumbs Up/Down, TiVo, 78
TiVo, 78-80

commercials, skipping (future video IEDs), 17-18

Compact Disk Data Base (CDDB), 212-214

Compaq iPaq Music Center, audio IED, 191

Compaq iPaq Music Center. *See* **iPaq Music Center**

compatibility
gaming IEDs, 118
multiple IEDs, 240
Rio Receiver, 193

components
gaming IEDs, 121-128
video cables, 28

composite video cables, 28

compression
data, hard disks (PCs), 99
MP3, 190
video, ATI, 104

configuring
AudioTron, 200
IED, 9
TiVo hard drives, 264

connecting
ARQ Pro, 212
IEDs, Web, 251
multiple IEDs, 239, 246
Perception Digital PD Hercules, 219
video IEDs, 30-31

connections
Internet, iPaq Music Center, 207
Universal Serial Bus (USB), 102
video IEDs, installing, 29-31
Web
multiple IEDs, 249-252
value proposition, 250-251

consoles
compatiblity, 118
gaming, 132
comparing, 119-121
Internet-capable, 124
interacting, 124
versus PCs, 117-119

controllers
Cube JoyBox, 149
GameCube, 142, 148
hardware
GameCube, 146, 149
Xbox, 162
remote
multple IEDs, 247-249
programmable, 248

controls
interface, GameCube, 142
regions, PlayStation 2, 176

copy protection
Macrovision, 242
multiple IEDs, 242-244
ReplayTV, 242
software, Macrovision, 244

costs
GameCube, 137
gaming IEDs, 137
TiVo, 64
UltimateTV, 6-7
video IEDs, 8, 18
Xbox, 137
ZapStation, 225

CPUs (central processing units)
AudioTron, 202
bit rates, 135
Flipper, GameCube, 143
gaming IEDs, 133
hardware
ReplayTV, 46
UltimateTV, 84
Gekko, GameCube, 142
overclocking, 270
utilitzation meter, ReplayTV, 48
Xbox, 156

Cube JoyBox, controllers, 149

custom channels, ReplayTV, 52, 58-59

Custom Record, features (TiVo), 88

customers
  support, IEDs, 10
  TiVo, 65-67

D

Dashboard, software (Xbox), 164

DAT (digital audiotape), 181

data compression, hard disks (PCs), 99

DCP (Digital Convergence Platform) 500 Series, 233

de100c (HP Digital Entertainment Center), audio IED, 285-286

delaying programming, timeshifting, 32

Depg, ShowShifter, 108

design, hardware
  GameCube, 141
  Xbox, 156

devices, integrated (set-top boxes), 229-230

DHCP (Dynamic Host Configuration Protocol), AudioTron, 200

diagnostics, UltimateTV, 89

Digishift, ShowShift, 108

digital
  audiotape (DAT), 181
  recordings, audio IED, 180-182
  video recorder (DVR). *See* video, IED

Digital Convergence Platform 500 Series (set-top box), 233

Digital Studio PCV-MXS10, 112-113

DigitalRecorder.tv Web site, 272

DigMedia MusicStore, audio IED, 219

DirecTiVo, hardware updates, 20

Dish Hack Web site, 266

Dishplayer, set-top boxes (future), 22

disks
  hard disks
    PCs, 99-100
    video storage, 100
    ZapStation, 225
  optical, GameCube, 146

displays, PCs, 101

Dreamcast, modems, 123

drives, formatting TiVo drives, 265. *See also* hard drives

dual-LNB dishes, 24

dual-tuner, software (UltimateTV), 87

DVDs
  gaming IED, 11
  Macrovision signals, filtering, 245
  players, MP3, 184
  playing, Xbox, 161
  ZapStation, 225

DVR (digital video recorder). *See* video, IED

Dynamic Host Configuration Protocol (DHCP), AudioTron, 200

E

e-mail, surfing (video IEDs), 277

Easter eggs
  ReplayTV, 63
  TiVo, 76

electric shock, risks (tweaking IEDs), 257

electrical outlets, installing video IEDs, 26

electronic gaming, 132

emulators, game IEDs (tweaking), 267

EPG, WinDVR, 111

Ethernet port, Xbox, 160

Extensible Markup Language (XML), ReplayTV, 51

F

factory dual-drive standalone TiVo, 262

feature creep, SAS (Swiss Army Syndrome), 136

features
  audio IEDs, 190
  AudioTron, 198, 201
  competitive, set-top boxes, 228
  Digital Convergence Platform 500 Series, 233
  Digital Studio PCV-MXS10, 112-113
  DigMedia MusicStore, 219

fit and finish, UltimateTV, 86

future, video IEDs, 17-19, 278, 281

gaming IEDs, 11, 136-137

HP Digital Entertainment Center (de100c), 286

iPaq Music Center, 204-206

online, ReplayTV, 59-60

ReplayTV 4000, 51

Rio Receiver, 195

security TiVo, 89

software, ReplayTV 4000, 51

SurfReady NTV-2500, 231

TiVo, 72, 88

UltimateTV, 84

files
  MP3
    audio IED, 12
    Rio Receiver, 197
  recording, tweaking video IED, 259
  transferring, tweaking video IED, 259
  video, MPEG-2 (Digital Studio PCV-MXS10), 113

Flipper, GameCube, 143

functions, ZapStation, 224

G

game loading, hard drives (Xbox), 162

GameCube (Nintendo), 8, 11, 138
  audio processing, 143
  buttons, 142
  consoles, comparing, 119
  control interface, 142
  controllers, 142, 148
  costs, 137
  Flipper, 143
  game cards, 142
  Gekko, 142
  hard drives, 122
  hardware, 140, 148
    controllers, 146, 149
    design, 141
    inputs, 144-146
    memory, 144
    outputs, 144-146
    processors, 142
    storage, 146
  inputs, 142
  Luigi's Mansion, tips, 151
  marketing, 140
  memory cards, 144
  modifications, 150
  online gaming, 127
  optical disk, 146

outputs, 142
polygons, 143
ports, 142
software, games, 149
Wave Race: Blue Storm for
    Nintendo GameCube, tips, 152

games
consoles, 132
IEDs, tweaking, 266-268
saving, Xbox, 159
software
    GameCube, 149
    gaming IEDs, 135
    Memory menu, 164
    Music menu, 165
    PlayStation 2, 173
    settings menu, 166
    Xbox, 163
top-selling, 2000, 174
Xbox, tips, 167

**GameShark Home Page Web site,
268**

Gamespy Web site, 124

gaming
electronic, 132
IEDs, 8, 11, 118, 138
    3D objects, 134
    caching, images, 135
    components, 121-128
    consoles, 117-119, 124
    costs, 137
    CPUs, 133
    features, 136-137
    *future, 128-130, 176-177, 281,
        284*
    GameCube. See GameCube
    *GPU (graphic processing unit),
        133*
    hard drives, 122-123
    Internet-capable consoles, 124
    modems, 123, 126-128
    patching, 126
    PCs, 116
    performance, 132, 135
    PlayStation 2. See PlayStation 2
    remote controllers, 247
    screens (loading), 122
    software, 135
    Web connections, 249-250
    Xbox. See Xbox
levels, storing, 123
multiplayer, 124-126
online, 124-125
    Microsoft Xbox, 127
    Nintendo GameCube, 127
    Sony PlayStation 2, 128

Gekko, GameCube, 142

GPU (graphic processing unit)
gaming IEDS, 133
polygons, 133-134
Xbox, 157

graphics card, displays, 101. *See also*
TVs, tuner cards

graphics. *See* **images**

H

hacking. *See also* **tweaking**
audio IEDs, 268
gaming IEDs, 267
video IEDs, 259
Xbox, 167-168

**Hacking the Rio Receiver Web site,
270**

hard
disks
    hardware, PCs, 99-100
    video storage, 100
    ZapStation, 225
drives
    *components, gaming IEDs,
        122-123*
    gaming IED, 11
    hardware, ReplayTV, 45
    ReplayTV, 59
    TiVo, 262-264
    tweaking, TiVo, 262
    updating, UltimateTV, 92
    Xbox, 122, 159, 162

hardware
ARQ Pro, 212-214
AudioTron, 198, 201-202
GameCube, 140, 148
    controllers, 146, 149
    design, 141
    inputs, 144-146
    memory, 144
    outputs, 144-146
    processors, 142
    storage, 146
iPaq Music Center, 206-208
PCs
    displays, 101
    hard disks, 99-100
    IEDs, 101
    memory, 97-99
    processors, 97-99
    TV tuner cards, 101, 106
    video IEDs, 97, 100, 103-106

PlayStation 2, 171-172
ReplayTV, 44
    CPU, 46
    hard drives, 45
    inputs, 45
    outputs, 45
    Philips 3139 Series TV tuner, 47
    Sony CXD1922, 46
    TV sound-processing IC, 46
    Xilinx Spartan-II XC2S40, 47
Rio Receiver, 193-197
TiVo
    *ASIC (application-specific inte-
        grated circuit), 70*
    inputs, 68
    modems, 70
    outputs, 68
tweaking, 269
UltimateTV, 81
    CPU, 84
    inputs, 83
    memory, 85
    outputs, 83
    Solo2, 84
updating, video IEDs, 20
Xbox, 154, 162
    controllers, 162
    design, 156
    input, 160-161
    memory, 158-160
    output, 160-161
    processors, 156
    storage, 161
ZapStation, 225

Hauppauge
TV tuner cards, 98, 103
WinTV-PVR, 103

Hi-Speed Port, GameCube, 144

hidden menu, ReplayTV, 48-49

**Home Phoneline Networking
Alliance (HPNA), audio IEDs, 195**

host systems, AudioTron, 202

**How to Upgrade Your Dishplayer's
Hard Drive Web site, 266**

**HP Digital Entertainment Center
(de100c), audio IED, 204, 285-286**

**HPNA (Home Phoneline
Networking Alliance)**
adapters, 193, 200, 207
audio IEDs, 195

I

I/O
ARQ Pro, 214
iPaq Music Center, 206
options, A/V receivers, 247

ID3, 197

IDC (International Data Corp), 11

IEDs (Interactive Entertainment Devices). *See also* **audio, IEDs; gaming, IEDS; video, IEDS**
advertising, 11
AudioRequest, 269
cables, 27-29
configuration, 9
connecting, Web, 251
connections, 29-31
customer support, 10
disadvantages, 9
game, tweaking, 266-268
installation, 9
Internet, accessing, 251
multiple, 238
A/V receiver, 246
compatibility, 240
connecting, 239, 246
copy protection, 242-244
customizing, 239-240, 243-249
future, 252
Macrovision, 244-246
remote controllers, 247-249
Web connections, 249-252
PCs
advantages, 96
disadvantages, 96
hardware, 101
setup, 9
set-top boxes, 227-230
Digital Convergence Platform 500 Series, 233
SimpleFi, 234-235
SurfReady NTV-2500, 230-231
Tuxia, 231-232
tweaking, 256
benefits, 258
professionally, 271-272
risks, 257
user interfaces, 9
viewers, advantages, 11
ZapStation, 224-227

images
caching, gaming IEDS, 135
quality, ATI, 103
Xbox, 157

information, satellite (UltimateTV), 90

infrared devices. *See* **remote controllers**

inputs
GameCube, 142
hardware
GameCube, 144-146
ReplayTV, 45
TiVo, 68
UltimateTV, 83
Xbox, 160-161
ZapStation, 225

installing
ATI, 103
considerations, video IEDs, 24, 27
Cube JoyBox (controllers), 149
IEDs, 9
multiswitches, 25
Rio Receiver, 193
video IEDs, 23-31

integrated devices, set-top boxes, 229-230

Interactive Entertainment Device. *See* **IEDs**

interactivity, recording options (video IEDs), 36-38

interfaces
ARQ Pro, 214-216
control, GameCube, 142
Perception Digital PD Hercules, 219
settings, ARQ Pro, 216
users
IED, 9
ReplayTV, 52, 55-56, 59-63
TiVo, 73-75

International Data Corp (IDC), 11

International Federation of the Phonographic Industry, 181

Internet
accessing, 37, 251
connections, iPaq Music Center, 207
consoles, gaming IEDs, 124
gaming IED, 12
radio, audio IED, 13
recording options, video IEDs, 36-38

Internet-Enabled set-top boxes. *See* **set-top boxes**

IP (Internet Protocol)
Auto, AudioTron, 200
iPaq Music Center, 208

iPaq Music Center, audio IED
customer service, 207-208
features, 204-206
hardware, 206-208
HPNA adapter, 207
I/O, 206
Internet connection, 207
IP (Internet Protocol), 208
LED readout, 209
OpenGlobe Entertainment Service, software, 209
remote controllers, setting up, 211
settings screen, 208
software, 209-211

IPQA Music Center, audio IED, 8

J-K

Jeff Mock Web site, 269

JReceiver Web site, 269

Keep Until, features (TiVo), 88

Kenwood, audio IED, 192

kernal (operating system), software, 135

L

law, risks (tweaking IEDs), 258

LCD readouts, AudioTron, 198

LED readout, iPaq Music Center, 209

levels, game (storing), 123

Lik-Sang Web site, 245

live buffering, hidden menu (ReplayTV), 48

lossless, recordings (video IED), 8

Luigi's Mansion, GameCube (tips), 151

M

MacAmp, MP3 player, 181

Macrovision
audio CDs, 246
copy protection, 242
fair use, 244-246
multiple IEDs, 244-246
signals, filtering, 245

managing TiVo, Web, 259

Matrox
    memory, 104
    picture-in-picture, 105
    resolutions, 104
    text decoding, 104
    timeshifting, 105
    TV tuner card, 104

Matrox Graphics, TV tuner card, 98

memory
    allocating, Xbox, 158
    ARQ Pro, 214
    AudioTron, 202
    cards, GameCube, 142-144
    CPU and GPU, Xbox, 159
    hardware
        GameCube, 144
        PCs, 97-99
        UltimateTV, 85
        Xbox, 158-160
    Matrox, 104
    segmented, Nintendo, 158
    SnapStream PVS, 109

menus, hidden menus (ReplayTV), 48-49

Mfs Tools, backing up TiVo hard drives, 263

Microsoft
    consoles, comparing, 120
    Xbox. *See* Xbox

Microsoft Developer Network, ID3, 197

mod chips, PlayStation 2, 176

models
    ReplayTV 4000, 50
    TiVo, 68
    UltimateTV, 81

modems
    components, gaming IEDs, 123, 126-128
    hardware, TiVo, 70

modes, backdoor (TiVo), 76

modules, Point-of-Deployment (POD), 228

Morpheus, MP3 files (sharing), 186

motherboards, ATI, 103

Motion Picture Experts Group (MPEG), 181

MP3, 181-182, 185, 190
    audio IED, 8
    AudioTron, 201
    DVD players, 184
    files, 12, 197
    portable players, 184
    Rio Receiver, 197
    sharing, 183

MPEG (Motion Picture Experts Group), 181

MPEG-2, WinDVR, 111-113

multiple IEDs, 238
    A/V receiver, 246
    compatibility, 240
    connecting, 239, 246
    copy protection, 242-244
    customizing, 239-240, 243-249
    future, 252
    Macrovision, 244-246
    remote controllers, 247-249
    Web connections, 249-252

multiswitches, 24-25

music, storing, 201

Music Mixer, ShowShifter, 109

MusicStore, audio IED, 219

MyReplayTV.com (ReplayTV), 59-62

N

Napster, piracy, 182

National Television Systems Committee (NTSC), video, 99

Neon Technology, 230

.NET Alert, video IED, 281

.NET Features, video IED, 281

Nintendo
    GameCube. *See* GameCube
    history, 139
    segmented memory, 158

Nomad Jukebox USB Protocol Web site, 271

NTSC (National Television Systems Committee) video, 99

nVidia, TV tuner card, 105

O

objects, 3D objects
    gaming IEDS, 134
    polygons, 135

OCAP (OpenCable Application Platform), 228

Official GameShark Discussion Board (The), Web site, 268

OGL (Online Gaming League) Web site, 124

online
    access, gaming IED, 8
    features, ReplayTV, 59-60
    gaming, 124-125
        IEDs, 12
        Microsoft Xbox, 127, 160
        Nintendo GameCube, 127
        Sony PlayStation 2, 128

Online Gaming League (OGL) Web site, 124

open architecture, gaming IEDs (PCs), 118

OpenCable, 227

OpenCable Application Platform (OCAP), 228

OpenGlobe Entertainment Service, iPaq Music Center (software), 209

operating future video IEDs, 19

operating systems (OS)
    ReplayTV, Sutter, 51
    TiVo, 71-73

optical disks, GameCube, 146

options
    I/O, A/V receivers, 247
    recording, video IEDs, 32-38

OS (operating systems)
    ReplayTV, Sutter, 51
    TiVo, 71-73

outlets, electrical (installing video IEDs), 26

outputs
    A/V, Xbox, 161
    GameCube, 142
    hardware
        GameCube, 144-146
        ReplayTV, 45
        TiVo, 68
        UltimateTV, 83
        Xbox, 160-161
    ZapStation, 225

overclocking
    AudioRequest, 270
    CPUs, 270

P-Q

parental controls, software (Xbox), 163

patching PCs, gaming IEDs, 126

pausing, recording options (video IEDs), 33

PCs
compatibility, 118
displays, 101
gaming IEDs, 116, 126
hard disks, data compression, 99
hardware, 97-106
IEDs, 96
iPaq Music Center, 206
processors, timeshifting, 98
software, video IEDs
CinePlayer DVR Plus, 110
ShowShifter, 108
VCR, 110
WinDVR, 111
TV tuner cards, 98
versus consoles, 117-119
video, *23*, *96-98*, *106-108*,
111-112

PD Hercules, audio IED, 217

**Perception Digital PD Hercules,
audio IED, 217**

performance, gaming, 132, 135

personal video recorder (PVR). *See*
video, IEDs

**Philips 3139 Series TV tuner,
hardware (ReplayTV), 47**

**phones, jacks (installing video
IEDs), 26**

picture-in-picture, Matrox, 105

piracy, Napster, 182

**playback, screens (TV tuner cards),
98**

players
DVD, MP3, 184
portable, MP3, 184

playlists, 203

**PlayStation 2 (Sony), gaming IED,
8, 11, 169**
consoles, comparing, 119
hard drives, 122
hardware, 171-172
mod chips, 176
modifications, 176
online gaming, 128
region controls, 176
software, 172-174

**POD (Point-of-Deployment) mod-
ule, 228**

polygons
3D objects, 135
GameCube, 143
GPU (graphic processing unit),
133-134

portable players, MP3, 184

ports
Ethernet, Xbox, 160
GameCube, 142

priority channels, ReplayTV, 56

**Prman's ReplayTV Advanced FAQ
Web site, 266**

processors
ATI, 104
hardware
GameCube, 142-143
PCs, 97-99
Xbox, 156
PCs, timeshifting, 98
video, PCs, 98
ZapStation, 225

**programmable remote controllers,
248**

programming
delaying, timeshifting, 32
navigating, video IEDs, 34
ReplayTV (away from home),
59-62
TiVo, 73

**PTVupgrade.com Web site, 266,
272**

PVR (personal video recorder). *See*
video, IEDs

R

**radio, Internet radio (audio IED),
13**

Rage Games Web site, 268

rates, bit rate, (CPUs), 135

**rebooting, glitches (video IEDs),
38**

**receivers, A/V, 246 (I/O options),
247**

**recorders, digital video
(ZapStation), 226**

recording
files, tweaking video IED, 259
options, video IEDs, 32-38

**Recording Industry Association of
America (RIAA), 181**

recordings
digital, audio IED, 180-182
lossless, video IED, 8

region controls, PlayStation 2, 176

Remote Central Web site, 248

remote controllers
multiple IEDs, 247-249
MyReplayTV.com, 62
programmable, 248
setting up, iPaq Music Center, 211
TiVo, 67
UltimateTV, 82

Replay
Guide, ReplayTV, 58
MyReplayTV.com, remote con-
trollers, 62
Zone, ReplayTV, 48

ReplayTV (video IED), 6, 43, 260
channels, deleting, 55-56
clocks, 48
commercials, skipping, 17-18
copy protection, 242
CPU utilization meter, 48
custom channels, 52, 58-59
Easter eggs, 63
features, online, 59-60
4000, 49-51
future, 62-63, 276
hard drives, 59
hardware, 44-47
hidden menu, 48-49
MyReplayTV.com, 59-60
operating system, Sutter, 51
priority channels, 56
programming (away from home),
59-62
Replay Guide, 58
Replay Zone, 48
show-based Replay channels, 56-58
software, 51-52
theme channels, 52
updates, 51
user interface, 52, 55-56, 59-63
Web site, 30, 110
XML (Extensible Markup
Language), 51

resolutions
displays, PCs, 101
Matrox, 104
TV signals, 101

resources, TiVo (tweaking), 265-266

**RIAA (Recording Industry
Association of America), 181**

Rio Receiver (audio IED), 8, 192, 198
compatibility, 193
CPU chips, 196
features, 195
hardware, 193-197
host systems, requirements, 196
ID3 tags, 197

installing, 193
MP3 files, 197
screen displays, 196
software, 197

ripping CDs, 181, 286

rumble, controllers (GameCube), 148

S

S-P-S-3-0-S, Tivo code, 79

S-P-S-Instant Replay-S, Tivo code, 78

S-P-S-Pause-S, Tivo code, 79

S-video cables, 27-28

SAS (Swiss Army Syndrome), gaming IED features, 136

satellites
information, UltimateTV, 90
signals, splitting, 25

saving games, Xbox, 159, 166

screen playback, TV tuner cards, 98

screens
ARQ Pro, 216
loading, 122
settings, iPaq Music Center, 208

searches, glitches (video IEDs), 38

security features, TiVo, 89

Sega Dreamcast, modems, 123

segmented memory, Nintendo, 158

Serial Port 1, GameCube, 144

Serial Port 2, GameCube, 144

set-top boxes, 227
competitive features, 228
Digital Convergence Platform 500
Series, 233
integrated devices, 229-230
Point-of-Deployment (POD)
modules, 228
SimpleFi, 234-235
SurfReady NTV-2500, 230-231
Tuxia, 231-232
video IEDs, future of, 22-23

setting up
remote controllers, iPaq Music
Center, 211
set-top boxes, 229

settings
interface, ARQ Pro, 216
screens (iPaq Music Center), 208

setups, IED, 9

Shagwell Easter egg, TiVo, 76

sharing MP3, 183

show-based Replay channels, ReplayTV, 56-58

ShowShifter
ACTiSYS IR200L Remote
Control, 109
Blue Skin, 109
Depg, 108
Music Mixer, 109
Web Scheduler, 108

signals
filtering, Macrovision, 245
Macrovision, filtering, 245
satellites, splitting, 25
TV, resolutions, 101

Sima Web site, 245

SimpleFi (set-top box), 234-235

sites. *See* Web, sites

SnapStream PVS, memory, 109

software
ARQ Pro, 214-216
AudioTron, 203-204
copy protection, Macrovision, 244
features, ReplayTV 4000, 51
fit and finish features, Windows
CE, 86
GameCube, games, 149
games, top-selling in 2000, 174
gaming IEDs, 135
iPaq Music Center, 209-211
Mfs Tools, 263
PCs, video IED, 106-112
Perception Digital PD Hercules,
219
PlayStation 2, 172-174
ReplayTV, 50-52
Rio Receiver, 197
TiVo, 70
TivoMad, 263
UltimateTV, 86-92
updating, video IEDs, 19
version, ReplayTV, 51
versions, TiVo, 71
Xbox, 163-166
ZapStation, 226

Solo2, hardware (UltimateTV), 84

SonicBlue, 269

**SonicBlue Rio Digital Audio
Receiver. *See* Rio Receiver**

**Sony CXD1922, hardware
(ReplayTV), 46**

Sony PlayStation 2. *See* PlayStation 2

speed, software (UltimateTV), 86

splitting satellite signals, 25

STARFIRE.tv Web site, 272

storage
glitches, video IEDs, 38
hardware
GameCube, 146
Xbox, 161
TiVo, adding, 260, 263-265
video, hard disks, 100

storing
game levels, 123
music, 201

streaming
audio, ZapStation, 224
video, ZapStation, 224

support, customer (IEDs), 10

SurfReady NTV-2500 (set-top box), 230-231

**Sutter, operating system
(ReplayTV), 51**

Swiss Army Syndrome (SAS), gaming IED features, 136

systems
host, AudioTron, 202
operating, ReplayTV (Sutter), 51

T

tags, ID3 (Rio Receiver), 197

TASTE, Tuxia (set-top boxes), 232

**TD-TD-TU-Instant Replay,
Thumbs Up/Down codes, 78**

**TD-TU-TD-Instant Replay,
Thumbs Up/Down codes, 78**

Techtronics (UK) Web site, 272

text decoding, Matrox, 104

theme channels, ReplayTV, 52

**Thumbs Up/Down codes, backdoor
codes (TiVo), 78**

Time Stretching, WinDVR, 112

timeshifting
ATI, 104
CinePlayer DVR Plus, 111
Matrox, 105
processors, PCs, 98
recording options, video IEDs, 32
TV tuner cards, 99
WinDVR, 111
WinTV-PVR, 103

tips
Luigi's Mansion, GameCube, 151
Wave Race: Blue Storm for
Nintendo GameCube, 152
Xbox games, 167

TiVo (video IED), 6
backdoor, 75-80
clocks, 78
codes, 78-80
costs, 64
customers, 65-67
Easter eggs, 76
factory dual-drive standalone, 262
features, 72, 88-89
front-panel controls, 68
future, 275
hard drives, configuring, 264
hardware, 20, 68-70
managing, Web, 259
models, 68
operating systems (OS), 71-73
programming, 73
rear-panel controls, 68
remote controllers, 67
security features, 89
set-top boxes, future of, 22
software, 70-71
storage space, adding, 260,
263-265
tweaking, 262, 265-266
types, deteriming, 261-262
user interface, 73-75
Web site, 259

Tivo Hack FAQ Web site, 266

TiVo Web Project, 259, 266

**TivoMad, backing up TiVo hard
drives, 263**

**transferring files, tweaking video
IED, 259**

troubleshooting, video IEDs, 31

tuner chips, TV tuner cards, 102

**tuners, single (multiple TVs),
24-25**

Turtle Beach AudioTron. *See*
AudioTron

Tuxia (set-top box), 231-232

**TV sound-processing IC, hardware
(ReplayTV), 46**

TV Wonder, 103

TVs
Internet, accessing, 37
iPaq Music Center, 209
multiple, single tuners, 24-25
signals, 24, 101
tuner cards
ATI, 103-104
hardware, PCs, 101, 106
Hauppauge, 103
Matrox, 104
nVidia, 105
screen playback, 98
timeshifting, 99
tuner chips, 102
*USB (Universal Serial Bus) con-
nections, 102*
video capture, 99

tweaking
audio IEDs, 268-271
game IEDs, 266-268
hardware, 269
IEDs, 256
benefits, 258
professionally, 271-272
risks, 257
TiVo
formatting drives, 265
hard drives, 262
making backups, 262, 265
resources, 265-266
testing backups, 265
video IEDs, 258-266

types, TiVo (determing), 261-262

U

**UltimateTV (UTV), video IED, 80,
93**
costs, 6-7
diagnostics, 89
features, 84
front panel controls, 82
future, 276
hard drives, updating, 92
hardware, 81-85
Internet recording option, video
IEDs, 37
remote controllers, 82
satellite informations, 90
software, 86-92
system tests, 91

**Universal Serial Bus (USB) connec-
tions, 102**

updating
hard drives, UltimateTV, 92
hardware, video IEDs, 20
ReplaytV, 51
software, video IEDs, 19

**upgradability, gaming IEDs (PCs),
118**

**USB (Universal Serial Bus) connec-
tions, 102**

user interfaces
ReplayTV, 52, 55-56, 59-63
TiVo, 73-75

users, interfaces (IEDs), 9

UTV. *See* **UltimateTV**

V

**value proposition, Web connec-
tions, 250-251**

VCRs, 16, 110

Vguys' Electronics Web site, 272

**VHS, Macrovision signals (filter-
ing), 245**

video
cables, 27-29
capture, TV tuner cards, 99
compression, ATI, 104
connections, 29-31
files, MPEG-2 (Digital Studio
PCV-MXS10), 113
IEDs, 6, 10-11
buffers, 33
cables (selecting), 28
connecting, 30-31
copy protection, 242-244
costs, 8, 18
customizing, 276
*Digital Studio JPCV-MXS10,
112-113*
*Digital Studio PCV-MXS10,
112-113*
future features, 17-19, 278, 281
*future, 19, 22-23, 113-114,
274-281*
glitches, 38
hardware updates, 20
installing, 23-31
lossless recording, 8
operations (future feature), 19
*PCs, 96-97, 100, 103-108,
111-112*

recording options, 32-38
remote controllers, 247
ReplayTV, 43-64
selecting, 42-43
skipping commercials (future feature), 17-18
software updates, 19
surfing, 276-277
TiVo, 64-80
tweaking, 258-266
UltimateTV, 80-83, 86-93
VCRs, 16
Web connections, 249-251
ZapStation, 226
NTSC (National Television Systems Committee), 99
processing, PCs, 98
storage, hard disks, 100
streaming, ZapStation, 224

virtual channels, 8

W

warranty, risks (tweaking IEDs), 257

Wave Race: Blue Storm for Nintendo GameCube, tips, 152

Wave/PC, audio IED, 220

Weakness.com Web site, 272

Web
connections, 249-252
IEDs, connecting, 251
sites
9th Tee, 266
Apex AD-600A Home, 271
ARQ1-20 Hacking Page, 270
Avs Forum, 266
Cheat Code Central, 268
Christopher Richmond, 269
DigitalRecorder.tv, 272
Dish Hack, 266
GameShark Home Page, 268
Gamespy, 124
Hacking the Rio Receiver, 270
How to Upgrade Your Displayer's Hard Drive, 266
Jeff Mock, 269
JReceiver, 269
lik-sang, 245
Nomad Jukebox USB Protocol, 271
Official GameShark Discussion Board (The), 268

Online Gaming League, 124
Prman's ReplayTv Advanced FAQ, 266
PtVupgrade, 266, 272
Rage Games, 268
Remote Central, 248
ReplayTV, 30, 110
Sima, 245
STARFIRE.tv, 272
Techtronics (UK), 272
TiVo, 259, 266
Vguys' Electronics, 272
Weakness.com, 272
ZapMedia, 225
surfing, video IEDs, 277
TiVo, managing, 259

Web Scheduler, ShowShifter, 108

WinAmp, MP3 player, 181

WinCinema, 111

WinCoder, WinCinema, 111

Windows CE, software (UltimateTV), 86

WinDTV, WinCinema, 111

WinDVD, WinCinema, 111

WinDVR, 111-112

WinProducer, WinCinema, 111

WinRip, WinCinema, 111

WinTV-PVR, 103

WinVCR (CinePlayer DVR Plus), 110-111

X-Z

Xbox (Microsoft), gaming IED, 8, 152
A/V output, 161
CDs, playing, 165-166
costs, 137
CPU (central processing unit), 156
DVDs, playing, 161
Ethernet port, 160
front panel, 156
games, 159, 166-167
GPU (graphic processing unit), 157
hacking, 167-168
hard drives, 122, 159, 162
hardware, 154-156
controllers, 162
design, 156
input, 160-161

memory, 158-160
output, 160-161
processors, 156
storage, 161
images, 157
linking, 126
memory, 158-159
modifications, 166-168
online, 160
online gaming, 127
software, 163-166

Xilinx Spartan-II XC2S40, hardware (ReplayTV), 47

XML (Extensible Markup Language), ReplayTV, 51

ZapMedia, 224-226

zapping, recording options (video IEDs), 34

Zapstation, 227
costs, 225
digital video recorders, 226
functions, 224
hard disks, 225
hardware, 225
inputs, 225
outputs, 225
processors, 225
software, 226
storage space, 224

ZapZone, software (ZapStation), 226